Land Law Reform

Achieving Development Polic

Law, Justice, and Development

The Law, Justice, and Development series is offered by the Legal Vice Presidency of the World Bank to provide insights into aspects of law and justice that are relevant to the development process. Works in the series present new legal and judicial reform activities related to the World Bank's work, as well as analyses of domestic and international law. The series is intended to be accessible to a broad audience as well as to legal practitioners.

Series Editor: Salman M. A. Salman
Editorial Board: Hassane Cisse, Alberto Ninio, Sophie Smyth, and Kishor Uprety

Land Law Reform

Achieving Development Policy Objectives

John W. Bruce
Senior Counsel
Legal Vice Presidency, World Bank

Renée Giovarelli
Staff Attorney
Rural Development Institute

Leonard Rolfes, Jr.
Senior Attorney
Rural Development Institute

David Bledsoe
Senior Attorney
Rural Development Institute

Robert Mitchell
Senior Attorney
Rural Development Institute

THE WORLD BANK
Washington, D.C.

© 2006 The International Bank for Reconstruction and Development / The World Bank
1818 H Street NW
Washington DC 20433
Telephone: 202-473-1000
Internet: www.worldbank.org
E-mail: feedback@worldbank.org

1 2 3 4 :: 09 08 07 06

This volume is a product of the staff of the International Bank for Reconstruction and Development / The World Bank. The findings, interpretations, and conclusions expressed in this volume do not necessarily reflect the views of the Executive Directors of The World Bank or the governments they represent.

The World Bank does not guarantee the accuracy of the data included in this work. The boundaries, colors, denominations, and other information shown on any map in this work do not imply any judgment on the part of The World Bank concerning the legal status of any territory or the endorsement or acceptance of such boundaries.

Rights and Permissions

ISBN-10: 0-8213-6468-5 e-ISBN: 0-8213-6469-3
ISBN-13: 978-0-8213-6468-0 DOI: 10.1596/978-0-8213-6468-0

Library of Congress Cataloging-in-Publication Data

Land law reform : achieving development policy objectives / John W. Bruce . . . [et al.].
  p. cm — (Law, justice, and development)
  Includes bibliographical references and index.
  ISBN-10: 0-8213-6468-5
  ISBN-13: 978-0-8213-6468-0
   1. Land reform—Law and legislation. I. Bruce, John W. II. Series

K3871.3.L36 2006
346.04'4—dc22

                2005057742

Contents

List of Tables and Boxes

Foreword

Land is a critical asset for economic growth, social development, and poverty alleviation. The terms on which land is held, used, and transferred have important consequences for economic growth, the distribution of wealth, and alleviation of poverty. We live in an age of profound and often rapid transitions in the economies and societies of nations. It is notable that in those transitional economies that are moving to rely more heavily on market forces, land law reform is commonly near the top of the national reform agenda. Difficult policy choices are required because land tenure serves a multitude of purposes. Land is valued by some as an investment opportunity, by others as a safety net, and by yet others as critical to their cultural identity.

Accordingly, land law reform is increasingly becoming a pressing need in many parts of the world. Many developing countries seek to move beyond the laws inherited from their colonial past or to update their land law in key areas like condominium law or the law relating to mortgages. Others grapple with the socially complex issue of the future of customary land tenure and the traditional institutions associated with it.

This book examines issues at the forefront of the debate on land law reform, pays particular attention to how reform options affect the poor and disadvantaged, and recommends strategies for alleviating poverty more effectively through land law reform. It reviews the role of the World Bank in land law reform, examining issues of process as well as substance. It also identifies key challenges and directions, and stresses the need to design law reforms in ways that suit diverse economic, legal, and institutional environments.

The Legal Vice Presidency is pleased to offer this publication and hopes it will deepen the understanding of the role of land law reform in poverty alleviation, gender equity, and environmental protection.

Scott B. White
Acting Vice President and General Counsel
World Bank

February 2006

Abstract

This book is a contribution to comparative thinking on reform of the law relating to land. It examines the implications for land law reform in the broadening of development goals beyond growth to include environmental protection, poverty eradication, and achievement of gender equity, and it reviews a broad range of experience in land law reform. After the introductory chapter, chapter 2 examines how land law reform is achieved through World Bank initiatives. It reviews steps the Bank has taken to achieve comprehensive reforms of land law in the context of natural resource management and land reform programs and land administration projects. It also analyzes lessons learned from various land law reform processes. Chapter 3 addresses reform of rules affecting women's access to and rights in land. The topic is one in which broad recommendations are not necessarily easy due to cultural and other norms governing women's rights and freedoms regarding land. Chapter 4 examines how to develop land markets while minimizing adverse effects and enhancing positive impacts on the poor. Chapter 5 discusses the importance of titling and registration of land rights, reviews concepts that are supported by the Bank in many of its land projects, and describes how titling and registration can affect economic growth and the alleviation of poverty. Chapter 7 deals with issues of equity and poverty in the context of conservation and environmental protection of farms and forests. It examines the role of individual property rights, as well as the legal tools that can be used to encourage conservation. The conclusion draws together significant aspects from all the chapters that are needed for effective land law reform.

Acknowledgments

The authors would like to acknowledge the help and support of a number of entities and individuals during the preparation of this study, which was carried out collaboratively by the Environmentally and Socially Sustainable Development (ESSD) and International Law Unit (LEGEN) of the Legal Vice Presidency of the World Bank and the Rural Development Institute (RDI) of Seattle, Washington.

The authors gratefully acknowledge the encouragement and advice provided throughout the process of preparation by Roberto Dañino, former Senior Vice President and General Counsel of the World Bank; David Freestone, Deputy General Counsel, Advisory Services; and Salman M. A. Salman, Lead Counsel (LEGEN). For managing this effort on the RDI end, our thanks go to David Bledsoe, Senior Attorney with RDI. Thanks are also due for the assistance provided by staff of both institutions, and in particular to Shéhan de Sayrah, Counsel (LEGEN), for his editorial assistance.

Several friends and colleagues reviewed drafts and their comments contributed greatly to the final product. Jon Lindsay, land law expert from the Food and Agriculture Organization's Development Law Service, as external reviewer for the entire volume made invaluable comments. Within the Bank, chapters were reviewed and commented upon by Gillian Brown, Malcolm Childress, Charles Di Leva, Isabel Lavadenz Paccieri, George Ledec, and Wael Zakout. Gershon Feder provided comments on a particular portion of one paper. We extend our thanks and appreciation to all of them.

Acronyms and Abbreviations

AusAID	Australian Agency for International Development
BP	Bank Procedure Notes
CAS	Country Assistance Strategies
CIS	Commonwealth of Independent States
DCA	Development Credit Agreement
DFID	Department for International Development
EU	European Union
FAO	Food and Agriculture Organization of the United Nations
GIS	Geographic Information System
GTZ	Deutsche Gesellschaft für Technische Zusammenarbeit GmbH
HRS	Household Responsibility System
IBRD	International Bank for Reconstruction and Development
ICCPR	International Covenant on Civil and Political Rights
IDA	International Development Association
IFAD	International Fund for Agricultural Development
ILC	International Land Commission
ILO	International Labour Organization
JSDF	Japan Social Development Fund
Lao PDR	Lao People's Democratic Republic
LDP	Letter of Development Policy
LWU	Lao Women's Union
MALR	Market-Assisted Land Reform
MDG	Millennium Development Goals
NGO	Nongovernmental organization
OD	Operational Directive of the World Bank
OP	Operational Policies of the World Bank

PAD	Project Appraisal Document
PNG	Papua New Guinea
PRR	Policy Research Report
PRSC	Poverty Reduction Support Credits
PRSP	Poverty Reduction Strategy Papers
PSIA	Poverty and Social Impact Analysis
RDI	Rural Development Institute
RPF	Resettlement Policy Framework
SAL	Structural Adjustment Loans
TA	Technical assistance
TPLF	Tigrean People's Liberation Front
UNDP	United Nations Development Programme
UNCED	United Nations Conference on Environment and Development
USAID	United States Agency for International Development
USDA	United States Department of Agriculture

CHAPTER 1

Introduction: Reforming Land Law to Achieve Development Goals

John W. Bruce*

1.1 The Potential of Land Law

The role of land tenure—property rights in land—has been a major preoccupation in development discourse from the time of giants like Adam Smith and Karl Marx through to today's luminaries, such as Hernando de Soto. In spite of their substantially different perspectives, none of these worthies ever doubted the critical importance of land and property rights in the development process. But because land issues are knotty and often political, the enthusiasm of development agencies for tackling them has waxed and waned.

Today at the World Bank, as in other international development organizations, the Millennium Development Goals (MDGs), with their emphasis on poverty alleviation, gender equality, and environmental conservation, have refocused attention on land issues. A substantial number of recent studies stress that differences not only in income but also in assets account for persistent poverty. In recent years several donor organizations have struggled with such issues as the appropriate roles for state and private actors, the implications of different patterns of distribution of land, and the relationship between property rights and incentives. The World Bank recently produced a Policy Research Report (PRR) on Land,[1] and the British[2] and German[3] aid agencies have published broad land-policy documents. The International Land Coalition (consisting of

---

* John W. Bruce is a former Senior Counsel and specialist in land law in the Environmentally and Socially Sustainable Development (ESSD) and International Law Unit of the Legal Vice Presidency of the World Bank. He is a former Director of the Land Tenure Center of the University of Wisconsin–Madison.

[1] World Bank & Klaus Deininger, *Land Policies for Growth and Poverty Reduction. A World Bank Policy Research Paper* (World Bank & Oxford Univ. Press 2003).

[2] Department for International Development (DFID), *Better Livelihoods for Poor People: The Role of Land Reform* (DFID 2003).

[3] Deutsche Gesellschaft für Technische Zusammenarbeit (GTZ) GmbH, *Land Tenure in Development Cooperation* (GTZ 1998).

Non-governmental Organizations [NGOs], multilateral organizations, and governments and based at the International Fund for Agricultural Development [IFAD]) has sought to define a common platform.[4]

What is the relationship between land policy and reform of the law relating to land? They are certainly not the same thing. Most land policy statements are so general that they provide only broad guidance for law reform; most laws relating to land leave obscure to readers the policies that lie behind them. They are nevertheless closely connected. The goods that land policy promises are, in the terminology current in the Bank's Legal Vice Presidency, "law-dependent public and private goods." The law relating to land is a critical tool in realizing land policies. Policy reform logically precedes law reform, but law reform seeks to translate those policies into action. A good law is a critical step, even though follow-through is equally important in determining whether the reform delivers the goods or fails to do so.

This is because, while policy determines broad directions, law answers the question, "What must be done to get us there?" The law provides commands to officials and citizens alike. It seeks to mobilize incentives and disincentives for behavior. Law must be far more specific than policy about what is expected, and it must balance the competing claims of different societal objectives in equally specific terms. For example, "land tenure security" is a staple objective in statements about land policy reform, but usually it is only in the subsequent work on law reform that competing claims of diverse stakeholders are accommodated and a balance stuck between security of tenure and other legitimate societal objectives, such as environmental protection, equitable land distribution, and the State's need for compulsory acquisition of land for public purposes.

It is difficult to overstate the extent to which laws relating to land affects the lives and welfare of citizens. These laws provide not only rules about land rights but also regulatory frameworks and administrative competences that are the basis for mobilizing nonlegal incentives. This book deals with this larger body of law rather than "land law" narrowly defined.[5] Through its legal enactments relating

---

[4] International Land Coalition (ILC), *Towards a Common Platform on Access to Land: The Catalyst to Reduce Rural Poverty and the Incentive for Sustainable Natural Resource Management* (ILC 2003).

[5] There is remarkably little in the literature on land law from a comparative development perspective, but two recent collections of essays give hope that the situation may be improving: *see Land Law in Comparative Perspective* (Maria Elena Sanchez Jordan & Antonio Gambaro, eds., Kluwer Law Intl. 2002); and Patrick McAuslan, *Bringing the Law Back In: Essays in Land, Law and Development* (Ashgate Publishing Ltd. 2003). An excellent recent synthesis is Jon Lindsay's "Chapter 8. Land" in *Law and Sustainable Development Since Rio: Legal Trends in Agriculture and Natural Resource Management*, FAO Legislative Study 73, 203–243 (FAO 2002).

to land, the State creates property rights, determines the scope of the rights and obligations that accompany them, and provides for regulating use of land. This body of law is fundamental in that it regulates our possession and use of the natural resource that underlies and supports much of the life of our planet, providing the physical underpinning of our environment, our productive activities, and our social and political constructs.

Land laws set the terms for transactions in land; in so doing they help determine the efficiency of land markets and shape patterns of land distribution. They in part determine the distribution of development opportunities and the incidence of poverty. The terms on which landholders hold their land affect their incentives to husband or neglect it. Land and property rights have deep, emotive social and cultural significance in the societies of many developing countries because access to land is intimately related to kinship and identity, and control of land is the basis of political and state power.

1.2   The Pressing Need for Reform

We are seeing unprecedented land law reform activity today. In part this is due to the broad trend toward market liberalization and the demand for stronger private property rights in land. The great competing political dispensations of the last century had quite different ideas about rights in land. Today the swing to privatization and expanded roles for markets in countries transitioning out of *dirigiste* economic management have created almost overnight the need for entire national systems of real property law. In framing these new systems, it is necessary to address not only the needs of economic growth, as important as these may be, but also new demands, such as gender equity, poverty alleviation, and environmental protection.

In countries where the State had appropriated and attempted direct management of natural resources—a much more common phenomenon—policymakers are rethinking the appropriateness of their property solutions in light of extensive failures in state natural resource management. At the same time there has emerged a more democratic ethos that requires that land tenure reflect popular choices rather than technocratic "fixes" or ideology-driven solutions. Decentralization holds out the promise not just of more effective implementation of national programs but also of legal regimes that better accommodate diversity and respond to local needs and preferences. In African and Southeast Asian countries, effective reconciliation of systems of statutory law and customary land law is the primary challenge for legal reform.

Beyond these driving forces, there is the more general need for modernization. Condominium law and community land trusts are examples of recent innovations in land law that are being widely emulated in the developing world. But many countries still work with colonial-era statutes. Africa is a veritable Valhalla for British statutes from the colonial period; though they may have been less than adequate in local circumstances, they nonetheless live on there long after they have been repealed in Britain.[6] Environmental and other values receiving greater attention in our time need to be factored into land policy and, where appropriate, embedded in the national law relating to land.

There is also a pressing need in many countries for simplification. One often finds layer upon layer of land legislation like geologic strata, piled upon each other without much attention to repeals or reconciliation and in desperate need of restructuring for accessibility and intelligibility.

Law reform during major transitions can be a contentious and complex process in any case, but there are special difficulties relating to land that tend to make law reform in this arena even longer and more difficult:

- Land is a multipurpose resource, providing the basis for both security and growth—purposes that are sometimes in competition.
- The stakeholders affected by land law reform are numerous and highly diverse; they value potential uses differently, so consensus is hard to obtain.
- Land issues have deep cultural and historical dimensions that make reform of the law relating to land a delicate matter in many societies.
- Those with vested interests, both private and bureaucratic, can be expected to resist reform.

Even where most stakeholders realize that reform is inevitable, struggles over changes in access to land and the power to control access can be intense.

Finally, it should be admitted that much remains to be learned about how to use law to achieve needed social and economic changes. Stipulating the desired situation in a law is not enough. The law must change incentives and structure a process of change. All of us who work in this area know of elegant laws that have had little impact on behavior, some for want of implementation and others in spite of serious implementation efforts. Political will, financial and institutional capacity, and beneficiary awareness all play important roles. What works in changing behavior through law will differ from one political and legal culture to the next; the question surfaces again and again in the chapters that follow.

---

[6] Patrick McAuslan, *Only the Name of the Country Changes: The Diaspora of "European" Land Law in Commonwealth Africa,* in McAuslan, *id.,* at 59–83, is very good value on this phenomenon.

1.3   New Development Goals

Because access to and use of land is central to the MDGs, they provide a convenient conceptual framework in which to discuss critical contemporary issues of land law reform, such as elimination of poverty, achievement of gender equality, and protection of natural resources. Chapter 2 below examines how one donor, the World Bank, in working with client countries uses land law reform as a tool for poverty reduction and growth. Chapter 3 looks at how land law reforms can achieve gender equity, while chapters 4 and 5 explore how land titling and land market reforms can be more sensitive to the needs of the poor. Chapter 6 examines how law reforms relating to natural resources and the environment impact the poor. Finally, chapter 7 brings together what has been learned to see what common themes emerge.

Chapter 2, "Reform of Land Law in the Context of World Bank Lending," considers how land law reform is achieved through World Bank initiatives. The Bank has not always clearly enunciated the policies behind such law reforms. There is no Operational Policy on Land, though a number of operational policies, such as those on Involuntary Resettlement and Indigenous Peoples, have land law content, spelling out rights that must be honored in the context of Bank projects. The thinking within the Bank on land policies was, however, restated in 2003 in a new PRR on *Land Policies for Growth and Poverty Reduction.*[7]

The Bank seeks policy changes and law reforms in the context of development policy lending (formerly called adjustment lending). The central purpose of such loans is reform of policy and law. Poverty Reduction Support Credits (PRSCs), the newest form of development policy lending, provide unique opportunities for the Bank to press for comprehensive legal reforms and may be the future of the Bank's involvement in law reform.

However, much of the interaction between Bank staff and client governments on reforms in land law still takes place in the course of investment lending, loans by the Bank to finance specific development activities. While the Bank sometimes has pursued reform of land law in the context of natural resource management or land reform programs, the primary opportunity for land law reform lies in the Bank's land administration projects. These projects assist governments in gaining control of their land resource and in implementing both policy and law reforms. Sometimes the Bank may require basic reforms even before a project will be considered, such as concentration in a single agency of all the competences needed for a successful program of systematic land titling and registration. It is also common for such projects to call for reforms in the legal framework for

---

[7] *See supra* n. 1.

titling and registration itself so that the project can go forward efficiently. While changes in law are sometimes made a condition of the loan, it is more common these days for the project to include a component that funds policy studies, policy reform, and legal reform. The project becomes a forum in which reform issues can be assessed, solutions devised, and policy makers persuaded that reforms are needed.

A final section of chapter 2 deals with lessons learned about process in land law reform. The thinking-out of policy reforms should precede and inform law reform, and the more participatory the law reform, the greater the ownership of the reform by both the implementing agency and those who will be affected. However, in the time frames of project cycles, there is a premium on attaining reforms sooner rather than later. Often the project manager must "seize the day." Political windows of opportunity for law reform can open and close in the space of a few months, and good practice in land law reform is frequently a casualty of the need to seize political opportunities.

In chapter 3, "Overcoming Gender Biases in Established and Transitional Property Rights Systems," Renée Giovarelli examines reform of rules affecting women's access to and rights in land. This is an area in which broad prescriptions are difficult, given the cultural embeddedness of inheritance and other rules governing women's roles and rights with regard to land. Few areas provide so many illustrations of the limits of law as an instrument of social change.

Analytically, the chapter deals with these issues as they arise in four situations:

- *The creation of new rights by state action:* This can come about when the State confers property rights, as in land settlement programs; privatization of state or collective lands in societies transitioning from communism to market economies; and the individualization of customary land tenure systems. The State must decide if it is conferring titles on individuals, on households, or even on the head of household as representing other household members. Its decisions often disadvantage women. Remarkably, these choices are often not spelled out clearly; the vagueness generally works to the disadvantage of women.
- *Recording of land rights:* The confirmation and recognition of existing rights by the State, for instance through land registration, is a process that is often said to simply record rights that already exist. In practice, the process has sometimes altered or simplified rights recorded, to the disadvantage of women and others. Recognition of informal unions and joint titling of husbands and wives are important measures for avoiding negative impacts on women.
- *The legal framework for land markets:* The impacts of the legal framework affect women's access to land and their participation in land markets.

Women may fare differently in informal and formal land markets, it is suggested, and a thoughtful approach to gendered impacts should accompany any liberalization of land markets.

- *Intrahousehold allocations of land:* It is here that the cultural element in land law makes itself felt most strongly, as women seek to gain and conserve land rights at critical life events, such as inheritance, divorce, and being widowed. Bride-price and dowry condition expectations. Reforms are hard-won in this area and nowhere are the limits of law as an instrument of coercion more evident. The task of reformers is to change minds as well as laws.

The new development goals stress poverty reduction, but are our policy and law reform prescriptions always compatible with poverty reduction? The Bank has been a major proponent of market liberalization, and more specifically land market liberalization. Does land market liberalization have a positive impact on the poor? There is lively debate on this both within and outside the Bank, and of course there is no pat answer that is correct for all times and places and time frames.

Leonard Rolfes, Jr., examines some answers in chapter 4, "A Framework for Land Market Law with the Poor in Mind." He asks how land markets can be developed while adverse effects on the poor are minimized and positive impacts are enhanced. The chapter first reviews the essentials required for effective development of land markets: a rule of law context, recognition of robust property rights, effective conflict resolution mechanisms, state restraint in taking private land rights, and effective documentation of land rights. It then goes on to examine ways to increase the efficiency of land markets. Since we know that smallholders can be highly efficient, markets that are better at recognizing efficiency and rewarding it should benefit the land-poor. Essential legal elements for various transactions (sales, mortgages, leases, etc.) are discussed.

Even if the legal framework for land markets is satisfactory, however, and land markets are relatively efficient, other factors often intervene to limit positive impacts on the poor. The most prominent of these are distortions in credit markets. Access to credit is commonly skewed against the poor, even those who have land. Special efforts are needed to help the poor access land through markets. Chapter 4 discusses restrictions of marketability and scale intended to help the smallholder, public education and legal aid, progressive land taxation, public land auctions, and land reform, including community-based—what the author calls "market-facilitated"—land reform. Rolfes discusses the importance to the poor of recent findings that land reform that provides small homestead and garden plots to the poor can be remarkably effective in raising incomes.

Rolfes reminds us that the poor have an interest in the efficiency of land markets because they are indeed efficient producers and efficient markets should move land to them. An adequate legal framework for land markets—not just ownership but leasehold markets as well—is part of the answer, but there is also need to recognize that credit market imperfections often prevent land markets from serving the interests of the poor and reducing poverty. Markets can be made friendlier to the poor, Rolfes indicates, but specific measures may be needed to assure positive impacts on the poor, and those impacts must be monitored carefully.

The importance of titling and registration of land rights that is noted in all the preceding chapters and is the focus of chapter 5, David Bledsoe's "Can Land Titling and Registration Reduce Poverty?" The Bank supports major land titling and registration programs around the world; twenty projects now active involve substantial titling activity. Titling is critical in the creation of new property systems in post-communist societies. It constitutes state recognition of the property rights of citizens. There has long been discussion of how titling may increase investment and growth, for instance by improving access to credit through mortgaging, and there is some empirical evidence to support this, but, as Bledsoe points out, there is little empirical evidence that titling and registration can improve the lot of the poor.

Bledsoe begins by reviewing the evidence on the impact of titling and registration on economic growth, noting how heavily it leans upon a single thirty-year-old study from Thailand. He goes on to look at evidence regarding titling and poverty alleviation, asking whether the poor benefit, whether they need titles, and whether some programs tend to exclude them from titling or at least disadvantage them, as in the case of sporadic titling. He urges the donor community to draw up common criteria and indicators for assessing the impact of titling and registration programs; include in any titling project assessment a poverty-targeting strategy and careful impact analysis; examine consistently any potential of projects to exclude women and others; and alter management and staffing of these projects to be more inclusive of women and others susceptible to exclusion or negative impacts.

Equity and poverty alleviation have a large role in the MDGs, but conservation and environmental protection have a high profile as well. Robert Mitchell in chapter 6, "Property Rights and Environmentally Sound Management of Farmland and Forests," asks whether, in addition to meeting growth and poverty alleviation objectives, the legal framework for property rights can also affect conservation. Much of the legal discourse about reforms to protect natural resources has been about regulation, but many developing country governments have weak governance systems and limited ability to enforce complex regulatory frameworks. Is it then necessary to rely on different mixes of incentive-creating property rights and regulations (backed by sanctions) in developing countries?

Mitchell first examines the legal framework for conservation: the role of individual property rights and the long-time horizons they provide to land users, increasing incentives for good husbandry; the relevance of group rights in property by communities and user groups (common property) in forests and other natural resources; and the regulatory tools available to governments, enhanced in recent years by international agreements that create new obligations on the part of national governments to regulate and conserve.

Mitchell then turns to policies and legal tools governments can use to promote conservation. For farmlands, these typically include strengthened property rights, policies affecting incentives to convert forests to farmland, zoning, and land reform, because placing land in the hands of smallholders with property rights encourages both intensive land use and good husbandry.

Mitchell moves on to review the poor record of the State as a conservator of forests in the Third World and the legal needs of the alternative, which is community resource management, such as group property rights, group definition, group legal personality, and delimitation of group territories. A cooperative agreement between the forestry agency and the community is a key legal instrument, usually requiring agreement to a management plan as a condition of access to and use of the resource.

Finally, chapter 6 looks at property rights in trees. Some legal systems that do not recognized private ownership of land do recognize ownership of trees. Indeed, planting trees under many customary land tenure systems can give rise to rights in the land where they are planted. Instead of property rights being needed to provide incentives for investment in land, as most economic models envisage, the prospect of gaining property rights is the incentive for the investment.

The key to natural resource management lies in finding a balance of incentives generated by property rights and disincentives, created by sanctions, for defying regulations. In countries with weak governance, at least, reliance on incentives needs to be maximized, making enforcement of regulations more manageable.

Chapter 7, the "Conclusion," seeks to draw out from the needs identified in the five papers basic implications for the coming generation of land law reforms.

CHAPTER 2

Reform of Land Law in the Context of World Bank Lending

John W. Bruce*

2.1   Introduction

In the course of their work, World Bank staff members are often confronted by the need for reform of laws relating to land. This may happen when they engage with national development officials on policies and strategies or, in narrower project contexts, when inadequacies in land law threaten to undermine achievement of project objectives and must therefore be addressed.

Issues of land law reform and implementation arise in the context both of conventional investment lending and of the development policy lending (including the new Poverty Reduction Support Credits [PRSCs]) that has in recent years come to represent a major proportion of Bank lending. This chapter explores some of the salient substantive issues in land law reform but its primary purpose is to explain how the Bank and its staff work through these issues with client countries in the context of Bank programs and projects.[1]

The chapter first examines the role that land law plays in accomplishing the development objectives of the Bank. It then asks where Bank staff turn for guidance on land policy to inform land law reform decisions. In this context it notes not only recent policy research publications relating to land but also operational policies of the Bank that have implications for land law reform. It then examines contractual approaches used by the Bank and its clients to agree on needed

---

* For this chapter the author has drawn upon his own project experience and reviewed documentation from recent Bank projects for further instances of law reform. Mr. Zhongzhi Gao, a legal intern from American University, Washington College of Law, provided invaluable assistance in this review. The picture painted here should be fairly representative but it is certainly not exhaustive, and some relevant examples may have escaped notice. The views expressed in this chapter are those of the author and do not necessarily reflect the views of the World Bank.

[1] The World Bank has long recognized the importance of the assistance with law reform that it provides to client countries, but the process has been documented only in general terms. *See* World Bank, *World Bank and Legal Technical Assistance: Initial Lessons* vol. 1, Policy Research Working Paper No. WPS 1414 (Legal Department) (World Bank 1995).

reforms, and how these are used in both nonproject and project contexts. Land administration projects funded by the Bank offer a substantial body of experience for this examination but natural resource management and other projects are considered as well. Looking beyond particular projects, the chapter then considers issues of process and style in land law reform that confront project managers, their clients, and lawyers. Finally, it attempts to identify what is needed to make Bank assistance to its clients on land law reform more effective.

The relationship between land law and the Bank's objectives of economic growth and poverty reduction are examined briefly as a prelude.

2.2   Land Law and the Bank's Objectives

From a broad land law and policy perspective, key tasks facing the Bank's client countries are strengthening private property rights; development and regulation of land markets; framing appropriate regimes for compulsory land acquisition for public purposes; reforming state land management; design of effective land use regulations; accommodating the legal diversity represented by customary, religious, and national law; reforming land administration institutions; and expanding access of disadvantaged groups to land.[2] While the Bank has concerned itself with all these areas in its many project contexts, its practice has prioritized the issues of robust property rights and their delivery to land users.

There is a well-developed body of legal and economic theory connecting property rights with economic growth. Strong property rights provide security of tenure, which in turn enhances incentives for investment. Property rights minimize externalities and allow landowners in market economies to pursue economic efficiency with fewer constraints. Rights to buy and sell land are the basis for a market in land, which can place land in the hands of more efficient users, those who are able to pay more for the land. Rights to mortgage land can improve access to credit and the terms of market access to land.

Economists associated with the Bank have played an important role in empirically substantiating these propositions and thinking through their implications for development policy.[3] Though this discussion has become increasing nuanced,

---

[2] *Law and Sustainable Development Since Rio: Legal Trends in Agriculture and Natural Resource Management,* FAO Legislative Study 73, particularly chapter 8, "Land," 203, 210 (FAO 2002).

[3] Gershon Feder, *Land Policies and Farm Productivity in Thailand* (Johns Hopkins University Press 1988); and Gershon Feder & D. Feeny, *Land Tenure and Property Rights: Theory and Implications for Development Policy,* 5(1) World Bank Economic Review 135–53 (1991). *See also* Frank F. K. Byamugisha, *How Land Registration Affects Financial Development and Economic Growth in Thailand,* World Bank Policy Research Working Paper 2241 (World Bank 1999).

it continues to reflect confidence in the fundamental importance of property rights and markets in them.[4]

There is broad consensus on these points, subject to important and obvious caveats with regard to their predictive value in specific circumstances. For example, the ability to mortgage land will not provide access to credit in the absence of lending institutions that can provide credit to landowners, and a market in land will not move land to efficient producers where those producers are unable to access credit. Land law reform, if it is to have its desired impact, must be sequenced in relation to, and coordinated with, other institutional, economic, and legal reforms.

There is less consensus with regard to the impact on the poor of the creation of more robust property rights systems—even on the "landed poor," the world's smallholders. Because many of the poor have weak land rights that are based on custom or occupation and are not recognized by national law, this debate has in recent years been couched in terms of "formality" and "informality."[5] The question then is whether the poor benefit from "formalizing" (recognizing by national law) their "informal" land rights. On the one hand, as Hernando de Soto suggests, the granting to the poor of formal and well-documented property rights in land not only confirms their rights but dramatically increases the value of the land and creates new opportunities for them.[6] On the other hand, it is less clear how well the poor and their land fare in land markets. Their poverty makes them subject to desperation sales, and the ability to market land is a two-edged sword. De Janvry *et al.*, reviewing the literature, conclude that while land sales markets are generally hostile to the poor, there are circumstances where land markets can work effectively to give them access to land.[7] The Bank's 2003 PRR on land is not optimistic about sales markets as a means for the poor to access land and suggests broader use of rental markets for this purpose.[8] No consensus on this seems likely to emerge soon. There is a pressing need for further studies to more adequately identify indicators that predict the impacts of land markets on the poor, in

---

[4] Klaus Deininger, *Land Policies for Growth and Poverty Reduction,* World Bank Policy Research Report (World Bank & Oxford University Press 2003). The primary focus of the report is on rural land policy.

[5] Characterization of customary land tenure as "informal" is common but misleading. Custom in fact represents an alternative formality, reflecting culturally embedded values and clear claims of right, managed by subnational social institutions with important interests and often political influence. The situation is quite different from that of squatters.

[6] *See* Hernando de Soto, *The Mystery of Capital: Why Capitalism Triumphs in the West and Fails Everywhere Else* 39–46 (Basic Books 2002).

[7] *See* Alain de Janvry, Gustavo Gordillo, Jean-Philippe Plateau & Elizabeth Sadoulet, *Access to Land, Rural Poverty and Public Action* 3 (Oxford University Press 2001).

[8] *See* Deininger, *supra* n. 4, at 84–98.

particular the poor who do have access to some land. These considerations should weigh heavily on those making land policy and designing land projects.

On the other hand, the case for strong property rights in land goes beyond the micro-impacts on households to creation of capital for development. As de Soto famously argues in *The Mystery of Capital,* land in many developing countries is "dead capital," capital that can only be made alive by legal reforms. In a developed economy, he writes, the rights in each piece of land are represented by a document, and through that document

> assets can live an invisible, parallel life alongside their material existence. They can be used as collateral for credit. . . . These assets can also provide a link to the owner's credit history, an accountable address for the collection of debts and taxes, the basis for the creation of reliable and universal public utilities, and a foundation for the creation of securities (like mortgage-backed bonds) that can then be rediscounted and sold in secondary markets.[9]

That may be the long-term future of land law in developing countries but in the short term careful attention to the phasing and sequencing of reforms is needed. There is need for direct attention to impacts on the poor. Vested interests, those of both property owners and land administration bureaucracies, demand accommodation. The legal task is not just stating where one wants to go (the legal objective) but how one gets there from where one is (the legal status quo). Because existing land tenure and institutions are so historically particularistic, varying greatly from country to country and even within countries, the task of planning this transformation, which is the task of land law reform, will never be simple or standardized. Because there will be winners and losers in the process, it will always be political.

Good policy makes for good law reform. The next sections of this chapter therefore consider the policy guidance available to Bank staff working on reform of the law relating to land.

2.3 General Guidance on Land Policy and Law Reform

Land policy and the law concerning land were not the subject of significant discussion at the Bretton Woods meetings that constituted the Bank; nor are they referred to in the Bank's Articles of Agreement (Bank's Articles). The Bank does not have an authoritative policy either on land or on property rights in land. This may in part be because the Bank is an international organization, part of the United Nations system, and land law and property rights were ideologically contested territory during the Cold War, the formative years of the Bank. They remain so, though to a lesser degree.

---

[9] *See* de Soto, *supra* n. 6, at 6.

International agreements and treaties often provide the basis for the Bank to work with its members on policy and law reform. This can be seen clearly in the case of environmental policy and law.[10] Many Bank clients are parties to these agreements; in the environmental area, international agreements have been accepted broadly enough to allow an argument that they are changing customary international law.

But property rights in land are, under international law, largely the business of the national state. A State has the right to establish its own property system so long as it is not repugnant to international law. While the Universal Declaration of Human Rights[11] states in Article 17 that "Everyone has the right to own property alone as well as in association with others" and that such right "shall not be arbitrarily deprived,"[12] international law does not dictate the content of property rights and the objects to which they apply. There is today no universally accepted standard for appropriate compensation for "takings" of land. This is a critical issue, since viability of property rights hinges heavily on the compensation that must be paid when the State expropriates them. Recognition of property rights without a guarantee of adequate compensation for taking has little meaning. Seidl-Hohenveldern *et al.*, chronicle the decline in the United Nations, after 1946, of an internationally protected right to compensation for the taking of property. More recently, however, due in part to the role played by the European Convention on Human Rights and Fundamental Freedoms,[13] some ground has been regained.[14]

---

[10] David Freestone, *Incorporating Sustainable Development Concerns into the Development and Investment Process—The World Bank Experience* in *Exploitation of Natural Resources in the 21st Century* 91 (M. Fitzmaurice & M. Szuniewicz, eds., Kluwer Law International 2003).

[11] Adopted and proclaimed by General Assembly Resolution 217 A (III) of December 10, 1948, U.N. Doc A/810 at 71 (1948).

[12] While art. 17(2) of the Universal Declaration of Human Rights of 1948 provides a guarantee against arbitrary deprivations of property, the section of the Secretariat draft that would have required just compensation did not appear in the final version. When the rights proclaimed in the Declaration were rendered operational in the International Covenants on Human Rights, all other rights were dealt with in these covenants except the guarantee against arbitrary deprivation of property. *See* Ignaz Seidl-Hohenveldern, *International Economic Law* 128 (3d rev. ed., Kluwer Law International 1999).

[13] *See* 213 U.N.T.S. 222, entered into force September 3, 1953, as amended by Protocols Nos. 3, 5, 8, and 11, which entered into force on September 21, 1970, December 20, 1971, January 1, 1990, and November 1, 1998, respectively.

[14] *See* Seidl-Hohenveldern, *supra* n. 12, at 126–28; *Oppenheim's International Law* vol. I: Peace, 921–26 (Robert Jennings & Arthur Watts eds., 9th ed., Longman 1992); and Rudolf Dolzer, *Expropriation and Nationalization*, in *Encyclopedia of Public International Law*, vol. II, 319–26 (Rudolf Bernhardt, ed., 1992). Seidl-Hohenveldern, writing most recently (1999), sees the work of the European Convention on Human Rights as representing a revitalization of the classic criteria for fair compensation (*see id.*, at 128).

The trend toward greater recognition of the critical role of property rights in land is reflected in a variety of recent declarations by international development agencies. Documents from the United Nations Conference on Environment and Development (UNCED) held in Rio, in particular Agenda 21, contain many references to land and property rights. Because indigenous peoples have been disadvantaged even in countries that offer private property rights in land, there are now a number of conventions that contain strong guarantees of their property rights in land. The International Labour Organization's (ILO) Convention No. C169, the Convention Concerning Indigenous and Tribal Peoples in Independent Countries, adopted in 1989 and ratified primarily by Latin American countries, requires recognition of the ownership rights of indigenous peoples over land traditionally occupied and calls on governments to take the necessary steps to identify and protect those rights.[15] Recent jurisprudence under the International Covenant on Civil and Political Rights (ICCPR)[16] interprets its provision on the right of indigenous people to enjoy their culture to include rights to land.[17] Similar trends are evident in the jurisprudence of the Inter-American Court of Human Rights in construing the American Convention on Human Rights.[18]

It must still be admitted that the development of clear and binding international norms in the area of property rights in land lags well behind that for environmental law. In the absence of such standards, where do Bank staff turn for policy prescriptions? They generally argue from first principles, such as the Bank's mandates to promote economic growth and fight poverty, mediated by economic understandings concerning land rights. Bank economists working with land issues have written important pieces on land policy;[19] these are distinguished from much other economic writing in the field by their sense of history. There has, however, been little *authoritative* guidance for staff.

---

[15] Article 14(2) of the Convention Concerning Indigenous and Tribal Peoples in Independent Countries, (ILO No. 169), 72 ILO Official Bull. 59, entered into force September 5, 1991.

[16] United Nations General Assembly Resolution 2200A (XXI), 21 U.N. GAOR Supp. (No. 16) at 52, U.N. Doc. A/6316 (1966), 999 U.N.T.S. 171, entered into force March 23, 1976.

[17] *See id.,* art. 27.

[18] *See supra* n. 2, at 209. *See also,* O.A.S. Treaty Series No. 36, 1144 U.N.T.S. 123, entered into force July 18, 1978.

[19] In particular *see* Klaus Deininger & Hans Binswanger, *The Evolution of the World Bank's Land Policy* in de Janvry *et al., supra* n. 7, at 407, which discusses the economic bases for Bank practice; in referring to the Bank's "land policy" in inverted commas it suggests that while this has not been officially declared, for instance in an Operational Policy, its outlines can be seen in numerous Bank documents and in Bank practice.

Recently, this position improved substantially with publication of a policy research report on "Land Policies for Growth and Poverty Reduction."[20] A PRR is not simply a statement of research findings; it also contains policy prescriptions discussed at the highest levels of the Bank. This report involved considerable consultation with both those outside the Bank and with the Bank's Land Policy and Administration Thematic Group,[21] composed largely of those who work on Bank land projects. These prescriptions are not binding on operational staff, but the Bank seeks to make the findings known among staff and clients, and the recommendations are influential.[22] Most Bank staff pursue objectives in land policy and land law reform roughly consistent with these principles.

In addition to these policy prescriptions, there is some guidance on specific issues that is binding on Bank staff. This is discussed in the following section on legal guidance.

2.4   Legal Guidance: The Operational Policies

The policies that bind Bank staff are Operational Policies (OPs) and Bank Procedure Notes (BPs). These are operational rules rather than general policy statements. The recently revised OP on Forestry (OP 4.36, November 2002), for example, does not attempt to say what are good or bad policies concerning forestry generally, except for brief recognition of consensus objectives, such as conservation and sustainable use. It instead says what the Bank does and does not do and how it does it. It specifies, for example, the circumstances under which the Bank will fund commercial logging. The trend in the drafting of these OPs is toward ever-greater operational specificity and away from broad statements of aspirations.

The Bank does not have an OP on land. Such a policy would be difficult to frame, given the diversity of national land situations and the substantial political and cultural content of land policy and law. There are, however, a few key policy statements regarding land in three OPs. These OPs constitute *binding* rules, though the texts must be carefully examined to answer the question, "Binding in what contexts?" They deal with land in the contexts of: (a) expropriation disputes

---

[20] *See* Deininger, *supra* n. 4.

[21] The Land Policy and Administration Thematic Group (TG) is a voluntary group of Bank staff working on land projects and policy. Attached to the Agricultural and Rural Development Department in the Bank, it is the primary vehicle for continuity in thinking on land issues in the Bank. Information and documentation from the TG can be accessed at http://www.worldbank.org/landpolicy.

[22] This seems to have been the fate of a 1975 sector policy report on land reform, of which few in the Bank are still aware—it appears to have fallen into what lawyers call "desuetude." *See* World Bank, *Land Reform: Sector Paper* (World Bank 1975).

among Bank members;[23] (b) involuntary resettlement;[24] and (c) dealings with indigenous peoples.[25] The latter two are designated as "safeguard policies," which are intended to avoid or mitigate possible negative impacts of Bank projects on those affected. The three policies are discussed here in turn.

The Bank's OP 7.40 (July 2001) on Disputes over Defaults on External Debt, Expropriation, and Breach of Contract, in paragraphs 5–8 dealing with disputes over expropriation, states a Bank policy on expropriation of land and other properties. Paragraph 5 provides that "The Bank recognizes that a member country may expropriate property of aliens in accordance with applicable legal procedures, in pursuance in good faith of a public purpose, without discrimination on the basis of nationality, and against payment of appropriate compensation." Paragraph 7 specifies that "The Bank does not lend for the purpose of enabling a country to expropriate an enterprise by providing the funds needed for compensation. However, if the question of compensation is satisfactorily settled, the fact of expropriation does not, of itself, prevent the Bank from lending, in appropriate cases, to enlarge or improve properties that have been expropriated."

The Bank's OP on Involuntary Resettlement (OP 4.12, December 2001, revised April 2004) seeks to avoid or mitigate loss by affected populations of assets, including land assets, due to activities funded by Bank projects. The policy was framed initially to cover physical displacement by infrastructure projects but has broader application. Involuntary resettlement is the problematic action, and loss of land a form of damage, that should be considered in framing a compensation package. Today, the OP provides protection for those who lose access to assets but are not actually displaced in the sense of being moved to a new location. Its protections (framed in terms of a taking of land) apply to those occupying the land without legal right under national law ("informal occupants," squatters, or holders under custom unrecognized by national law).

OP 4.12 states, in paragraph 3, that the policy covers "direct economic and social impacts that both result from Bank-assisted investment projects, and are caused by (a) the involuntary taking of land." Paragraph 6(a)(iii) requires a resettlement policy framework or plan that calls for "prompt and effective compensation at full replacement cost for losses of assets attributable directly to the project." The preference in the case of land assets, stated in paragraph 11, is for provision of replacement land "for which a combination of productive potential,

---

[23] OP 7.40, Disputes over Defaults on External Debt, Expropriation, and Breach of Contract (July 2001).

[24] OP 4.12, Involuntary Resettlement (April 2004).

[25] OP 4.10, Indigenous Peoples (May 2005).

locational advantage, and other factors is at least equivalent to the advantages of the land taken."[26]

Similarly, the Bank's OP 4.10 on Indigenous People (May 2005)[27] seeks to ensure that indigenous peoples reap full benefits from Bank projects and are not inadvertently disadvantaged by them. The OP recognizes that "the identities and cultures of Indigenous Peoples are inextricably linked to the lands on which they live and the natural resources on which they depend."[28] It defines indigenous peoples in part by reference to their "collective attachment to geographically distinct habitats or ancestral territories . . . and to the natural resources in those habitats and territories."[29] In carrying out the Social Assessment and preparing the Indigenous Peoples Plan or Planning Framework, particular attention must be paid to "the customary rights of indigenous peoples, both individual and collective."[30]

Paragraph 17 further provides:

17.   If the project involves: (a) activities that are contingent on establishing legally recognized rights to lands and territories that Indigenous Peoples traditionally owned, or customarily used or occupied (such as land titling projects); or (b) the acquisition of such lands, the IPP sets forth an action plan for the legal recognition of such ownership, occupation, or usage. Normally, the action plan is undertaken prior to project implementation; in some cases, however, the action plan may need to be carried out concurrently with the project itself. Such legal recognition may take the form of:

(a) full legal recognition of existing customary land tenure systems of Indigenous Peoples; or
(b) conversion of customary usage rights to communal and/or individual ownership rights.

If neither option is possible under domestic law, the IPP includes measures for legal recognition of perpetual or long-term, renewable custodial or use rights.

These operational policies on involuntary resettlement and indigenous peoples can raise issues of land law reform during the design of Bank investment projects,

---

[26] The standards of compensation required here are reminiscent of those required by international law when the property of citizens of one nation is compulsorily acquired by the government of another nation. The classical formulation requires prompt compensation at market or replacement value, but recent practice has diverged from this, *see* Dolzer, *supra* n. 14, at 323–24, and Oppenheim, *supra* n. 14, at 926. International law does not hold governments to this standard for their own citizens.

[27] A revision of the previous Operational Directive (OD) on Indigenous Peoples, under discussion since 1999, was approved in 2005 as OP 4.10.

[28] *See id.,* paragraph 2.

[29] *See id.,* paragraph 4(b).

[30] *See id.,* paragraph 16(a).

but even when the Bank is not supporting legal reform, the good example pro-vided by the requirements of the OPs can be contagious. Compensation paid in one government project to displaced landholders can raise questions in the minds of those affected by other government projects as to whether they in fairness deserve the same treatment. The experience with the Involuntary Resettlement OP in Lesotho illustrates this: The standards for compensation for land under the Bank-funded Lesotho Highlands Water Project 1A 1991 (P001396) and 1B 1998 (P001409), which was provided for in a project-specific regulation,[31] raised expectations and generated demands that this become the national standard for compensation in cases of resettlement.[32]

A new OP may increase efforts to reconcile national law and standards in Bank safeguard policies. In 2005 the Bank approved an OP on Piloting the Use of Borrower Systems to Address Environmental and Social Safeguard Issues in Bank-Supported Projects (OP 4.00). Client countries whose national laws meet the objectives of those safeguard policies can be certified as such and will then need to worry only about their own laws in implementing Bank-funded projects.

How, then, does the Bank engage client countries in reform of the law relating to land? This can be done in an investment project context, in policy-based lend-ing contexts, and in policy development contexts outside lending programs. These are examined in the following sections.

2.5 Policy and Law Reform Outside the Project Context

The Bank has struggled over the years to find the right "door" through which to enter into dialogue with client countries on topics as sensitive as land policy reform. Deininger and Binswanger give some sense of the evolution in thinking on this matter:

> [T]he Bank discovered that the past approach of initiating narrow inter-ventions in individual areas (such as titling) to establish the basis for a broader policy dialogue did not reach this objective. It was gradually

---

[31] Lesotho Highlands Water Project Compensation (Amendment) Regulations, 1992.

[32] Kingdom of Lesotho, *Report of the Land Policy Review Commission* (Government Printer 2000). The report states, at page 43: "The issue of compensation for lost land has become a problem because there are no standard compensation rates to be followed. For instance the Lesotho Highlands Development Authority (LHDA) uses different compen-sation rates as compared to those used by Lesotho Housing and Land Development Corporation (LHDC). In recent times people have indicated that they want LHDA com-pensation rates to be used as they are relatively higher than the others. In some cases people who were given compensation some years back have come back claiming more compensation as soon as they discover that LHDA is paying more compensation."

replaced by a strategy that aims to base land market interventions on a broad and encompassing policy dialogue and consensus in the client country. In countries where land issues have in the past been the cause of wars, revolutions, and civil strife, reaching such a consensus requires time and a sustained dialogue on key policy issues between government, Non-governmental Organizations (NGOs), and civil society at large. Initiating such a process, ensuring its integration into a broader framework of rural development interventions, and strengthening the capacity of key players has become a critical component of the Bank's 'land policy.'[33]

It is in this context that the Bank and client governments have begun to address land law and policy issues as part of a systematic policy reform process. In this process, the Bank develops its lending program in countries by preparing Country Assistance Strategies (CAS) and Poverty Reduction Strategy Papers (PRSPs) with the client governments. These planning documents often identify certain areas of national land policy and law as requiring reform. The Bank assists clients in pursuing these reforms in a variety of project and program contexts, especially in connection with "policy lending." Policy lending, which is nonproject lending, includes both traditional Structural Adjustment Loans (SALs) and the new PRSCs. Because these loans have as their primary purpose changes in policy, they are an important vehicle for Bank support of policy and law reform.

Land law reform in both project and policy-lending situations will be discussed below, but to facilitate understanding of how this process works in Bank-funded efforts, it is important to introduce briefly the contractual tools available to the Bank and its clients in reaching agreement on law reforms.

2.6   Covenants and Conditions as Contractual Tools

The Bank and its clients use Bank funds to support important policy and legal reforms. Though the Bank cannot compel legal change by sovereign states, it does create incentives for governments to change laws: Funding for a project or part of a project may be conditioned on certain legal reforms. The ministry or other government agency that receives the funds often champions the legal reforms, though other government agencies and civil society may also support them.

---

[33] *See* Deininger and Binswanger, *supra* n. 19, at 406–40 (in particular 407).

In such cases, the Bank will usually require a change not just in policy but also in law, because policies bind only the government of the day, and only for so long as that government says that it is policy. Indeed in some national contexts, it is difficult to know what is necessary to authoritatively enunciate or change a government policy. There may be no tradition of governments making authoritative policy declarations, nor any standardized formalities for doing so. Bank staff familiar with the British/European Union model of a "green paper" for a draft policy and a "white paper" for a final authoritative policy statement will find that this is unknown in many countries. In one African client country recently, an attempt by consultants to press for a "white paper" was greeted with the sentiment that there was perhaps something racist about the notion. It may be that, if it is to become regular practice, the notion of a "policy declaration" requires some element of democracy in the political culture, with a citizenry that can demand to know what the government is going to do. Why else should the government tie its hands?

Changes in the law are a different matter. These are legally binding not only on the current government but also on the next government, unless they are repealed. They are far more reliable as indicators of success in the policy reform process than policy reform statements themselves, which can prove ephemeral.

In the Bank's lending instruments, the Bank and its clients can record their mutual commitments to legal reform in two ways, conditions or covenants. A *condition* is simply a future event that, if it does not happen as required, has consequences. It is a requirement that must be met before something happens, often before the loan is made. There may be, for instance, a condition of appraisal, a condition of negotiations, or a condition of disbursement. Sometimes legal reforms are called for as conditions: If the law reform is not accomplished, something specific will not happen. The consequence may be, for example, that the effective date of the loan is delayed, or that disbursement will not begin. Failure to meet the condition is not a breach, however, and does not trigger the responses triggered by a breach. Because a *covenant,* on the other hand, is a commitment undertaken by a party, failure to meet the commitment is a breach that may trigger a number of possible responses by the Bank, including suspension of the loan.

The Bank discourages the use of covenants to require law reforms because to do so would require the client government to commit its legislative branch to enact a law. In many countries this is not constitutional; nor is it generally desirable. Paragraph 14 of OP 7.00 on Lending Operations: Choice of Borrower and Contractual Arrangements (February 2001) states that rather than using covenants, where a change in law is necessary to achieve the objectives of the project, the change should be made the subject of a condition of negotiation,

Board presentation, effectiveness, or disbursement.[34] In both policy lending and investment lending, Bank managers and clients have recourse to conditions in the loan agreement or other agreements (e.g., letters of development policy, agreed minutes of negotiations). Nevertheless, covenants, in particular dated covenants (a particular reform by a specified date), are[35] sometimes included in loan agreements; there are references to several in this chapter.

In recent years Bank management has urged restraint in the use of conditions and covenants. Conditionality, it is appreciated, is no substitute for government ownership of reforms. Based on recognition of the importance of such ownership, the Bank has since the late 1990s sought to reduce the number of conditions in its programs. There has thus been a decline in conditionality, most strongly for policy and law reform conditions and to a lesser extent for conditions related to financial management.

2.7   Reform in the Context of Development Policy Lending

Casual observers of the Bank may think of its work in terms of investment projects, such as those that fund roads and dams, and even social and economic infrastructures, such as schools and government offices. In fact an ever-larger part of Bank lending, more than a fourth of new commitments in the most recent fiscal year, falls outside traditional investment projects and into the realm of

---

[34] The Bank's OP 7.00 on Lending Operations: Choice of Borrower and Contractual Arrangements (February 2001) provides in paragraph 14 that:

> The Bank does not stipulate covenants that require the member to enact legislation, and tries to work within existing law to the extent possible [footnote omitted]. If enactment of particular legislation is necessary to achieve the project's objectives, the appropriate steps to be taken for such enactment should be clearly defined; and such enactment is made a condition of negotiation, Board presentation, effectiveness, or disbursement, rather than a covenant.

Footnote 14 to paragraph 14 goes on to explain that:

> Development policy loans require often [sic] entail significant changes in existing laws, regulations, and administrative practices. The legislative steps to be undertaken are normally described in the Letter of Development Policy (see para.16), but may also be part of the specific actions incorporated in the Loan Agreement as conditions of Board presentation or conditions of disbursement of particular loan tranches, rather than as covenants.

[35] Zhanar Abdildina & Jaime Jaramillo-Vallejo, *Streamlining Conditionality in World Bank—and International Monetary Fund—Supported Programs,* in *Conditionality Revisited, Concepts, Experiences, and Lessons* 85–91 (Stefan Koeberle, Harold Bedoya, Peter Silarszky & Gero Verheyen, eds., World Bank 2005). Unfortunately, no figures are available for earlier and more recent levels of conditionality in land projects.

"development policy lending." This includes both the older SALs and new vehicles like PRSCs.[36]

The framework for this is set out in OP 8.60 on Development Policy Lending (2004). The purpose of such lending is "to help a borrower achieve sustainable reductions in poverty through a program of policy and institutional actions that promote growth and enhance the well-being and increase the income of poor people."[37] Such lending aims, *inter alia,* "to promote competitive market structures (for example, [through] legal and regulatory reform)."[38] Because policy change and support of its implementation are the *raison d'être* for development policy lending, conditions often involve legal reforms. "The legislative steps to be undertaken are normally described in the Letter of Development Policy (see para. 16) but may also be part of the specific actions incorporated in the Loan Agreement as conditions of Board presentation or conditions of disbursement of particular loan tranches, rather than as covenants."[39] The Letter of Development is written by a client government official to the World Bank as part of the lead-up to the loan, for instance a PRSC. Progress in achieving reforms will later be reviewed in the Program Document for the PRSC. As countries usually have a succession of PRSCs, this process repeats itself: a statement of intention followed by an assessment of progress in the program document, followed by a further policy letter, and so on.

For example, the Bank is currently working with the Government of Vietnam on land policy and legal development, which are dealt with under the Vietnam Second Poverty Reduction Support Credit, 2003 (P075398). The Letter of Development Policy (LDP)[40] for the credit provides, in paragraph 54, that the program

---

[36] FY 2005 new commitments consisted of US$16,215.44 million for investment projects and US$6,604.68 for development policy projects. *See* http://web/worldbank.org/external/projects/main?page.

[37] OP 8.60, Development Policy Lending (August 2004), para. 2. The decision to proceed to development policy lending with a client country is made in the context of the Country Assistance Strategy (CAS) preparation; factors considered include the overall soundness of the macroeconomic framework, the strength of the policy development program, the strength of the government's commitment to the program, the ability of the government to implement the program, and the country's track record on policy reform. The Bank consults on such programs through CAS discussions and through discussions of other country strategies, such as the Poverty Reduction Strategy Paper (PRSP) in International Development Association (IDA) countries and the country overall and sectoral development policies in IBRD countries (OP 8.60, paras. 3 and 6).

[38] World Bank, *World Bank Lending Instruments; Resources for Development* (World Bank 2003).

[39] *See supra* n. 34.

[40] Letter of Development Policy (May 30, 2003), from the Governor of the Bank of Vietnam to the President of the World Bank, available at http://www.worldbank.org.

will support issuance of land tenure certificates, noting that land-use rights that can be traded and mortgaged provide several benefits, especially for the poor. The Development Credit Agreement (DCA) for the project, in schedule 2, notes progress made to date: issuance of land-use right certificates to (i) about 35 percent of users of urban residential land; and (ii) in forest areas, about 60 percent of households and individual land users who have received or rented forest land directly from the State. The Letter goes on to state, in paragraph 80, that under future PRSCs:

> [T]he National Assembly is expected to adopt a new, substantially revised Land Law, which will provide greater land-tenure security and equal access to land by all sectors, that is correspondent with the customs and habits of the communities that are using the land legally. Registration and other civil transactions relating to land use rights will be simplified. Especially, land use rights and project bidding methods will be applied widely for the cases when credit organizations fail to collect their debts. Issuance of Land Tenure Certificates will be continued under PRSCs.

In Rwanda, the Bank is again working for legal reform relating to land. This is dealt with in the Rwanda Institutional Reform Credit Project (Structural Adjustment), 2003 (P066385). In this case, the medium-term (through 2005) policy and institutional objectives as set out in the Program Document called for improving productivity of rural assets while recapitalizing these assets and aimed for "a land policy and land law that provides security of tenure, gives women land inheritance and ownership rights, and provides overall land use."[41] Immediate benchmarks were adoption of a land policy by October 2002 and submission of a land law to the National Assembly by 2003.[42]

The experience under two successive Uganda Poverty Reduction Support Credits (1 and 2) (P050438 (2001) and P073671 (2002)) provides insight into some of the opportunities and limitations of Bank assistance using the PRSC mechanism. The Bank, through loans for the Agricultural Secretariat in the Bank of Uganda, played an important role in the development of post-Amin land policy, largely through funding for a research and policy development exercise involving the Makerere Institute of Social Research at Makerere University and the Land Tenure Center of the University of Wisconsin–Madison. The process culminated in the detailed provisions on land in the 1995 Constitution and the

---

[41] Program Document, Rwanda Institutional Reform Credit Program (Structural Adjustment), 2003 (P066385), annex A.

[42] *See id.*

constitutionally mandated Land Act of 1998.[43] The UK's Department for International Development (DFID) carried the burden of technical assistance for preparation of the Act and later for public education and amendment of the Act to scale down a too ambitious and ultimately unaffordable administrative framework for its implementation.[44]

The Land Act and its implementation figured prominently in the Uganda PRSC discussion, which initially targeted amendment of the Land Act, approval of a Land Sector Strategic Plan, and implementation of the Land Act. In particular, amendment of the Act was required to address women's limited rights in land and the fact that the original Act had prescribed a staffing pattern for decentralized land administration that the country could not afford. The Act was amended and the Strategic Plan adopted as envisaged, but implementation has been very limited. For a third PRSC, 2003 (P074081), implementation objectives were stated more specifically and narrowly, focusing on actual staffing and decentralized financial arrangements, and on completion of pilot work. A new law on mortgages was encouraged.[45]

The slow progress is largely the result of inadequacy of the resources for implementation committed by the Government of Uganda. This reflects the political weakness of the Ministry of Water, Lands and Environment. Policy loans, while they state targets for law and policy reform or their implementation, do not directly support those processes. The funding provided is in the nature of general budgetary support; in Uganda, this has not strengthened the capacity of that Ministry.

In Tanzania, the 2003 PRSC (P074072) and Grant[46] identified a number of inadequacies in the Land Acts, particularly related to collateralization, foreclosure, consent by spouse, customary and small mortgages, default notice, and third-party mortgages. Under this initial PRSC, the Ministry of Lands prepared a position paper on changes that may be needed in the laws. Drafting of amendments to the Land Act and their delivery to parliament for approval were made

---

[43] Patrick McAuslan recounts the making of the 1998 Land Act from his perspective as one involved in the drafting, in "As Good as It Gets: Politics and Markets in the Making of Uganda's Land Act, 1998," in Patrick McAuslan, *Bringing the Law Back In: Essays in Land, Law and Development* 275–309 (Ashgate Publishing Ltd. 2003).

[44] McAuslan gives his personal view of the history of the DFID's Securing Sustainable Livelihoods Through Land Reform Project in "Men Behaving Badly: A Narrative of Land Reform," *see id.,* at 310–52.

[45] The Letter of Development Policy from the Minister of Finance, Planning and Development to the President of the World Bank, July 23, 2003, noted progress made to date and focused on financial planning for decentralized land administration and on passage of a Mortgage Decree.

[46] Program Document, Tanzania PRSC 2003, at 33.

trigger conditions for the 2004 PRSC (P074073). The LDP for this Second PRSC[47] noted that the act was amended in February 2004, clearing the way for individuals and firms to use their land as collateral. For a proposed Third PRSC, the Bank and the Government are discussing preparation and approval by the Government of regulations for implementing the amended Land Act.

Policy lending, while a powerful tool for law reform because governments desire these effectively untied funds, may be less effective in ensuring a good legislative result or implementation of new law. First, in contrast to land investment projects, project preparation sometimes does not mobilize effectively expertise on land law and policy, within and outside the Bank, at the time the conditionality is designed. Second, it does not allow focused application of loan funds to support particular activities; the assistance consists of broad budgetary support to the client government. Third, the policy loan may not adequately provide for effective technical assistance to the client government in meeting its policy and law reform obligations. (This may be mitigated where there is also an investment project in place to support these activities, or such support is available from another donor.)

Let us turn now to experiences with investment projects where Bank loan funds support specific activities that include land policy and law reform.

2.8   Reform in the Investment Project Context

During preparation of any investment project, the Task Team should (and usually will) ask, in light of the objectives of the project, whether there is an adequate legal framework for the planned activities. If the project concerns or relies upon significant mobilization of land as a resource, for instance in an infrastructure or agricultural project, then the adequacy of the law relating to land must be investigated. How rights are defined and distributed can affect how intended beneficiaries respond to the opportunities offered by a project. Land rights also play an important role in determining who benefits from projects; an inadequate legal framework can create serious risk of failure to attain such project objectives as poverty alleviation.

It may be that if fundamental legal reforms are needed to achieve the objectives of an investment project, it is better not to proceed to negotiation of the loan; the time may not be ripe for the project. It might be possible to condition Board presentation or loan effectiveness on legal reforms, but passing laws take time, which could entail extended periods of uncertainty. If the project team is confident that a needed reform will be forthcoming shortly, they may recommend conditioning disbursement of funds on the legal reform.

---

[47] Letter of Development Policy from the Minister of Finance of Tanzania to the President of the World Bank, June 30, 2004.

In most cases, the flaw in the legal framework affects some subset of activities under the project, so the condition on disbursement may be only for the affected component. Recognizing the need for government to respect the legislative branch's prerogatives, the condition usually takes the form of a commitment by government to prepare and submit legislation to the legislative branch by a particular date rather than a commitment to enact the legislation. Where all that is needed is a change in regulations that need not go to the legislature but can be accomplished by the executive, the condition may require the change.

The most common investment project contexts for engagement with client governments on reforms of the law relating to land are, not surprisingly, "land projects." These fall into three major categories:

1. The numerous land administration projects, which generally seek to build the capacity of government to administer property systems, assist in implementation of land privatization, and support the survey and titling of land-holdings.
2. Land reform projects, through which the Bank seeks to improve access of the poor to land and to increase efficiency by downscaling to more manageable operating units, often family-operated units.
3. Natural resource management projects, in which land law issues often arise, especially common property issues.

In the sections that follow, the issues raised in each project type are explored and a few projects in each category are examined in detail.

2.9   Land Administration Projects

Land administration projects account for the majority of "land lending" by the Bank. Because they have produced a rich body of experience, they are discussed at some length here.

The Bank helps client governments to provide their citizens with greater security of tenure and more open land markets. It loans exclusively to governments, for which land administration—the provision of a legal framework and the public infrastructure for private markets in land rights—is an appropriate task. The main thrust of Bank funding in this area has been to support the provision and documentation of land rights. In some contexts, like Eastern Europe and the former Soviet Union, this involves *titling,* the conferring upon landholders by the State of a right to land. In others, property rights exist but have not been effectively documented. In these circumstances, the Bank has often supported registration of those rights.

In both contexts, the Bank has often used a system of recording land rights known as *systematic title registration*.[48] Systematic title registration is based upon a careful mapping of parcels that creates a registry organized by parcel; each parcel is shown on a large map with its unique number, with a register of land rights for that parcel identified by the same unique number. The basis for registration is a field operation for demarcation and survey of boundaries and adjudication of rights. That process moves from parcel to parcel in a locale officially declared an "adjudication area," gathering the needed information and informally mediating or adjudicating disputes, subject to appeal to the courts. The systematic process is in some cases compulsory, in others voluntary; but because people are generally anxious to have their rights registered and only nominal fees are charged, normally almost all parcels in an area can be adjudicated in a single field operation. This systematic approach works well for registration of existing rights and is also very effective where the client government wants to grant new land rights: to "title" as well as register land.

Because the process is painstaking, participatory, and very reliable, its registration of a title can be given extraordinary legal effect: it is often provided that the title cannot be affected by any right not shown on the register or that it is "indefeasible." Often it is said that the State guarantees the title shown on such a register, which is literally true in some but not all national systems. The certainty created allows anyone contemplating a transaction to rely confidently on the register to show who is the legal owner of the land.[49]

Bank projects generally prefer to support systematic ("mass") registration of titles rather than registration in response to the request of individuals ("sporadic registration"). Great efficiencies stem from avoidance of repeated trips to the field by surveyors and other staff involved in the process. The systematic

---

[48] *See* Deininger, *supra* n. 4, at 71. This system of registering title is called "Torrens Title" after its inventor, Sir Robert Torrens, the first Premier of the State of South Australia. This system of titling is now used in many parts of the world, having been transferred during the colonial period by the British and French and more recently through the efforts of donor agencies. It makes registration of a title conclusive of right to the property. This means that any person checking the title register can be sure that the party who is shown on the register as the owner is indeed legally the owner.

[49] Deeds registration, an older system, allows right-holders to record the document on which their rights are based (their deeds) in a register. The entry is made only at the initiative of the owner of the land. This is called "sporadic" registration to distinguish it from "systematic registration." Not all parcels or transactions get on the register, and registration does not confirm the title, so it is a much less reliable source of information on ownership. The entries are usually chronological and connected only to a map of the parcel itself that is appended to the deed. Key publications on systems of titling include the classic S. Rowton Simpson, *Land Law and Registration* (Cambridge University Press 1976) and, more recent and more technical, Peter F. Dale & John D. McLaughlin, *Land Administration* (Oxford University Press 1999).

approach is especially useful in major transitions, as when: (1) customary or informal rights are to be formalized; (2) state or collective land is being broken up into smaller holdings and privatized; or (3) it is simply desired to bring all land in an area onto a single efficient rights database.

Where the project is not just registering an existing right but conferring and documenting that right, it is engaged in "titling" rather than just registration. Systematic titling and registration, as practiced in Bank projects, is generally highly participatory and, because of the scale of operations, efficient. It is also fairer. Because everyone's land is registered at the same time, in a highly public venue with broad community involvement, the likelihood that boundaries of properties will be demarcated correctly is greater, and the chances are minimized that someone might, by fraud, get his neighbor's land registered in his name.

Systematic registration and titling, because it is a rigorous field operation involving checks and rechecks of the results, is expensive. Its appropriateness in deep rural areas and areas of low land value where markets are undeveloped is questionable. In such areas the system has often proven unsustainable.[50] Most titling under Bank projects is therefore focused on urban and peri-urban land and on high-value agricultural land, areas where land and credit markets are developing. This allows the system to generate fees based on transactions, which can help sustain the system.

While most Bank-funded land administration projects focus on systematic registration, they are often asked to support in addition some sporadic registration, where land is registered in response to requests from landholders. While this is a less efficient use of Bank funds, systematic titling may take fifteen or twenty years to cover a country, and in areas not yet reached by the process, there is a need to meet urgent demands from individuals.

A variety of legal issues concerning land arise in these land administration projects.

2.9.1   The Legal Framework for Land Registration

Almost all land administration projects have a component that supports strengthening the legal and regulatory framework for project activities, and almost all of those components seek some reform of the legal framework for land registration.[51] Where these reforms may be absolutely necessary for the project to

---

[50] *Searching for Land Tenure Security in Africa* (John Bruce & Shem Migot-Adholla, eds., Kendall-Hunt Publishing 1993).

[51] An interesting exception is the Bank's prototype land administration project for Asia, the three-stage Thailand Land Titling Project. The project is still cited as best practice in the Bank. The first two stages managed to work within existing laws and regulations with no discussion of legal reform; only in the PAD for the third project (Thailand Land Titling Project III, 1995 (P004803)) is there a suggestion of a need for modest changes in the regulatory frameworks.

achieve its objectives, they are most likely the subject of conditions. In land administration projects, the first step is to ensure that laws governing the three basic tasks—adjudication, survey, and titling—are adequate.[52]

Experienced Bank task managers are quite familiar with the legal issues and models in this area. The key statutes are usually a Land Registration Act, a Land Adjudication Act, and a Land Survey Act, plus the regulations under these laws. But there are variations in the pattern; sometimes two of the acts are merged in one or the acts arranged differently in terms of the national hierarchy of laws. Some laws include considerable procedural detail, while in others these are left to regulations.

In Cambodia, for example, the Land Law of 2001 contains the basic legal framework for title registration, adjudication, and survey but few details.[53] The details are spelled out in substantial subdecrees and regulations. The Bank's Cambodia Land Management and Administration Project has focused its legal reform assistance on elaboration of the subsidiary legislation related to adjudication and titling.[54] If that

---

[52] For example, the Bank's Armenia Title Registration Project, 1999 (P057560), argued for a new Land Registration Law but had to make do with a 1979 enactment it considered marginal. The Moldova First Cadastre Project, 1999 (P035771), made enactment of such a law and implementing regulations a condition of presentation of the loan to the Bank's Board. The Ukraine Rural Land Titling and Cadastral Project, 2003 (P035777), made passage of a land law satisfactory to the Bank a precondition for the loan, and Parliament did pass such a law. Under the project, efforts will focus on drafting of a new mortgage law and procedures for implementing the Land Code. The Bank had also sought creation of a unified cadastre and title registry. As an interim measure, amendment of Cabinet of Ministers Resolution No. 689 dated May 15, 2003, provides for the gradual consolidation within the Cadastral Commission (CC) of registration activities carried out by a number of agencies. This was a precondition for disbursement of the cadastral development component of the project; passage of a cadastre and/or title registry law satisfactory to the Bank is a condition for disbursement of Phase 3 of the cadastral system development component of the loan. The Nicaragua Land Administration Project, 2002 (P056018), sought new laws, and a disbursement condition for the second tranche of the Nicaragua PRSC I, 2004 (P082885), is passage of the two laws by Congress.

[53] Land Law, promulgated as Royal Decree NS/RKM/0801/14, August 30, 2001, arts. 226–46.

[54] The Cambodia Land Management and Administration Project, 2002 (P070875), supported preparation of the following: Sub-Decree No. 46 ANK/BK of May 31, 2002, on the Procedures of Establishment Cadastral Index Map and Land Register; Sub-Decree No. 47 ANK/BK of May 31, 2002, on the Organization and Functioning of the Cadastral Commission; Sub-Decree No. 48 ANK/BK of May 31, 2002, on the Sporadic Land Registration; Prakas (regulation) of the Ministry of Land Management, Urban Planning and Construction No. 112 DNS/BrK of August 21, 2002, on the Guidelines and Procedures of the Cadastral Commission; and Ministry of Land Management, Urban Planning and Construction, No. 001DNS/SD, Instructive Circular Relating to the Implementation of the Procedure of Establishing the Cadastral Index Map and the Land Register (Systematic Registration), August 19, 2002.

does not require amendment, Bank attention will then turn to regulation that further detail key processes.[55]

Often there are specific deficiencies that prompt remedial legislation or regulations. Some issues that recur across projects (those listed here are only illustrative) are

(a) the need to restructure land administration institutions to avoid overlapping mandates, turf battles, and unnecessarily complex procedures that have high transaction costs, as in the Ghana Land Administration Project, 2004 (P071157) and the Philippines Land Administration Project, 2000 (P066069);

(b) the need to strengthen provisions on the legal conclusiveness of titling, an important issue in the Cambodia Land Management and Administration Project, 2002 (P070875);

(c) the need to provide more adequately for systematic adjudication of land rights, notably in the Guatemala Land Administration Project, 2000 (P049616), where the Bank conditioned effectiveness on satisfactory amendment by executive accord of the Peten Land Law with regard to adjudication;

(d) public access to the land register, notably in the Romania General Cadastre Project, 1998 (P034213);

(e) ways to register communal and community land assets, notably in the Cambodia Land Management and Administration Project, 2002 (P070875) and the Laos Second Land Titling Project, 1996 (P075006);

(f) ways to register co-owned land, in the Sri Lanka Land Titling and Related Services Project, 2001(P050738);

(g) the ability of adjudication officers to make decisions based on incomplete documentary evidence and to rely upon oral evidence, in the Sri Lanka Land Titling and Related Services Project, 2001 (P050738); and

---

[55] For example, the Bulgaria Registration and Cadastre Project, 2001 (P055021); the Slovenia Real Estate Registration Modernization Project, 2000 (P055304); the Indonesia Land Administration Project, 1994 (P003984); the Kyrgyz Republic Land and Real Estate Registration Project, 2000 (P049719); the Romania General Cadastre and Land Registration Project, 1998 (P034213); the Lao Land Titling Project, 1997 (P004208); and the Sri Lanka Land Titling and Related Services Project, 2001 (P050738). The Russian Federation Land Reform Implementation Support Project, 1995 (P034579), has a land registration component, and the conditions of effectiveness under VI in the DCA include "(d) issuance of procedures on registration of land and real estate acceptable to the Bank."

(h) the need for a clearer statement of the conditions under which errors in the register may be corrected, and by whom, an issue in the Cambodia Land Management and Administration Project, 2002 (P070875).

Bank land administration projects have generally had good success in improving the legal framework for land registration, but reforming land registration law is not easy. Opposition comes primarily from the vested interests of attorneys and notaries, whose income may be threatened by simpler, cheaper approaches. The seemingly technical nature of these laws is in fact misleading; apparently innocuous provisions can have controversial outcomes, for instance on the gender distribution of land rights.

One issue that has definite political resonance is the objection that legally conclusive titling confirms the ill-gotten gains of land-grabbers, frustrating future restitution claims. Where legal remedies are available, as where concessions can be terminated or reduced for failure to fulfill development conditions in the concession agreement, these injustices can be remedied without challenging efforts to protect security of tenure. But in many cases the rights will have been acquired legally and with due legal formalities, however much land-allocating officials may have abused their discretion. Confirmation of those rights is sometimes the price of confirming the rights of the poor and vulnerable as well.

2.9.2 Security of Tenure: Content of the Rights to be Registered

A threshold question in a land administration project is: what property rights in land are available, and are they robust enough to be worth registering? If the property rights available are anemic, the considerable cost to record them will not be worthwhile. To take an extreme example, it would hardly make sense to invest in systematic registration under a tenure system based on nontransferable one-year leases from government, subject to arbitrary revocation.

This issue is fundamental: as with computerization, simple registration of weak rights is "garbage in, garbage out." A Bank-funded project seeking to support security of tenure through title registration cannot ignore the fact that the State can take property without compensation, and if the project seeks to support development of land markets, it cannot ignore the fact that transactions in land are subject to onerous official consents. It must therefore seek to strengthen tenure as well as register it.

For example, the loan agreement concluded for the Ghana Land Administration Project, 2003 (P071157) reflects a concern with security of tenure through a disbursement condition that requires clarification satisfactory to the Bank of a constitutional issue concerning the continued validity of customary land rights.[56] A similar stress on robust rights for land administration projects can be seen in other countries as well, for instance in Indonesia,[57] Nicaragua,[58] and Bolivia.[59]

How much security of tenure is enough? There was a time when Bank task managers would have been comfortable with nothing less than full private ownership, with all the freedom of action that confers. However, experience and research have in recent years provided evidence that use rights, customary rights, and leasehold rights can provide farmers with security of tenure sufficient to their needs. In Southeast Asia, for example, Bank land administration projects often title land still under ultimate state ownership, so long as beneficiaries have relatively substantial and secure (and even inheritable and transferable) use rights in the land.[60] Recent Bank projects in Africa are registering not only formal tenures less than ownership but also customary rights in land—not seeking to transform them to private ownership, as was done in Kenya[61] in the 1960s and Malawi[62] in the 1980s, but registering the customary right on its own terms, as

---

[56] The PAD for the Ghana Land Administration Project, 2003 (P071157), in Part G(2)(iii), contains a condition of disbursement on specified components that requires the Government to provide "assurances, satisfactory to IDA, with respect to the continuing validity of customary freeholds and other traditional allocations of land." Article 267(5) of the 1992 Constitution placed this in doubt with a provision prohibiting the creation of any "freehold interest howsoever described" from chief's land, which some commentators have interpreted as outlawing the creation of, and possibly even undermining the validity of, "customary freeholds," as Ghana's common law courts call the primary right of use under customary law.

[57] The Indonesia Land Administration Project, 1994 (P003984), systematically reviewed existing laws on land, but with very limited impact. Reform of the legal and regulatory framework is a continuing concern of the Indonesia Land Management and Policy Development Project, 2004 (P064728).

[58] The Nicaragua Agricultural Technology and Land Management Project, 2002 (P056018), supported a national Committee for the Study of Agrarian Legislation in the hope of drafting a new law to consolidate and guarantee property rights, relying in part on a conditionality on the second tranche of an Agricultural Sector Loan from the Inter-American Development Bank (IADB) for passage of the law.

[59] The DCA (June 26, 1995) for the Bolivia National Land Administration Project, 1995 (P006197) in art. 5.01(a) requires amendment of several laws to achieve this end; the details are discussed thoroughly in the Letter of Land Policy of March 15, 1995, from the National Land Agency to the Bank.

[60] The Laos Land Titling Project, 1997 (P004208): the Cambodia Land Management and Administration Project, 2002 (P070875); and the Indonesian Land Administration Project, 1994 (P003984).

[61] The Bank supported registration of Kenyan agriculturalists under the Land Settlement Project, 1960 (P001219), and of groups of ranches in pastoralist areas under the Kenya Livestock Project (01), 1968 (P001228).

[62] Lilongwe Land Development Project (03), 1980 (P001598).

defined by customary law. The Côte d'Ivoire Rural Land Management and Community Infrastructure Project, 1998 (P001194) registered rights of households derived from customary law,[63] and the Ghana Land Administration Project, 2004 (P071157) will, on a pilot basis, register rights of customary land authorities and supports traditional land administration.[64]

Most Bank land administration projects address the issue of tenure more directly by supporting not just registration of existing rights but the conferring of new rights. These are land titling projects in which land registration has a "constitutive function," creating new land rights as it registers them. One important context in which land registration performs a titling function is the creation of new systems of property rights in land for citizens of states that are in transition out of systems of state or collective ownership of land resources. Bank land administration projects in Eastern Europe and the Commonwealth of Independent States (CIS) countries are examples. Here the adoption of western property rights systems is driven in part by the desire to be more competitive within Europe and may figure in EU accession discussions.[65] Because of the economic

---

[63] The experience with this project highlights a potential problem of basing titles too exclusively on customary rights: the danger of excluding immigrant communities, who may have weak or nonexistent customary rights. Land access for recent immigrants is a critical factor in the ethnic tensions underlying the current insurrection in Côte d'Ivoire. Similar complex problems of custom exist with insecurity of tenure under custom for former slave communities, or "guest lineages," whose ancestors "borrowed" land from older families in times of land plenty; and for women, who in some lineage systems have access to land only through husbands, not in their own right. *See* Jean-Pierre Chauveau, *The Land Question in Côte d'Ivoire,* Issue Paper No. 95, Drylands Program (International Institute for Environment and Development, August 2000); and Volker Stamm, *The Rural Land Plan: An Innovative Approach from Cote d'Ivoire,* Issue Paper No. 91, Drylands Program (International Institute for Environment and Development, March 2000).

[64] The project will pilot the titling of customary allodial rights (the ultimate ownership by the tribe or extended family, rather than individual or household rights) in Accra and Kumasi, where most urban land is under customary tenure. Implementation will raise complex issues of: (a) exactly what title is registered; (b) whether it is registered in the name of the community, the chief, or the chief as trustee for the community; and (c) who will prevail when there are disputes between a principal chief with primary allodial rights over a large territory and subchiefs who claim subsidiary allodial rights over subterritories. The project aims to support and reform the work of traditional land administrators, standardize procedures, make them more transparent and participatory, and improve record keeping. Implementation has just begun.

[65] The basic membership criteria for the EU as laid down at the Copenhagen Summit in June 1993 do not include reform of land law; indeed art. 259 of the Treaty Establishing the European Community states that "This treaty shall in no way prejudice the rules in Member States governing the system of property ownership." But once it has been agreed that an Eastern European country has met the basic membership criteria, accession discussions may raise land law issues: Poland's land acquisition policy became an issue, as did Hungary's discriminatory policies against foreign land ownership.

benefit, because of the desire to integrate with Europe, and because of prerevo-
lutionary traditions of private ownership of land, the Eastern European countries
have opted quite decisively for private ownership; some, such as Poland,
Yugoslavia, and Hungary, had retained a limited amount of land under private
ownership (household food plots, for instance) even under the Communist dis-
pensation. The Bank has sought robust property rights in these countries in order
to have tenure that is adequate to title.[66]

The needed reforms have perhaps come hardest in Central Asia. Some countries, such as the Kyrgyz Republic, have made the transition to private property
relatively quickly, but in others, such as Azerbaijan, Kazakhstan, Tajikistan, and
Uzbekistan, the reform process has been more halting. An anticipated land
administration project in Kazakhstan was cancelled in part because an earlier
project failed in its attempt to obtain a revision of the 1994 Land Code, which left
landholders vulnerable to revocation of their land rights by officials and was not
adequate for a market-oriented land economy.[67]

Some projects reflect narrower, more specific, concerns about property rights.
While security of tenure is important to investment, the economic model used by
the Bank to explain the productive impacts of titling[68] makes it clear that these
are best achieved through credit access and investment impacts, so land must be
mortgageable, and to be mortgageable, it must be marketable. The Bulgaria
Cadastral Project, 2001 (P055021), for example, focuses on problems with foreclosure under existing mortgage law and the condominium provisions of the law

---

[66] For some projects, passage of a land law with robust property rights has been treated as
a precondition for Bank involvement. The PADs for the projects for the Ukraine (Ukraine
Rural Land Titling and Cadastre Development Project, 2004 (P035777)) and the Kyrgyz
Republic (Kyrgyz Republic Land and Real Estate Registration Project, 2000 (P049719))
reflect the importance of such laws being passed before projects could be undertaken.

[67] The Kazakhstan Registration and Real Estate Rights Pilot Project, 1997 (P046044),
noted the need for reducing the ease with which officials could revoke land rights under
the 1994 Land Code and features of the existing law that limited transactions; the DCA
(May 16, 1997) (Schedule 5), had a number of conditions regarding institutional arrangements to ensure coordination between the cadastre and the land registry. The 1995 Structural Adjustment Loan (SAL) (P008502) to the Kazakh government contained a condition
in the DCA of June 12, 1995 (Schedule 4), concerning revision of the Code to simplify
procedures for land privatization and land transactions. The SAL required acceptance of
a new law by the Cabinet for submission to Parliament rather than actual passage. According to the Implementation Completion Report for the Registration and Real Estate Project
(June 1, 2001, at 13), a revised Land Code prepared with the participation of Bank-funded
legal consultants was submitted to Parliament but had to be retracted after severe political criticism: The institutional arrangements for the pilot had not functioned well, and
implementation of coordination between the cadastre and land registry had not been satisfactory. An anticipated follow-on project, Kazakhstan Registration and Real Estate
Rights Project 2, did not go forward. The Land Code was enacted in 2003.

[68] *See* Feder, *supra* n. 3, and Feder & Feeny, *supra* n. 3.

on ownership; the Kazakhstan Registration and Real Estate Rights Pilot Project, 1997 (P046044), on transferability of land rights; the Moldova First Cadastre Project, 1999 (P035771), on ending a moratorium on sales of agricultural land and eliminating a requirement that banks that were foreclosing had to resettle the owners of the land foreclosed; in the Kyrgyz Republic Land and Real Estate Registration Project, 2000 (P049719), on clarification and possible easing of a moratorium on land sales; and in the Ukraine Rural Land Titling and Cadastre Project, 2003 (P035777), on the need for a law on mortgages. The Sri Lanka Land Titling and Related Services Project, 2001 (P050738), which is also concerned with the removal of legal limits on the marketability of land, adopts an unusual approach to agreed-upon law reforms.[69]

2.9.3   Institutions: Getting Key Functions Under One Authority

One of the difficulties projects face—one that is especially serious for projects that seek to support systematic titling and registration of land—is that in some countries the involvement of several government agencies is required. For instance, the tasks of demarcation and survey of landholdings and the keeping of survey records may be the responsibility of one government agency, perhaps a Cadastral Institute, while the machinery for registration is housed in another, perhaps the Ministry of Lands, Interior, or Justice. This tends to cause serious inefficiencies when systematic titling and registration are attempted. It also substantially increases the costs and time required for registration of transactions.

The Bank has urged that key land administration functions be consolidated under one authority. It has generally sought to persuade client governments to remove registration (though not adjudication of land disputes) from the courts and even from the Ministry of Justice and consolidate it with the cadastral function in a single land agency. It is sometimes argued that while involving the judiciary as a second institution provides checks and balances, which reduce corruption, in some countries where the Bank is working on these issues, judges are

---

[69] The PAD describes the need for such reforms and anticipates dialogue on them during the project, but the DCA sets out no conditions, just a general statement in 4(2)(c) that government will "undertake" legal reforms regarding restrictions on land transactions and organization according to an agreed list. "Undertake" appears to refer to a good faith effort rather than enactment, and the list is detailed in the Minutes of Negotiation, which are not disclosed. Listing there does not create a legal obligation on the part of the client; it is simply a statement of shared intention. The list of legal reforms needed can be adjusted by agreement of the parties without amendment of the DCA, since they are not specified there but only incorporated by reference to the minutes.

poorly trained and corrupt and their involvement adds nothing but another hurdle to be negotiated.[70]

The fragmentation of land administration functions among several government agencies has been a particular problem in countries of Eastern Europe and the former Soviet Union. What is known in the region as the "One Agency" issue has been a major concern of Bank staff. While projects in One Agency countries (Armenia, Moldova, and Kyrgyz Republic) are performing well, projects in Two Agency countries (Bulgaria, Croatia, and Romania) perform less well. Some reforms have, however, been forthcoming. Bulgaria has passed a law that transfers the registration function out of the courts into the Ministry of Justice; Croatia has taken the same function away from judges and given it to clerks; and Romania has shifted the function out of the courts and the Ministry of Justice into the cadastral agency. Nevertheless, the issue continues to be a concern in other countries in transition, including Russia, Slovenia, and Ukraine.

The issue of fragmentation of land administration functions arises in other parts of the world as well. It has been addressed by the Bank and its clients successfully in Cambodia, El Salvador, and the Lao Peoples Democratic Republic (Lao PDR), where the Bank refused to move forward with the design of a project until land administration functions were consolidated in a single agency. While the issue is less often addressed in the Latin American context, legislation for a National Land Institute was sought under the Bolivia National Land Administration Project, 1995 (P006197).

Such a shift to a single institution can be contentious, especially in long-established systems. Because change threatens vested interests it can be difficult to achieve. The experience under the Philippines Land Administration and Management Project, 2000 (P066069) is illuminating. The project pursued one of its objectives, the unification of land administration functions in a single agency, by supporting the development of proposals along this line by the Ministry of Natural Resources. That Ministry did land titling and already operated a title registry. Its unification proposals were resisted by the Ministry of Justice, which operated a parallel judicial titling system, and the Agrarian Reform Agency, which also granted land rights. Power to reorganize units of government was vested in the Office of the President, and initially Presidential backing for the change seemed to insure success. However, it was determined that this reorganization was sufficiently contentious that it had to be sent to Congress, with the prospect of long delays. In the interim, the Ministry of Natural Resources

---

[70] This issue has sometimes been the subject of contention among donors. Some European donors, Germany in particular, manage efficient dual-agency systems that involve the courts. The EU, with both systems in use among its members, has not taken a position. Bank experts acknowledge that the German system works well but are skeptical that it can be replicated in countries in transition and so favor the single-agency model.

adopted a *de facto* "one stop shop" approach, setting up in each pilot titling area a land office which had space for each of the government agencies involved, hoping that proximity and encouragement could help achieve cooperation and efficiency without a legal consolidation. Late in the project, it was clear that this had not happened to the extent hoped, and the Ministry redoubled its efforts to move the unifying legislation that had been submitted to Congress out of committee and onto the floor for a vote. They failed to do so because of strong opposition from judges and lawyers. The Bank then embarked on a Land Administration and Management II Project, 2005 (P073206), with this need still on the agenda.

A similar issue arose in the Bank's urban titling work in Ghana under Ghana Urban II—Secondary Cities, 1990 (P000910). There, the older deed registry system, which covered scattered parcels around the country (primarily in urban areas), was to be replaced by a modern title registration system. It will take twenty to thirty years to expand the title registration system to cover the whole country. In the meantime, the older deed registry system remains operative in areas that have not been reached by systematic work because it is the only mechanism by which to obtain title in those areas and therefore cannot be done away with. The relationship between the two systems was not well spelled out in the law, and confused and competitive relations between the systems and agencies developed. Under a land-titling component in Ghana Urban II, the older Deeds Registry, based in the Ministry of Justice, failed to make available to the Title Registry the deed information for areas of Accra to be titled systematically. Because the systematic titling went forward without that information, there are contradictions between ownership records in the two systems.

The two systems continue to coexist. In cases of conflict, the courts in Accra tend to investigate the rights involved from scratch, undermining the usefulness of both systems and public confidence in the conclusiveness of title registration. Now that the Deeds Registry has been shifted to the Ministry of Lands, the Ghana Land Administration Project, 2004 (P071157), should not face similar problems. One lesson from this experience is that title registration laws should specifically provide for how old and new systems should relate during the transition and specify the ultimate authority of the title registry where conflicts arise.

2.9.4 The World Bank Operational Policy on Involuntary Resettlement

It was noted earlier[71] that the Bank OP on Involuntary Resettlement has land law content; task teams working on land administration projects must consider how this interacts with their projects.

---

[71] *See supra* section 2.4.

Discussions during the revision of the Involuntary Resettlement OP (OP 4.12, December 2001, revised April 2004) dealt explicitly with whether the titling components of land administration projects "triggered" the OP. It was suggested that when one claimant was adjudicated as owning the parcel rather than another, the losing party is displaced ("involuntarily resettled," in the language of the OP), in which case the OP would be triggered and its requirements of compensation for land and support for resettlement costs might apply. After task managers for land administration projects in the Bank's Land Policy and Administration Thematic Group argued vigorously that no adjudication system, including the courts, could work under such requirements, a footnote was added to the OP explicitly excluding land disputes between private individuals from the operation of the OP.[72]

Disputes between government and private individuals, however, were not excluded, and so are covered. A government, under a Bank-supported land administration project, must either (i) allow squatters to remain as squatters on the land it owns; preferably, (ii) provide them with secure rights to that land; or, if it evicts them, (iii) resettle them and compensate them. Some such cases will arise under almost any land administration project; they will be common where government owns extensive lands, which will invariably have some illegal occupants. Issues also commonly arise around methods of registering occupied public rights of way, which were often occupied before they were declared rights of way. A Resettlement Policy Framework (RPF), which is referenced in the credit agreement and thus commits the Bank and Government to an approach to resettlement consistent with the OP standards, can provide a basis for handling such cases as they arise.[73]

While an RPF can address this concern,[74] in most cases task managers and governments seek to design the project to avoid the possibility that displacements

---

[72] Footnote 8 to paragraph 3(a) of the OP states: "This policy also does not apply to disputes between private parties under titling projects, although it is good practice for the borrower to undertake a social assessment and implement measures to mitigate adverse social impacts, especially those affecting poor and vulnerable groups."

[73] There may be other reasons why an RPF needs to be done in a land administration project that has a public works component, such as construction of offices that will displace land users.

[74] The Involuntary Resettlement OP was triggered and addressed in the following land administration projects: Ghana Land Administration, 2004 (P071157) (for civil works, with a resettlement policy framework (RPF) prepared); Cambodia Land Management and Administration, 2002 (P070875) (by concerns re displacement, with an RPF prepared); Lao PDR Second Land Titling, 2003 (P071007) (for civil works, with an RPF prepared); and Panama Land Administration, 2001 (P050595), Nicaragua Land Administration, 2002 (P056018), and Honduras Land Administration, 2004 (P055991), all three of which prepared process frameworks to deal with livelihood impacts due to delimitation of protected areas and indigenous territories. Only in the Cambodia case does the applicability of the OP to government-private disputes seem to have been a consideration in addressing involuntary resettlement.

will occur that would trigger the OP. This understanding may be embodied in the Credit Agreement as conditions. For example, the Sri Lanka Land Titling and Related Services Project, 2001 (P050738) in Schedule 4 of the DCA provides that the government will not cause displacement or restrict access through titling of government land under the project (DCA, 4.3(a)). In other cases, where government land is occupied and an accommodation for the occupants cannot be reached, the land is simply not registered. Either approach avoids triggering the OP. Unfortunately, monitoring mechanisms are often not in place to ensure compliance with these understandings. Such approaches may avoid complications and speed the titling process, and may be consistent with the letter of the OP, but they potentially exclude vulnerable land users from the benefits of the project.

2.9.5   The World Bank Operational Policy on Indigenous Peoples

OP 4.10 provides that Bank-funded projects must seek to respect the rights and concerns of indigenous communities, even more than those of other land users. Paragraph 17 of the OP, which deals specifically with land titling projects, indicates a preference for legal recognition of those rights as either customary rights or individual and communal ownership rights, but where neither option is available under national law, it will accept legal recognition as "perpetual or long-term renewable custodial or use rights."

Few land administration projects have so far confronted these issues, primarily for two reasons:

1. Most indigenous peoples live at the fringe of development, in the mountains or in the rain forest, far from the high-value, increasingly commercialized land targeted for land registration.
2. The land rights of indigenous peoples are largely customary and there often does not exist, under national law, an adequate legal framework for recording customary land rights. Indeed the communities that own such land may not even be recognized as legal persons under national law, making it difficult to register land in their name.

These are problems for state provision of security of tenure to any community that relies on customary land tenure rights, whether or not the group meets the Bank's criteria for an indigenous people.

In these circumstances, the land administration project is often designed to avoid areas where customary law, including that of indigenous peoples, applies— task managers may be particularly cautious because early titling projects in

Africa have been roundly criticized as having botched the conversion of customary land to individual titles[75]—but some projects attempt to develop a policy and legal framework for registration of land affected by customary tenure.

A phased approach, for instance, is spelled out in the Project Appraisal Document (PAD) for the Indonesia Land Administration Project, 1994 (P003984):

1. Exclude areas with *hak ulayat* (customary communal land rights) from areas for systematic adjudication under the project.
2. Do not register systematically any *hak ulayat* land if such is found in the project area.
3. Examine the feasibility, desirability, and methodology of registering *hak ulayat* in three selected areas through *adat* [customary] land right studies.
4. Identify issues related to such rights.

Toward the end of the project, in part as a result of these discussions, Government enacted a regulation providing for registration of communal land rights.[76]

Another project dealing with this issue is the Cambodia Land Management and Administration Project, 2002 (P070875). Here there is a legal basis for titling: the Land Act 2001 provides for the ownership of land by indigenous peoples and for the titling of that land.[77] The NGO community has given effective

---

[75] Parker Shipton, *The Kenyan Land Tenure Reform: Misunderstandings in the Public Creation of Private Property,* in *Land and Society in Contemporary Africa* (R.E. Downs & S.P. Reyna, eds., University of New Hampshire Press 1988); Simon Coldham, *The Effect of Registration of Title upon Customary Land Rights in Kenya,* 22(2) Journal of African Law 91–111 (1978); and Shem Migot-Adholla *et al., Security of Tenure and Land Productivity in Kenya* in Bruce & Migot-Adholla (eds.) *supra* n. 50, at 119–40.

[76] Regulation of Minister of State for Agrarian Affairs/Head of BPN, No. 5 of 1999, Guide to Settlement of Issues Related to Adat Law, Communities' Ulayat Rights, in art. 4. This is a less than comprehensive legal solution to the issue, however, and the extent of implementation is unclear. The issue remains on the agendas of both the client and the Bank, and will be highlighted if current plans for decentralization of land administration in Indonesia move forward.

[77] The rights of indigenous communities are dealt with in arts. 23–28, particularly art. 26, which states: "Ownership of the immovable properties described in Article 25 [land traditionally used] is granted by the State to the indigenous communities as collective ownership. This collective ownership includes all of the rights and protections of ownership as are enjoyed by private owners. But the community does not have the right to dispose of any collective ownership that is State public property to any person or group. The exercise of all ownership rights related to immovable properties of a community and the specific conditions of the land use shall be subject to the responsibility of the traditional authorities and mechanisms for decision-making of the community, according to their customs, and shall be subject to the laws of general enforcement related to immovable properties, such as the law on environmental protection."

voice to the demands of indigenous peoples in the mountainous areas in the west of the country for protection of their land. GTZ[78] technical assistance under the project is now supporting a pilot study, with demarcation and adjudication, in two indigenous communities. The current project does not plan to title these lands, as they are outside the project provinces, but the communities may elect to do so on the basis of the pilot work carried out. The experience of the pilot will inform the development of detailed regulations on titling of customary lands, to supplement the single authorizing article in the Land Law.

2.9.6   Gender and Land

The World Bank has an OP 4.20 on Gender and Development[79] that, while it calls for nondiscrimination, does not specifically mention property rights. Nor does it provide explicit guidance on how to operationalize nondiscrimination in project contexts. Task managers of land administration projects do, however, confront important land law issues that affect women differently than men. Land administration projects can influence the initial gender distribution of land rights at watershed transitions in property systems, for instance from state to private ownership or from customary to state systems. Failure to provide wives with land rights can affect their standing in the community, their bargaining power within their households, and their sense of self-worth. It can also result in real landlessness and poverty when women are widowed, divorced, or abandoned. Any serious attempt to address poverty issues in the land sector must deal with this problem.[80]

For state or collective ownership systems, initial land distributions to households during reform normally are based on household size and household members are listed on distribution documents. Specific shares in hectares may be allocated for each household member. But there is a tendency for the State to then deal with the new farm family as a household through the household head, usually a man, and for the title to be issued in the name only of the head of household.[81]

---

[78] Deutsche Gesellschaft für Technische Zusammenarbeit (GTZ) GmbH is a nonprofit international corporation for sustainable development with worldwide operations; it implements much of Germany's development assistance program (*see* http://www.gtz.de/english).

[79] OP 4.20, Gender and Development (March 2003).

[80] For a classic examination of these issues for Latin America, *see* C. D. Deere & M. León, *Empowering Women: Land and Property Rights in Latin America* (University of Pittsburgh Press 2001).

[81] A thorough study exists for Albania: Susana Lastarria-Cornhiel & Rachel Wheeler, *Gender, Ethnicity and Landed Property in Albania,* Working Paper No. 18, Albania Series (Land Tenure Center, U. Wisconsin–Madison 1998). While a number of unpublished reports on the gender impacts of privatization have been done by units within the Bank, they are largely anecdotal, with little data on outcomes.

In the transition from customary land tenure to formalized systems, similar problems arise. Often this transition involves individualization, with greater rights to sell or mortgage, and the titling process commonly vests rights exclusively in the male head of household. In the patrilineal systems that predominate in most of Africa, the man does "own" the household land, but wives have protections under custom that tend to be neglected in the adjudication process, such as the obligation of a husband to provide his wife with land to farm, which is common in many systems.

How do these issues arise in the context of land administration projects? In land titling women may be given titles, jointly titled with their husbands, or titled only when they are household heads. In systematic adjudication of rights, such rights as women have in land may either be recorded or they may be neglected. In a title registration system, where unregistered rights are ineffective, this creates the risk that women's rights will be lost because they are not recorded. These issues are not often confronted directly by land administration projects. It is commonly assumed that national law is adequate if it does not *de jure* discriminate against women in landholding, but experience shows that even where women have valid legal claims upon land, they can be lost in the registration process if adjudication staff do not take affirmative action.

The Bank has not sponsored major reform legislation on this issue, but it has encouraged greater gender inclusiveness in the rights registration process through reform of implementation procedures. In the Philippines, for instance, the Land Administration and Management Project, 2000 (P066069) played a major role in obtaining the 2002 repeal of a 1936 administrative order; the repeal removed gender bias in the acceptance and processing of applications for homestead patents and other applications for public lands.[82]

A number of other land administration projects, while not seeking changes in law, have been proactive in ensuring that the rights women do have are not lost when rights are adjudicated. This is a serious concern, because even when the law gives women rights to land, in practice there are cultural reasons and reasons related to authority within the household that may lead to failure to record women's rights during adjudication.

Two East Asian efforts supported by the Bank have recently addressed these issues and been recognized as good practice. The first is the Lao PDR Land Titling Project, 1996 (P004208), which incorporated gender sensitivity training

---

[82] Para. 8 of the Land Administrative Order 7–1 (April 30, 1936), "Rules and Regulations Governing the Filing and Disposition of Applications of Alienable Lands of the Public Domain or for Real Properties in the Commonwealth of the Philippines," was repealed by Department of Natural Resources Administration Order No. 13, Series of 2002.

for field adjudication staff and public education campaigns that covered, *inter alia,* women's land rights issues. Moreover, the Lao Women's Union (LWU) has been integrated into implementation of the project.[83]

The second good practice case comes from Vietnam, where the 2001 Decree No. 70 on Implementation of the Marriage and Family Law required that all registrations of land use rights must be in the names of both spouses. The Bank supported a pilot program that focused on such activities as ensuring that forms used in adjudication were appropriate for joint titling and that requirements of documentation (for example, tax receipts, usually in the husband's name) did not stand in the way of women asserting their rights. The project substantially increased the number of parcels registered to women, especially the number of parcels registered jointly to husbands and wives. The case makes the point that simply reframing forms can have a major impact.[84]

The Land Policy and Administration Thematic Group and the Gender and Development Thematic Group in the Bank recently completed a portfolio review of gender in land administration projects and sponsored four case studies of land administration and reform projects (in Azerbaijan, Bolivia, Ghana, and Lao PDR). The Bank has now published a document synthesizing these studies.[85]

How far can the Bank and its clients go in promoting women's land rights as part of the titling process? The project must comply with national law and cannot force the registration of rights that women do not have. But in the field adjudication process, there are opportunities for convincing beneficiary families to register their land jointly. Husbands and wives may agree to joint titling of land even where it is not required under national law, and projects can quite legitimately encourage them to do so through public education activities, pointing out the legal advantages of joint titling for the family.[86]

---

[83] Zongmin Li, *The Lao People's Democratic Republic: Preserving Women's Rights in Land Titling* (*Module 9, Investments in Land Administration, Policy and Markets*), in *Agricultural Investment Sourcebook,* 411–12 Agricultural and Rural Development Department (World Bank 2004).

[84] Kabir Kumar, *Land Use Rights and Gender Equality in Vietnam,* Engendering Development No. 1 (World Bank 2002).

[85] World Bank, *Gender Issues and Best Practices in Land Administration Projects, A Synthesis Report* (World Bank 2005), prepared by consultants Renée Giovarelli, Susana Lastarria, Elizabeth Katz, and Sue Nichols, is an unusually thorough and frank look at the handling of gender issues in four Bank land projects.

[86] The experience of three countries with joint titling is reviewed in Susana Lastarria-Cornhiel *et al., Joint Titling in Nicaragua, Indonesia and Honduras: Rapid Appraisal Synthesis* (Land Tenure Center, U. Wisconsin–Madison 2003).

2.9.7 Settling Land Disputes

Land administration projects support adjudication of land disputes in the process of systematic field operations to resolve conflicting claims to land. Though this is of great importance to the success of these projects, it can only be treated summarily here; it deserves a paper of its own. The law governing systematic adjudication generally provides for a field mediation procedure, which may be carried out by an adjudication officer (a member of the government team), possibly assisted by local assessors or by a local mediation committee created for the purpose. The committee is in some cases given the status of a local court; it may even be chaired by a judge. Where the court system is seriously inadequate, projects sometimes support a second level of mediation institutions for cases where local mediation fails. They may even fund legal assistance for the poor and disadvantaged to help level the playing field.

For example, the Cambodia Land Management and Administration Project, 2002 (P070875), supports a system of Cadastral Commissions at the district, provincial, and national levels to hear appeals of field adjudications. Replacing an older dispute settlement commission structure in the Ministry of Interior, the system brings this function under the Ministry of Lands. The Cadastral Commission was created pursuant to Article 47 of the 2001 Land Law. Where local mediation fails, the parties can take their dispute to the district and then the provincial commission, each of which again mediates. The National Commission, if a dispute reaches it, is mandated by Article 47 to render a decision, which is subject to judicial review at the request of a dissatisfied party.[87]

The project has funded the drafting of regulations to govern the proceedings of these commissions[88] as well as training and equipping them. That support, provided initially only to areas being titled under the project, was recently expanded to the Cadastral Commission nationwide, if on a more modest scale. The project is also providing funding for an NGO, Legal Aid of Cambodia, to expand its activities to provide poor and disadvantaged parties with advice and representation before the commissions. The disputes for which legal aid is being provided in the pilot phase involve villages or other groups of claimants that have been expelled from land they claim by government agencies, in particular the military and the forestry department. It is too early to assess the success of this program. [89]

---

[87] Unfortunately, art. 47 does not state to which courts appeals should be taken from decisions of the National Cadastral Commission, a subject being discussed by the Ministry of Lands and the Ministry of Justice.

[88] Sub-Decree No. 47 ANK/BK of May 31, 2002, on the Organization and Functioning of the Cadastral Commission.

[89] The courts may be reluctant to share the dispute settlement function. The Cambodian Ministry of Justice unsuccessfully raised the issue of whether the national law on the judiciary or even the Constitution had by assigning this competence to the judiciary precluded nonjudicial settlement of disputes.

There are other cases of support by land administration projects for dispute settlement beyond the field adjudication work, especially in Bolivia, Guatemala, and Nicaragua, and in the case of Guatemala, for the provision of free legal services.[90]

2.10   Land Reform

The Bank has for some time been involved in land reform in a variety of contexts; its work on land reform has received new impetus from the recent emphasis on poverty alleviation. The World Development Report 2000/1 emphasizes the vulnerability created by a lack of assets: "Lack of adequate assets can set up a vicious spiral in which actions to cope in the short term [such as distress sales of land] worsen deprivation in the long run."[91] The Bank's 2004 PRR on Land emphasizes that land is both the major element of wealth for most rural households and the basis for attempts by most of those households to escape poverty.[92] Poverty is thus as much about lack of assets as it is about income; to place a durable productive asset in the hands of the poor is a remarkably effective way to fight poverty.

Donor support for land reform has waxed and waned since World War II. The optimism engendered by the East Asia reforms of the 1950s gave way to pessimism in the wake of problematic reforms in Latin America in the 1960s and 1970s, reforms that were politically deeply divisive and were often rolled back when the party in power changed. In some countries, land reform gave rise to large bureaucracies that failed to efficiently deliver land and needed support for beneficiaries.[93] Though economists in the Bank have argued the economic case for land reform since at least the mid-1970s,[94] finding the right implementation strategies has been difficult. In the 1980s and 1990s, land reform meant the breakup of collective and state enterprises in the postsocialist world—a process the Bank has assisted primarily through titling and registration projects for new private landholders, as for example in the Kyrgyz Republic Land and Real Estate Registration

---

[90] Bolivia National Land Administration Project, 1995 (P006197), Guatemala Land Administration Project, 2000 (P049616), and Nicaragua Land Administration Project, 2002 (P056018).

[91] World Bank, *World Development Report 2000/2001, Attacking Poverty; Opportunity, Empowerment and Security* 34 and 39 (World Bank 2001).

[92] World Bank & Klaus Deininger, *Land Policies for Growth and Poverty Reduction. A World Bank Policy Research Paper xx* (World Bank & Oxford University Press 2003).

[93] The Latin American reforms of the 1960s and 1970s were evaluated during the 1980s. *See* Alain de Janvry, *The Agrarian Question and Agrarian Reformism in Latin America* (Johns Hopkins University Press 1981); *Searching for Agrarian Reform in Latin America* (William C. Thiesenhusen, ed., Unwin Hyman 1989); and Peter Dorner, *Latin American Land Reforms in Theory and Practice: A Retrospective Analysis* (University of Wisconsin Press 1992).

[94] World Bank, *Land Reform: Sector Paper* (World Bank 1975).

Project, 2000 (P049719). The Bank has, however, sometimes been involved in designing the regulatory framework for implementing the land reform itself, as in the Tajikistan Farm and Privatization Support Project, 1999 (P049718).

Today a new generation of Bank land reform projects is implementing an alternative approach, "community-based land reform," in which Bank funds are provided to groups of beneficiaries to purchase land. The Bank's pilot work with this concept had earlier been hampered by a Bank rule against disbursement against land,[95] but in 2003 the Managing Director exempted community-based land reform projects from this prohibition and set up a Community Land Purchase Committee within the Bank to vet projects and monitor success. In August 2004, the "expenditure eligibility" reforms, designed to loosen a variety of restrictions on the activities the Bank can fund, did away more broadly with the prohibition of use of Bank funds for land purchases. However, it maintained a Land Purchase Committee both to review projects seeking approval for land purchases and to craft guidance for Bank staff on use of land purchases in a much broader range of contexts.

The community-based land reform approach, with its reliance on the market mechanism, is not (as is sometimes suggested) grounded in an idealization of markets but rather on a recognition that land sale markets will not, left to themselves, move land to those who have too little, although the land-poor are efficient producers.[96] Early experience suggests that this reform model is a relatively efficient way to move land to the poor because it reduces political tensions, bureaucratic inefficiencies and corruption, and court disputes.

The legal issues that arise in the community-based land reform projects are of quite a different nature than those arising in compulsory land acquisition programs. Under the criteria applied by the Land Purchase Committee, a project will be approved to purchase land only where the purchase is for a productive purpose, where the land market is sufficiently developed to provide an efficient means of transferring land, and where mechanisms are in place to ensure safe handling of funds. These requirements, originating with the mandates of productivity and efficiency in the Bank's Articles,[97] are legal rather than merely practical requirements. They necessitate careful inquiry into (a) the forms of

---

[95] The prohibition was included in para. 2(b) of OP 12.00 on Disbursement (February 1997), now repealed, where land was listed among items against which Bank funds could not be disbursed.

[96] There are a number of reasons why markets do not move land to the poor, even though smallholders are remarkably efficient producers; the most important involve distortions in the credit market that deny the poor access to credit to purchase land. In addition, the value of land in agriculture is inflated by its potential value in other uses to levels that farmers cannot afford. *See* Deininger, *supra* n. 4, 96–97.

[97] *See* art. 1, International Bank of Reconstruction and Development, Articles of Agreement (as amended, effective February 16, 1989).

tenure available; (b) whether the seller has good title to the land to be purchased; (c) the efficiency of the land market (including regulatory restrictions, credit market imperfections, and the distortions that both introduce into the land market itself); and (d) the forms of organization available for beneficiary groups, which must provide the juridical personality required to hold land.

The flagship project is the Brazil Land-Based Poverty Alleviation Project, 2001 (P050772). It was possible to acquire this experience before there was an exemption for land purchases using Bank funds because the client governments were able and willing to provide the purchase funds while the Bank covered relocation and investment costs. This project extends to several Brazilian states a program piloted in 1996–97 in the State of Ceara (Ceara Rural Poverty Alleviation Project (Ln 3918-BR)). The pilot showed that the process used was effective and agile, beneficiaries responded well to the opportunity, and the prices obtained compared favorably with those paid in compulsory acquisitions. Early experience with loan repayments, after a five-year grace period expired, has been positive. Concerns of land reform advocates about the impact of the new project on the federal compulsory acquisition program were alleviated by a decision that the new project will not fund purchases of any land eligible for taking under the federal program of compulsory acquisition, establishing a complementary relationship between the two programs.

The PADs and the DCAs for both the pilot and the new project are devoid of concerns, conditions, or covenants relating to reform of the law relating to land. This is because the large holdings to be purchased under this program belong to a formalized land sector, one in which full private ownership is well established, land is registered, and the legal framework for land transactions is relatively well developed. Unlike compulsory acquisition programs, there is not a series of legal hurdles to be surmounted under this model—just the normal requirements for valid land transactions. There is a good deal of legal work required under such a project in terms of drawing up articles of association or incorporation of the group, the loan agreement to the community for the purchase, land conveyancing, registration of sales, the mortgage burdening the initial group title, arrangements for titling when the mortgage is repaid by the beneficiaries, and arrangements for legal subdivision of the land once the group has title (*de facto* subdivision will usually have been accomplished earlier). But these are all relatively routine matters in the Brazilian legal system.

The first project operating under the exception allowing the purchase of land with Bank funds for community-based land reform is the Andhra Pradesh Rural Poverty Reduction Project, 2003 (IDA-37320/P071272). Land purchases are budgeted at $4 million, with land purchase being one possible use of funds under the project's Community Investment Fund. Investment funds will also be provided to beneficiary groups. The project commissioned studies of the operation of land markets and the land administration machinery prior to appraisal and concluded that, with precautions, these could safely be used. The project benefited from two detailed legal reviews of the arrangements, one by a legal consultant hired by the project design team and the other as part of the external review process used by the Land Purchase Committee.

The Andhra Pradesh Project has an Operational Manual for Land (OM)[98] dealing with land purchases, referenced in the paragraph 4.3 of the DCA. One of its requirements is striking: While membership in the beneficiary group is not limited to women, it is specified that land purchased "will be given in the name of women only," presumably referring to the titling. The project may deviate from this general rule in one project district in order to conduct a comparison study (OM II.C.7). The OM also states eligibility requirements for land that seek to confirm that productivity will be increased, responding to a requirement of the Bank's Articles. A condition in the DCA requires assessment of the productive impact of the project (schedule 2(2)(iii)). The DCA also requires that the land not be occupied by households that would be involuntarily displaced in case of a purchase (OM II.C.3(a)). Annex 4 to the OM includes forms for Memoranda of Understanding between different levels of local government regarding responsibilities under the program, between local government and the beneficiary group covering the loan, and between the lender and the borrower regarding the mortgage.

A second project, the Malawi Community-Based Rural Land Development Project, 2004 (P075247), has been approved and implementation has begun. The project will provide funds for land purchases by communities from freehold and long-term leasehold estates in southern Malawi. In this case, the funding was provided to the government in the form of an IDA grant. During appraisal of the project, several legal issues arose:

1. Most of the land to be purchased will come from estates established decades ago and registered under an old Deeds Registry system. Malawi also has a more recent Title Registry system running in parallel. It was decided that to provide adequate security of tenure, the land purchased should be moved into the Title Registry system.
2. Some of the estates to be purchased are under long-term leasehold from the State; it was decided that the beneficiaries should receive a renewal of the term (40–99 years).
3. An issue arose as to whether the beneficiary group could decide that it wanted to take the purchased land back into the customary land tenure system. It was decided that this should be an option and could be done by a transaction on their part in the case of freeholds, or by the Minister degazetting the land as government land in the case of leases.

---

[98] State of Andhra Pradesh and Society for the Eradication of Rural Poverty, *Operational Manual for Land,* December 12, 2002.

4. The form of association for the purchasing group was debated; the Ministry preferred a trust arrangement but it was decided to leave this open so that purchasers could experiment with a number of possible forms.

Unlike the projects in Andhra Pradesh and Brazil, the Malawi project contains a land administration component, in recognition of the weakness of the Ministry's capability in the Southern Region. In this case the legal framework for land administration is adequate (it had been used by an earlier Bank project),[99] so the project focuses on capacity-building, especially in the regional title registration office that will need to register the new holdings.

While these early community-based land reform projects represent an important departure for the Bank and raise important legal issues for consideration during the design process, they seem not to have required much by way of reform of the law relating to land. They do have one obvious need, however, and that is need for a legal framework that allows secure transactions in land rights. This has been present in both the Andhra Pradesh and Malawi projects, which have targeted land that has been titled where the legal framework is fairly well developed and a reasonably efficient land market is functioning. The lack of need for legal reform, as a precondition and in terms of effective land delivery, has been part of the beauty of this approach.

On the other hand, the task team must do due diligence to establish that there are no problems. An assessment of the legal framework should be funded during pre-appraisal to look at freedom to transfer land rights, formalities to transfer land, and registration of transactions under national law. It will also be important to examine regulatory distortions of the land market. In any given case, legal reforms might be needed to ensure efficiency in land acquisition before there is an adequate legal framework for community-based land reform in place.

2.11   Natural Resource Management

One of the most systematic and substantial reforms of land policy and law supported by the Bank was in the context of a forestry project, the Tanzania Forest Resources Management Project, 1992 (P002785).[100] The work built upon a landmark public consultation and report by the Presidential Commission of Inquiry

---

[99] The relevant laws are the Land Act, 1965, and the Registered Land Act, 1967, both of which had been used for land titling and registration under the Bank's Lilongwe Land Development Project, 1980 (P001598).

[100] Tanzania Land Act, 1999, and Village Land Act, 1999. The role of the Bank in supporting the policy reform and subsequent legal reforms is described online at http://web.worldbank.org/external/projects/main?pagePK=64312881&piPK=64302848&theSitePK=40941&Projectid=P002785.

into Land Matters.[101] The study and policy development process under the project produced a new Land Policy in 1995 and, with DFID technical assistance, a new Land Law in 1999, the final year of the project.[102] The new law, *inter alia,* affirms the right of villages to use by-laws to manage their natural resources; these are facilitating the replication of a number of the household and community forestry initiatives developed under the project.[103]

This, however, is unusual. Normally the managers of a natural resource management project, like managers of land administration projects, tend to focus on the specific legal reform needs of the project itself. Under the Bank-supported Colombia Natural Resource Management Program, 1993 (P006868), local communities in Colombia's Choco Region on the Pacific were, according to the PAD, unable to manage their natural resources as the project envisaged because the entire region was classified as a forest reserve: "Clarification of the land ownership situation is essential for the design of resource management and conservation policies, in order to assess the convergence of interests of the parties affected and involved, [and] the distribution of economic benefits and costs." A legal regime for titling indigenous reservations had existed for some time, and land was titled both to individuals and the Amerindian communities. New reservations were created and existing reservations expanded and their boundaries demarcated. Under the 1991 Constitution and Law 70, 1993, passed just as the project began, it also became possible to provide collective titles to land to Afro-Colombian communities.[104] The project did not occasion major law reforms but worked on regulations and contractual arrangements for implementation of these legal reforms in the Choco Region. The project eventually issued 83 titles

---

[101] Better known as "The Shivji Report" after its Chair, Professor Issa Shivji of the Faculty of Law, University of Dar Es Salaam, the report is an extraordinarily frank and thoughtful consideration of national land tenure policy. Its proposals were radical, and the Bank-funded effort became the context in which the Tanzanian land administration bureaucracy, heavily criticized in the report, had to come to terms with its recommendations and define a new land policy. The report has been published as Government of the United Republic of Tanzania (Ministry of Lands, Housing and Urban Development), *Report of the Presidential Commission of Inquiry into Land Matters,* vol. I, (Scandinavian Institute for African Studies 1994).

[102] The process is recounted by the drafter in McAuslan, *supra* n. 43, at 267–272, and commented upon by the former chairman of the Commission of Inquiry in Issa G. Shivji, *Not Yet Democracy: Reforming Land Tenure in Tanzania* (International Institute for Environment and Development 1998).

[103] *See* Liz Wiley, *Finding the Right Legal and Institutional Framework for Community-Based Natural Forest Management: The Tanzania Case,* CIFOR Special Publication (CIFOR 1997).

[104] *See* Transitory Article 55 of the Political Constitution of Colombia, 1991. In 1993, Congress enacted Law 70/93, The Law of Black Communities, implementing the Transitory Article.

covering 404 communities containing nearly 40,000 families and covering nearly 2 million acres. In its later years, however, project implementation was seriously disrupted by the growing insurgency and violence in the region, and as a result there was no follow-on project.[105]

Forestry projects raise similar issues. Most forestland in Bank client countries is owned by the State and administered by a forestry department, so there is often no legal framework for individual or community property rights in forestland. Alternatively, there may be a system of property rights different from those that apply to farmland. It has been suggested that stronger property rights regimes are needed for communities occupying forestland to create the security and incentives that promote good husbandry of the forest resource by these communities and their members.[106] However, forestry departments cling resolutely to their control of these resources. Commercial and other production on this forestland, legally or illegally, provides major income streams to forestry departments and their employees.

Where a property rights option has been available for local communities to secure control of their natural resources, including forests, the Bank may seize the opportunity, as in the Colombia project. Where a property option is not present, natural resource management projects (except for the Tanzania case) have generally not sought to establish one through law reform. Instead they have attempted to work with contractual solutions that involve agreement between the forestry department and a community or resource user group on a forest management plan.[107] For example, the Lao PDR Forestry Management and Conservation Project, 1994 (P004169), funded the launching of a pilot program for participatory management of production forests in sixty villages in two provinces. The Forestry Law of 1996 (Article 7) allowed for the organization of village forestry associations, agreement between governments and associations

---

[105] *See* a study documenting the land work under this project that gives considerable attention to the legislative framework: Bettina Ng'weno, *On Titling Collective Property, Participation, and Natural Resource Management: Implementing Indigenous and Afro-Colombian Demands: A Review of Bank Experience in Colombia* (September 2000) available at http://lnweb18.worldbank.org/External/lac/lac.nsf/0/d56de267ed9a073985256a 320063a78d?OpenDocument.

[106] *See* John Bruce, *Property Rights Issues in Common Property Regimes for Forestry,* in 1 World Bank Legal Review: Law and Justice for Development 257 (World Bank 2003); and John Bruce & Robin Mearns, *Natural Resource Management and Land Policy in Developing Countries: Lessons Learned and New Challenges for the World Bank,* IIED Issue Paper No. 115 (International Institute for Environment and Development 2002).

[107] The variety of contractual solutions used in Asia is reviewed by Owen J. Lynch & K. Talbott, *Balancing Acts: Community-Based Forestry Management and National Law in East Asia and the Pacific* (World Resources Institute 1995).

on ten-year management plans, and fifty-year management contracts between the State and associations for association use of state forest land, with sharing of revenues. Because the viability of the relationship depends on the ten-year plan, as pointed out by an evaluator, an association's secure expectation concerning use of the land is effectively limited to ten years, despite the fifty-year term of the contract. The sustainability of the program will depend on the decisions of the officials of the day.[108]

Usually these agreements do not confer property rights, and they often fall short of providing secure tenure. China and the Philippines have done better, using long-term leaseholds for community forestry management.[109] A similar approach is being pursued by the Bank-supported Vietnam Forest Sector Development Project, 2004 (P066051). Forest plantations (fast-growing trees, mixed plantations, and fruit trees) are to be established on state land (all land in Vietnam being state land) with forty- to fifty-year Land Use Certificates, using a participatory approach involving village consultations, land allocation, and certification of land use rights.

In the arid pastures context, a context common in Bank client countries in Africa and Asia, the Bank has faced similar issues of State land ownership and a reluctance to accord use rights to users or user communities.[110] Progress is not always easy. In Mongolia, through a Japan Social Development Fund (JSDF) grant and a Sustainable Livelihoods Project, 2002 (P067770), the Bank encouraged the government to pursue a system of community-access commons, which were allowed under the 1994 Land Law. In an unfortunate regression, a 2003 Land Law in effect returned pastureland to the status of an open access resource.

Bank projects on natural resource management and forestry have not been very active in seeking property rights and titles for land users, though communities may be as badly in need of these for their forests and pastures as individuals for their residences and farms. Nor have these needs for tenure and title been addressed in Bank-funded land administration projects. These have avoided titling on forestland, given the lack of a legal framework for property rights there, rather than confronting that lack as a legal reform issue. There is in fact often a serious and unfortunate disconnect between the Bank's work on land law reform and reform of the law relating to natural resource management, perhaps partly as

---

[108] Paula Williams, *Draft Evaluation Summary, Evaluation of Three Pilot Models for Participation Forest Management: Village Involvement in Production Forestry in Lao PDR* (World Bank 2000).

[109] John Bruce, *Legal Bases for the Management of Forest Resources as Common Property,* 89–91 and 103–107 (FAO 1999).

[110] *See* Bruce & Mearns, *supra* n. 106.

a result of the way the Bank organizes itself: The first falls under Agriculture and Rural Development, the second under Environment, and two different thematic groups of Bank staff deal with these issues.

2.12   Process and Style in Land Law Reform

Bank task managers do not usually set out on a project development mission with reform of the law relating to land in mind. Rather, they discover in the course of scoping and pre-appraisal activities that it may be impossible to attain the objectives of the project without such reform. If clearly necessary, disbursement of funds or perhaps execution of the project may be made contingent upon the reforms. But because legal reforms are seen as time-consuming and unpredictable, task managers are reluctant to make projects conditional on legal changes or rely on them for project success. Rather, they will try to find ways, which may be less than optimal, to achieve project objectives without reform. The project can then go forward and if law reform would clearly ease project implementation or enhance project impacts, it can be folded into the project, usually into a "policy development and legal framework" component. Studies may be funded and a process initiated to reconsider problematic elements in the law concerning land. Once the Bank is involved in pressing for law reform, however, it has a legitimate interest in the process by which government seeks to accomplish it. The success of a reform initiative depends on how the project negotiates the difficulties encountered in the process. It is therefore worth reviewing here some important issues of timing and process that regularly confront Bank clients and task managers. These are legal issues. While the list is not exhaustive, the following deal with some of the more common situations.

2.12.1   Getting the Timing Right

Bank task managers need to understand the procedures required to get laws and regulations enacted so that they can address the delay and other risks involved in law reform. The Bank's country lawyers and legal consultants hired by the project help make these processes understandable. Managers must, for example, be sensitive to election schedules and how they relate to the project cycle. In most countries no controversial legislation is likely to pass in the year before an election, or in the year following as a new government organizes itself. The appearance of a potential champion for land law reform in a key government position may create a window of opportunity that must be seized. Reformers in government, and those from the Bank who support them, must plan conservatively and avoid setting unrealistically short-term targets for legislation, as well as being alert and flexible enough to respond when windows of opportunity open. As any task manager is aware, this is a tall order.

There are larger timing issues as well. Is it too early to make reform of the law relating to land a priority? New property rights or titling laws will not achieve much of their potential impact on productivity unless product and credit markets are functioning satisfactorily. Creating legal mortgageability of land, for example, is not much help unless there are viable credit markets and credit institutions willing to lend against land. It has been suggested, based on the experience in Africa,[111] that pushing property rights reform too far out ahead of reforms in other sectors may not be productive.

The fact that in many developing countries market forces will be in very different stages of evolution in different parts of the country complicates these timing issues. Urban and peri-urban or coastal areas will exhibit conditions very different from those in interior and deep rural areas. One of the strengths of the systematic title registration approach in the Bank's land administration projects is that it can be applied only in areas where the necessary preconditions for positive impacts exist.

A final timing issue involves establishing the appropriate relationship between reforms in land law and distributive decisions. Should a new property rights system be deployed early in transitional situations, in spite of inequities and even the alarming appropriations of land by the powerful that often occur in these fluid situations? Or should it be held back until these distributional issues can be addressed, in the meantime leaving smallholders without legal protections? Getting the necessary political support for property rights for some may require providing it for the others. This issue has been raised often in the context of legal reforms associated with land administration projects.

Carpe diem? Perhaps, but ultimately the decision to move ahead with law reform is one for national counterparts. The economic urgency of land law reform is a technical issue on which the Bank can provide good value to its clients, as it can on the costs and benefits of potential reforms. By providing consultants and drawing on the expertise of its own Legal Vice Presidency, it can provide effective assistance in the actual drafting of laws. Task managers, however, will usually need to rely on colleagues in the cooperating national institution and on the Bank's country office director and local staff for advice on the political lay of the land and the political prospects of proposals for reform.

There are obviously no fail-safe strategies with regard to the timing of land law reform initiatives—only the lessons that timing is crucial and that sensitivity to a variety of factors in recognizing and seizing opportunities for reform is essential.

---

[111] *See* Bruce & Migot-Adholla, *supra* n. 50.

2.12.2   Sequencing Policy Reform and Law Reform

The reform of land policy and law potentially involves several stages:

- Identification of problem areas
- Policy discussions and public consultations
- Preparation of a policy document and its endorsement by government
- Assessments of existing law in relation to new policy directions
- The drafting of the law itself
- Approval of drafts by the cabinet
- Public discussions of drafts
- Finally, enactment into law by the legislature or the executive.

Most staff of the Bank would agree that the ideal process begins with a systematic and thoughtful review of problems, proceeds through development of policy, and culminates in law reform. In practice, often these are telescoped into a land law preparation process in which fundamental land policy issues are debated and resolved in the drafting committee. This is a poor process largely because participation is limited in terms of both disciplinary perspectives and stakeholder input. Experts from one discipline should never make land policy alone; their perspectives tend to be narrow and they often opt too readily for the solutions their own disciplines provide.[112] Failure to proceed systematically can draw fire from the press, politicians, and the NGO community.

Though most Bank staff understand this, they nonetheless find themselves supporting less than ideal land law reform processes. They may be driven by the need to make the loan within a reasonable time and not drag out the project development process indefinitely. Or they may be deferring to the advice of national champions of reform, who may be more concerned with where they are going than how they will get there.

In 2002 the Government of Cambodia, with support from the Asian Development Bank and the World Bank, enacted a new Land Law. The law was seen as urgently needed to deal with extensive land grabbing and endemic land disputes.

---

[112] Julio Faudez remarks:

> [W]hen foreign legal experts assess the legal needs of developing countries they almost always seem to assume that the problems they have identified can be resolved by the enactment of new legal rules. While in some occasions this diagnosis is correct, quite often it is not . . . In fact, it is often the case that new legal rules are not the best solution either because there is no agreement in society as to the content of the rules or because the rules simply do not reach the groups that the rules are meant to reach.

See Julio Faudez, *Legal Reform in Developing and Transition Countries; Making Haste Slowly, in Comprehensive Legal and Judicial Development: Towards an Agenda for a Just and Equitable Society in the 21ˢᵗ Century* 374 (Rudolf V. Van Puymbroeck, ed., World Bank 2001).

While the draft was not subject to broad public review as it was developed, it was subject to intensive review and redrafting by key stakeholders. The broadcasting on national television of the lively, sometime contentious, parliamentary debates on the draft was a milestone in legal development in Cambodia. Only once the Land Law was in place was the Government willing to be drawn by the multilaterals into a broad land policy development process.[113]

In the interest of rapid progress, Bank task managers and their counterparts may seek to work as far down in the hierarchy of legislation as possible and will sometimes stretch a point, taking advantage of a lack of rigor concerning the hierarchy in the national legal system to accomplish quickly in a regulation what should rightly be done in a law. Legal experts working with the project must sometimes make difficult choices between "doing good law" and "making the project work."

2.12.3   Public Participation and Consultation

The law relating to land affects the interests of a broader range of stakeholders than many other bodies of law and they should have the chance to articulate their needs. In recent years, local "Land NGOs" have helped give them voice. Public participation and consultation are important not only to the quality of policy and law but also to the prospects for implementation, and the Bank can often do a great deal to encourage adequate public consultation, if only by making funding available. The Bank has considerable experience in public consultation for projects.[114]

Broad public consultation works best at the land policy stage, but due to the "telescoping" already mentioned, there are often demands for public consultation on the law rather than the policy. A highly technical law will make this difficult. Brevity and simplicity in drafting, eschewing jargon and leaving details that may need adjustment to regulations, can greatly facilitate stakeholder input. Otherwise, the law can be summarized (and of course translated) for public discussion. In Cambodia a broad public debate ensued while the National Assem-

---

[113] Land Law, promulgated as Royal Decree NS/RKM/0801/14, August 30, 2001. This law covers both property rights and land administration. Though not elegantly drafted, it is adequate and clear; more important, it is Cambodian and enjoys exceptional "ownership" among Cambodians, official and unofficial. This is reflected in the Government's very serious public education and implementation efforts. A new Civil Code drafted by JICA TA for the Ministry of Justice is under consideration, and discussions are underway on alignment of the Land Law and the immovable property provisions of the draft Code.

[114] *See,* for example, chapter 4 on Consultation and Disclosure in Kenneth M. Green & Alison Raphael, *Third Environmental Assessment Review (FY 96-00),* Environment Department, 62–86 (World Bank 2002); and Shelton Davis & Nightingale Rukuba-Ngaiza, *Meaningful Consultation in Environmental Assessment,* Social Development Note 39 (World Bank 1998). The thinking about public consultation supported by the Bank has focused on environmental and social assessments for project design, rather than policy and law reform.

bly was considering the draft, thanks to the commendable decision of government to broadcast the entire Assembly debate, lasting some weeks, on national television. Consultation after a law is drafted is thus not too late, but how it is done will depend on the complexity and accessibility of the law.

It is easier to deal with some of these issues if it is recognized and accepted at the outset that a major land law reform takes a number of years: Most practitioners of land law reform would accept two years as fast and five years as more the norm. Because the process is important to the ultimate success not just of enactment but also of effective implementation, the rewards of patience and persistence can be large. This suggests that fundamental land law reform can best be handled in the context of policy lending or of an investment project that does not immediately require the reforms and can afford to target enactment late in the life of the project. Where the law is more technical and less political, such as a title registration law, progress may be more rapid, and if regulations will meet the need, they can sometimes be done within months and usually within a year, depending in part on whether regulations can be approved by the Minister concerned or, as in some countries, must go to the Cabinet or the President for approval.

In Tanzania, the Bank in the 1990s was able to support the later stages of a much more considered land-policy-to-land-law process. The Presidential Commission on Land Matters (the Shivji Commission) had used a broad and rigorous public consultation process effectively to substantiate the needs for wide-ranging reforms. The public consultations by that Commission should be consulted as an example of best practice.[115]

2.12.4   Funding Technical Assistance for Law Reform: Commissions and Consultants

The Bank often supports law reform by funding studies of the existing legal framework, commonly by a commission of local experts though sometimes by an individual legal consultant. Though these processes can be drawn out, they effectively mobilize local expertise. If there are policy directives, the study can provide indications of what laws need to be changed to achieve them. On the technical side, one of the payoffs of a comprehensive study should be a rigorous review of existing legislation that can support a solid repeals provision, specifying laws and sections of laws to be repealed, rather than depending exclusively on a boilerplate formulation, such as "Any provisions of law in conflict with this law are hereby repealed." (Few who administer the law will have the expertise to determine what other laws are affected, and to what extent.)

---

[115] *See* Government of Tanzania, *supra* n. 101.

The Bank also supports international consultants who work with a local drafting committee on new laws. Bank staff may suggest capable consultants and provide funds to hire them, if this can be done under national rules. (In some countries, Ministry of Finance rules do not allow the use of loan funds for technical assistance, and the task manager might then either use grant "trust funds" for this purpose or seek a partnership with a bilateral donor who can provide a grant.) If handled badly, this can result in the consultant drafting the law and the local drafting committee merely acting as a sounding board. This may produce a more elegant (though not a better) statute but can erode any sense of local ownership of the law. Normally the local drafting committee should be in the driver's seat and the consultant should come in periodically to review and comment on their work. The consultant can appropriately contribute to the outline for the law by providing models of best practice and by suggesting modifications in drafts and even language for modifications. A local legal drafter should be used, with the international consultant acting as an advisor. This will do a great deal to avoid unintended interactions with other laws, violation of local legal drafting conventions, and the confusion these mistakes can cause.

The selection of international legal consultants calls for close collaboration between the Bank's task managers and staff of the Legal Vice Presidency. Often, indeed, the legal consultant for a project will actually be hired by a bilateral donor that is partnering the Bank on the project where the country's rules do not permit use of loan funds for technical assistance (TA).

2.12.5 Cutting Clothes to Fit the Cloth: Financial and Human Resources as a Constraint

In many developing countries that came to independence in the 1960s and 1970s—Africa provides many examples—the independence government's succession to the State's "monopoly of law" was a heady experience that inspired a generation of land laws that were never implemented. Most often, those governments aspired to take over control of land allocation from traditional authorities, a task well beyond their financial and staff resources. This is less common today, but caution is still needed.

In Uganda, a new Land Act was enacted in 1998, in compliance with a mandate for a new land law in the 1995 Constitution.[116] The World Bank had financed a joint program of studies by the Makerere Institute for Social Research and the Land Tenure Center of the University of Wisconsin–Madison that built an impressive consensus on fundamentals for a new law. While not involved in the drafting of the bill, the Bank was supportive of its enactment. DFID provided technical assistance for the drafting.

---

[116] *See* art. 237 of the Constitution of the Republic of Uganda, 1995.

The Act provided for an admirable decentralization of land administration to District Land Boards, with District Land Offices, and for a system of Land Tribunals. It became clear in the first year after enactment, however, that legislation of these structures did not mean that the Ministry of Finance had to fund them. Because funding only very gradually became available, this left a lacuna in the area of land dispute resolution. The amendments that were required to bring the Act into line with the resources available were not made until six years later, in 2004, at the considerable cost of loss of momentum for implementation.

These problems are not confined to Africa. Unimplemented legislation is a major issue in countries in transition, where legal reforms have been broad and rapid but the institutions needed to enforce new laws may be weak or lacking entirely.[117]

A better practice can be illustrated from the Bank's Lesotho Agricultural Policy and Capacity Building Project, 1998 (P001402). There, DFID provided technical assistance for drafting of a new Land Law, but in this case the TA team involved both economists and lawyers and, as the shape of the new law became clear, they gave government a clear picture of the cost implications of options under discussion.[118]

2.12.6   The Long and Short of It: Styles of Legislative Drafting[119]

Some dimensions of the drafting task are fairly straightforward. In a civil law jurisdiction, basic property rights will be delineated in the Immovable Property chapter of the civil code. There will then often be additional laws on specific areas of land law, for example land registration or condominiums or mortgages

---

[117] Kathryn Hedley, *Law and Development in Russia: A Misguided Enterprise?* 90 American Society of International Law Proceedings 237.17 (1996).

[118] Lala Steyn & Michael Aliber, *Resources and Finances Required for the Implementation of a New Land Act in Lesotho,* Lesotho Land Policy and Law Harmonization and Strategic Plan Project, Agricultural Policy and Capacity Building Project (DFID June 2003). The draft law is still under consideration at Cabinet level.

[119] Ann and Robert Seidman, with their collaborators, have produced a number of valuable resources for anyone who wishes to better understand the legislative drafting process and the issues that arise in drafting for developing countries: *Making Development Work: Legislative Reform for Institutional Transformation and Good Governance* (Ann Seidman, Robert B. Seidman, & Thomas W. Wilde, eds., Kluwer Law International 1999); and Ann Seidman, Robert B. Seidman, & Nalin Abeyesekere, *Legislative Drafting for Democratic Social Change; A Manual for Drafters* (Kluwer Law International 2001). The Seidmans have also written a thorough review of their experience in legal drafting with a UNDP project in China, in Ann Seidman & Robert B. Seidman, *Drafting Legislation for Development: Lessons from a Chinese Project,* 44 American Journal of Comparative Law 101 (1996).

that supplement the fundamental provisions of the code. In a civil code drafting tradition, even these supplementary laws will tend to be relatively succinct.

In common law jurisdictions, the situation is less uniform. There may not be a "land law" *per se*; case law is treated as the foundational law and only specific matters are legislated upon. Alternatively, there may be land laws that combine property provisions with provisions on land administration. These are quite common in countries where governments have rejected the received colonial law and sought to replace it through legislation.[120] They may exist as well in some civil law countries, as they do in Cambodia.[121]

In recent years there has been considerable discussion of the pros and cons of brevity in the drafting of land legislation. Conventional wisdom in both civil and common law countries is that economy and precision are primary virtues in legislative drafting. Key matters should be covered in the law and secondary matters expanded upon in regulations under the law or in administrative instructions. A relatively simple law will be more easily understood by all concerned; changes in matters of detail, which may often be necessary, need not go back to the legislature for approval if they are in regulations. In recent years, however, McAuslan has argued the contrary: that the increased complexity of a market economy requires longer laws and laws that incorporate substantial amounts of administrative law to ensure their proper implementation and limit arbitrariness on the part of administrators.[122]

Another key issue in drafting has to do with borrowing from foreign statutes. Faundez warns against "reckless copying of foreign legal texts."[123] This is generally good advice. It is an axiom of legal sociology that the same rule addressed to role-occupants in different contexts will often not produce the same result. On the other hand, the nature of a given drafting task may make a difference in whether copying is "reckless." For example, copying substantive legislation on property rights in land may be highly problematic, since attitudes toward land tend to be culturally embedded and are often the product of local histories. Wholesale borrowing of laws in such a case can produce charges of "legal colonialism," with some justification.[124] But working from a foreign law or regulations to develop first drafts of title registration statutes or regulations, which are quite technical,

---

[120] I. Ajani & U. Mattei, *Codifying Property Law in the Process of Transition: Some Suggestions from Comparative Law and Economics,* 19 Hastings Int'l & Comp. L. Rev., 117–37 and 131–32 (1995).

[121] *See supra* n. 53.

[122] *See* McAuslan, *supra* n. 43, at 255–58, specifically 257. He cites, with approval, the National Land Code of Malaysia, which has 501 sections and 11 schedules in 400 pages.

[123] *See* Faundez, *supra* n. 112, at 369–95.

[124] *See* T. W. Wade & J. L. Gunderson, *Legislative Reform in Transition Economies: A Short-Cut to Social Market Economy Status,* in *Making Development Work* (A. Seidman, R. B. Seidman & T. W. Wade, eds., Kluwer Law International 1999).

is not such a bad idea—though care must always be taken to make adjustments to the local social and economic context.[125]

2.13   New Frontiers: Into the Land Market

To date, the World Bank's experience with land has been largely in the contexts of policy and legal reform and land titling. This may soon change dramatically. In 2004, in a review of eligible Bank expenditures, the Directors approved elimination of the prohibitions of land purchases contained in various OPs. Those OPs have now been amended.[126]

The Land Purchase Committee created to work with community-based land reform projects remains in place to approve project proposals for land purchases, and the committee is working with the Land Policy and Administration Thematic Group to draft guidance for task managers and their teams. In that context, a whole range of new contexts for land purchases is being discussed, among them

- Purchases to accommodate those being voluntarily resettled, as in the case of disaster management projects;
- Purchases to accommodate those being involuntarily resettled, for instance by urban redevelopment or infrastructure projects;
- Purchases of land to add to protected areas, opening the way for land trust arrangements; and
- Purchases of land for urban renewal.

---

[125] Legal transplants have sometimes been effective, as noted by Alan Watson, *Aspects of the Reception of Law,* 44(2) Am. J. Comp. L. 335 (1996). The impact of a specific legal transplant in a country in transition is examined in Philip M. Nichols, *The Viability of Transplanted Law: Kazakhstani Reception of a Transplanted Foreign Investment Code,* 18 U. Pa. J. Int'l Econ. L. 1235 (1997). For the developing world in the civil law context, Rene David's recounting of his work on a Civil Code for Ethiopia is a classic about a thoughtful effort to take customary land tenure law into account: Rene David, *A Civil Code for Ethiopia: Considerations on the Codification of the Civil Law in African Countries,* 37 Tul. L. Rev. 189 (1963).

[126] Disbursement OP 12.00 (February, 1997), which in para. 2(b) prohibited disbursement of Bank funds against land, has been replaced by OP 6.00 (April, 2004) on Bank Financing, which contains no such prohibition. The Involuntary Resettlement OP 4.12 (April, 2004) was amended at the same time to remove a parallel prohibition from para. 34 of the December 2001 text. Today, the only similar prohibition is in para. 7 in OP 7.40 on Disputes over Defaults on External Debt, Expropriation, and Breach of Contract (July 2001): "The Bank does not lend for the purpose of enabling a country to expropriate an enterprise by providing the funds needed for compensation." This is read as applying to "enterprises" rather than land and, from the context in this OP, as applying only to takings of properties of aliens and only in the context of major expropriation events such as the Suez Canal seizure and the nationalization of the Iranian oil fields, events that prompted the promulgation of this OP.

Since the elimination of the prohibition on land purchases, the committee has been approached about land purchases in a wide range of projects, including community-based land reform projects, a project for the promotion of transgenerational land transfers (to place land in the hands of younger farmers), and infrastructure projects that involve the compulsory acquisition of land. The last point is interesting: the Bank would normally have a preference for market acquisitions, where possible, but there is nothing in its policies or other rules that would preclude use of Bank funds for a compulsory acquisition where this is the most efficient way to obtain the land.

This new opening for land purchases by Bank projects has implications for Bank work on the law relating to land. Land markets and the law governing land transactions will no longer be the province of a small, specialized subset of Bank staff dealing with land projects. Many more Bank operational staff will need to gain experience with land transactions and markets, and that experience will hopefully feed back into land law reform thinking in helpful ways. As a participant in land markets, the Bank may learn lessons that have escaped its attention as an advocate of land markets.

2.14   Conclusion

The World Bank is making important contributions to reform of the laws concerning land in client countries, in both the area of property rights and the sphere of land administration. These legal reforms are made on the basis of an increasingly nuanced set of policy prescriptions and with greater flexibility as to forms of property in land and systems of land registration. It seems clear that much future law reform sponsored by the Bank in this area will be developed though policy lending processes and, in the case of investment projects, during the implementation of the project rather than at the outset. Focusing adequate legal expertise on these issues in the policy lending context is an important challenge. At the same time, the range of projects affected by land law issues and that can potentially generate initiatives for legal reforms is growing. While land administration has been the front line for the Bank in land law reform, opportunities for land law reform are posed in natural resource development projects and in a new generation of projects that can now use Bank funds to purchase land.

In these circumstances, and given the pressures involved in project development, the important challenges for the Bank are:

- Provision of useful training opportunities for both legal and operational Bank staff in the reform of land law, including, in light of the new ability to purchase land with Bank funds, the law dealing with transactions in land

- Ensuring that adequate legal advice is provided to task team leaders and client governments in the context of both investment and development policy lending, both through specialized legal staff within the Bank and external legal consultants
- Relying more on persuasion than on conditionality, which will require use of tools that create conviction of reform needs, such as policy research (free-standing and within projects) or programs that generate feedback on felt needs for legal reforms, such as public consultation and legal assistance programs
- Finding space in the crowded project design and implementation time frame for policy and law reform processes that involve broad public participation, create stronger local ownership of a new law, and provide for public education on new rights and responsibilities.

CHAPTER 3

Overcoming Gender Biases in Established and Transitional Property Rights Systems

Renée Giovarelli*

3.1 Introduction

Rights to land are critical to economic development for women. In the developing world, more than half of all women still work in agriculture. In India, 86 percent of rural women workers work in agriculture compared with 74 percent of rural male workers. In addition, females head a large percentage of households: 20 percent in Bangladesh and India and 30 percent in sub-Saharan Africa.[1] Among the poor, women and women-headed households are most vulnerable and account for a growing majority of the extreme poor.[2]

Land rights that are taken for granted by men often do not exist for women.[3] Women may either lose rights to land or not gain rights to land as a result of: (1) a

---

* Renée Giovarelli, a lawyer, is the principal of International Partners in Development in Seattle, Washington, U.S.A. She previously was Staff Attorney at the Rural Development Institute (RDI) in Seattle, Washington. The views expressed in this chapter are the views of the author.

[1] United Nations Department of Economic & Social Affairs, *1999 World Survey on the Role of Women in Development: Globalization, Gender and Work* 85 (United Nations 1999) [hereafter the *1999 World Survey*].

[2] International Land Coalition, *Towards a Common Platform on Access to Land: The Catalyst to Reduce Rural Poverty and the Incentive for Sustainable Natural Resource Management* 4 (ILC 2003), available at: http://www.landcoalition.org/pdf/CPe.pdf (report of the World Bank Regional Workshop on Land Issues in Asia, Phnom Penh, Cambodia, June 3–6, 2002).

[3] In the Near East, for example, women rarely own arable land, although civil and religious law permits them not only to own but also to buy and sell land. For example, in Jordan, women own 28.6 percent of the land; in the United Arab Emirates, 4.9 percent of land; and in Oman, 0.4 percent of land. In some regions of Egypt, 24 percent of landowners are women; in Morocco, 14.3 percent; and in Lebanon, 1 percent. Cyprus is an exception, with 51.4 percent of the land owned by women. Female holdings are generally smaller than male holdings. *See* Food & Agriculture Organization of the United Nations, *Women, Agriculture, and Rural Development: A Synthesis Report of the Near East Region* (FAO 1995), available at: http://www.fao.org/documents/show_cdr.asp?url_file=/docrep/X0176E/X0176E00.htm.

cultural or legal inability to acquire land rights through markets, inheritance, transfer, or gift; (2) barriers to rights created by marriage, divorce, bride price and dowry, or polygamy; (3) privatization or individualization of land; or (4) failure to formalize women's rights in titling programs. In many countries, while women have access to land through their husbands or fathers, they do not own land or have ownership-like rights to it. Cultural prohibitions against women's ownership of land are often more powerful than the written law allowing women to own land. In other cases, customary law or cultural norms determine which rights to land a woman may freely exercise. For example, in sub-Saharan Africa, women may have a right to cultivate and dispose of a crop, but rarely do they have a right to allocate or alienate land, although their husbands and fathers can do so.[4]

In addition to cultural norms and customary law, women may have inferior rights to land as a result of outright discriminatory policies at the central or local level, or because of poorly drafted regulations governing land and property rights. Since rights to land and property must be recognized both legally and socially to be usable and enforceable, overcoming gender biases in property rights systems requires overcoming gender biases within the social and cultural context of those systems. Legislation alone cannot do this, though that is not to say that legislation does not make a difference.

In the face of entrenched customary law and cultural norms, what is the value of legislation that rejects such customs or norms?

Laws legitimize the possibility of change. While legislation does not itself change custom, it allows those who are brave enough or desperate enough or organized enough to use the law to work to effect change. There are many examples of the effect law can have on custom.[5] In Uganda, women who were trained about land rights, including rights established by international protocols and treaties, were pleased that their country had signed protocols and treaties agreeing to provide women with equal rights. These protocols did not have an immediate and binding affect on Ugandan legislation, but did give active women a specific platform from which to argue for change.

In the past, donor projects have sometimes contributed to gender biases by supporting those who are already advantaged by wealth, power, or custom, to the disadvantage of those who are poor and vulnerable. Future donor projects must be

---

[4] M. Kevane & L. C. Gray, *A Woman's Field Is Made at Night: Gendered Land Rights and Norms in Burkina Faso,* 5(3) Feminist Economics 1, 2 (1999).

[5] In the Kyrgyz Republic, the Governor of the State of Osh Oblast passed an initiative to reduce expenses at festivities. Families were being economically stressed by the cultural requirements for food and gifts for weddings and funerals. The initiative limited what could be offered in terms of number of sheep or horses slaughtered. This legal initiative gave the community a framework to agree on how many slaughtered animals would be respectful to the deceased without being a burden on the family.

designed in a way that goes beyond "doing no harm" to women's rights but rather affirmatively empowers women. In transitional economies, the introduction of individual rights to land and a land market necessarily changes the traditions and customs of a society to some extent. Part of this change should be an effort to empower the poor, the disadvantaged, and women through ownership rights to land and property. When women's rights are explicitly taken into account and they participate in the design of a policy, equity is increased. In many cases, increased gender equality can also lead to increased economic equality.[6] Certainly women's access to land is a major component of the success of agricultural sector policies.[7]

Reform policies must address gender biases by: (1) identifying the issues and their sources; (2) drafting legislation that creates property rights systems under which women and men have equal rights; and (3) accounting for the social and cultural factors and limitations in each setting that constrain women's property rights and addressing them, as appropriate, through legislation or social and cultural programs.

The World Bank has initiated a review of the Bank's land portfolio to assess the impact Bank land programs have had on women. An initial review done between 2003 and 2004 determined the range of project experiences that incorporated gender issues in World Bank projects related to land administration.[8] It was the first stage of a larger study that continued with four in-depth project impact studies: the Ghana Urban II Project, 1999 (P000910); the Lao Land Titling Project, 1996 (P004208); the Azerbaijan Farm Privatization Project, 1997 (P040544); and the Bolivia National Land Administration Project, 1995 (P006197). The Bank's land administration portfolio is young, in that only one reviewed project was started before 1990. This early review, it is hoped, will influence current and future land projects.

This chapter contributes to the Bank's review of its own projects by setting out the larger experience with these issues. The chapter (1) examines comparative examples that demonstrate unique constraints on women's property rights to agricultural land within the context of the issues listed above; and (2) provides recommendations based on these examples that should be factored into any future national reform policies or donor programs related to agricultural land to ensure

---

[6] *See generally,* P. Moock, *The Efficiency of Women as Farm Managers: Kenya*, 58 Am. J. Agric. Econ. (December 1976); R. S. Meinzen-Dick, L. R. Brown, H. S. Feldstein & A. S. Quisumbing, *Gender, Property Rights, and Natural Resources,* 25(8) World Dev. 1303 (1997).

[7] M. Fong, *Gender Analysis in Sector Wide Assistance in Agriculture Productivity* in *Women Farmers: Enhancing Rights, Recognition and Productivity,* 23 Development Economics and Policy 251 (P. Webb & K. Weinberger, eds., Peter Lang Publishing 2001).

[8] Hild Rygnestad, *Land Administration and Gender Issues Portfolio Review* (prepared for the World Bank Group 2004).

that women's rights are recognized and respected. The chapter is not a literature review. It relies primarily on material from four diverse countries where the Rural Development Institute (RDI) has had recent involvement with these issues, referring to other countries only to illustrate specific points.[9] It addresses ideas for both better policies and better project design.

The second part of the chapter considers gender issues in the context of programs that create new rights to land, both through privatization of state land and changes from customary to individual tenure. The third part reviews joint titling and co-ownership provisions and the fourth part discusses women's access and barriers to the land market. The fifth part discusses how intrahousehold transactions, including divorce and inheritance, affect women. Gender biases occur in practice and within both statutory and customary law, and this chapter addresses each of these issues within each section. Recommendations for overcoming gender biases in land reform programs are offered in the last section.

3.2   Creating New Rights to Land

"New" land rights are created in two basic ways: (1) grants of rights by the State through distribution to individuals or groups, or (2) individualization of customary, communal tenure. However, "in the process of privatization and reducing the complex bundles of rights into a single unitary right, many women and marginal users lose out."[10] Women can lose out in two primary ways: (1) they may lose use rights or rights of occupation to the new owner; or (2) they may receive title but may not have the resources to produce, and therefore lose their ownership rights over time. This section will discuss how privatization and individualization programs affect women's rights to land.

3.2.1   Privatization and Individualization of State Land

Privatization of land is generally undertaken to increase investment in and productivity of land, to encourage efficient use and allocation of land, and to empower recipients by providing them with a valuable asset. Government privatization of state land has occurred throughout the transitional economies of the former Soviet

---

[9] The four countries are China, India, the Kyrgyz Republic, and Uganda. RDI has been working in China since 1987 and most recently advised the government on the drafting of the Rural Land Contracting Law with an eye not only to improving the land tenure security of all farmers but also ensuring that women's land use rights are protected. Work in India has included field studies in several states on women's land rights and recommendations on how to enhance women's access and rights to land, especially in government land distribution programs. Similarly, in the Kyrgyz Republic and Uganda, RDI has conducted field research on women's land rights and recommended changes to the land policies of both countries.

[10] *See* Meinzen-Dick *et al., supra* n. 6, at 5.

Union and Eastern Europe. In China, while land has not been privatized, decollectivization of agriculture under the Household Responsibility System (HRS) reforms of the late 1970s and early 1980s resulted in the creation of household-based use rights to land. In India, many states have allocated to landless laborers land that was either state-owned or taken from large landowners.[11]

In privatization programs, legal title to land is distributed to the individual, the household, or the head of household, depending on the country. Each of these choices affects women and their immediate and future rights to land.

3.2.1.1 Household Distribution of Land

Generally, land is distributed and titled to households when the unit of operation in the culture is the household and not the individual or when there is a concern about fragmentation of land. In China and the Kyrgyz Republic, the household is the unit of operation and the population-to-land ratio is quite high.[12] A distribution to individuals would have created very small plots of land, which would in turn have created even more serious fragmentation problems.

While both China and the Kyrgyz Republic distributed land to families on a per capita basis, the individual's rights within the family were not clearly defined, due at least partially to cultural norms, which do not emphasize individual ownership rights. In both countries, distributing land to the household often means that the male head of household has greater actual rights to the land than his wife or daughter, even though on its face the law does not discriminate against women.

In China, where land contracts are issued, they are issued in the name of the head of household. Household members' names may or may not be listed in the contract, but no specific land parcel or parcels are attributed to individual members. In some villages in China, under the 1998 Land Management Law that provides farmers with a thirty-year use right to land, young men receive more land on the assumption that they will bring a woman to their household; similarly, other communities do not give unmarried young women land because they will

---

[11] *See, for example,* Robin Mearns, *Access to Land in Rural India: Policy Issues and Options,* World Bank Working Paper No. 2123, 31 (World Bank 1999).

[12] In China, average per capita land allocation was approximately 1.32 mu (approximately 0.086 hectares) according to a national survey in 1999; *see* R. Prosterman, B. Schwarzwalder & J. Ye, *Implementation of 30-Year Land Use Rights for Farmers Under China's 1998 Land Management Law: An Analysis and Recommendations Based on a 17 Province Survey,* 9(3) Pac. Rim L. & Pol'y J. 507, 516 (2000). In the Kyrgyz Republic, per capita distribution was approximately 0.75 to 1.5 hectares in northern provinces and 0.1 to 0.3 hectares in southern provinces; *see* R. Giovarelli, C. Aidarbekova, J. Duncan, K. Rasmussen & A. Tabyshalieva, *Women's Rights to Land in the Kyrgyz Republic* 10 (World Bank 2001).

probably marry and leave their families within the thirty years.[13] A 1,200-household survey in 60 villages in 2001 found that only 6 percent of women could receive land rights in their husbands' villages immediately after they married; 60 percent had to wait until a land reallocation in the village; and 24 percent were never able to receive land[14]—in spite of the fact that in China the United Nations Development Programme (UNDP) estimates that women now constitute approximately 80 percent of the agricultural work force and perform more than 80 percent of the routine farm labor.[15]

Although land use rights in China were theoretically allocated to farm households for a period of years, approximately 80 percent of Chinese villages adopted the practice of periodically readjusting landholdings in accordance with changes in household makeup as part of the HRS. As the system was originally implemented, any change in the number of members in a household, as by birth, death, or marriage, was to be followed by an immediate adjustment of the size of a family's landholding. This system of immediate readjustment was hard to manage. It was replaced in most villages by a system of reassessment and readjustment of the entire village every few years.[16]

Not all land readjustments were of the same magnitude. "Big" or comprehensive readjustments involved a change in the landholdings of all households in the village. In a big readjustment, all farmland in the village was given back to the collective management and reallocated among village households so each household received entirely different land. A "small" or partial readjustment consisted of adding to or taking from a household's existing landholding when that household's size changed. Small readjustments could take place continually as household sizes changed, or every few years to reflect changes that occurred in the intervening years. Under small readjustments, households that neither added nor lost members continued to farm the same landholding.[17]

In most cases, these land readjustments ensured that women did not lose their right to a share of household land upon marriage, since their husbands' households would be entitled to receive additional shares of village land upon their

---

[13] Z. Li, *Women's Land Rights in Rural China: A Synthesis* 6 (Working Paper for the Ford Foundation 2002). *See also* Z. Li and J. Bruce, *Gender, Landlessness and Equity in Rural China,* in *Developmental Dilemmas: Land Reform and Institutional Change in China* (Peter Ho, ed., Routledge 2005).

[14] *See id.* at 7.

[15] *See id.* at 3.

[16] R. Prosterman, T. Hanstad, B. Schwarzwalder & L. Ping, *Legal and Institutional Reforms in China's Rural Land System* (unpublished report 2001) (copy on file with RDI). *See also* Prosterman *et al., supra* n. 12, at 548.

[17] *See* Prosterman *et al., supra* n. 12, at 508.

marrying into the households. However, even the practice of land readjustments did not ensure that all women received land shares in their husbands' villages. In fact, in a survey in Shanxi Province, 8.5 percent of women did not gain access through readjustment to land in the villages in which they were living.[18] Women who were divorced were particularly vulnerable. By custom, they return to their families, but their land shares may have already been readjusted away from their families in that community, causing them to create land pressure on their parents or brothers. This does not mean that women do not have access to land; it does mean that they have less land security than men.[19] The proportion of households surveyed that contained landless women ranged from 16 to 23 percent.[20]

While women generally favored readjustments, it is important to recognize that the practice of frequently readjusting landholdings has led to a significant overall reduction in land tenure security on all farmland in China. Since households cannot be certain when readjustments will occur, and households that will lose land as a result of readjustments cannot be certain which land they will lose, long-term investment in land has been greatly discouraged. In addition, many local officials have taken the opportunity of readjustments to take land out of production for economic development for their own personal gain, further eroding farmers' confidence in their land use rights.[21]

The Rural Land Contracting Law that went into effect on March 1, 2003, protects contracted land rights from readjustments while allowing villages to reserve land to help populations newly added to the village. Women are also able to keep the portion of the land belonging to their birth families that was allocated for them, although as in the Kyrgyz Republic, according to interviews with women farmers, few women will exercise this right.[22]

In the Kyrgyz Republic, while the legal rules provided for individual rights within the family, there were no regulations allowing for division of the household parcel for the first nine years after the land law was implemented. Nearly ten years after the land reform began, clarifying legislation was finally passed to

---

[18] L. Zhu & Z. Jiang, *Gender Inequality in the Land Tenure System of China*, in *Women Farmers, Enhancing Rights, Recognition and Productivity Women Farmers: Enhancing Rights, Recognition and Productivity*, 23 Development Economics and Policy 203, 206 (P. Webb & K. Weinberger, eds., Peter Lang Pub. 2001).

[19] *See id*. at 206.

[20] *See id*.

[21] *See* Prosterman *et al., supra* n. 12, at 513.

[22] Author's unpublished field research. This law has not yet been fully implemented, and readjustments are still occurring. Field research indicated that where land was scarce women did not favor the new law.

allow individuals the right to the value of their portion of the land, though not to demarcate or partition it.[23] In the Kyrgyz Republic, as in China, upon marriage women leave their households to join their husbands' families. If a woman is to receive the value of the land she leaves, the remaining co-owners of the land plot must purchase the land from her.

The primary impetus for this rule was a concern about fragmentation of land, but cultural norms played an important role as well. Very few women request the value of their land when they leave their household to join their husbands' households because it would be shameful for them and their families if they were to do so.[24]

In both China and the Kyrgyz Republic, even when women were not disadvantaged in the initial land distribution, problems occurred as populations grew and women left their families of origin to live in their husbands' villages and on their husbands' families' land, as is the custom. When household rights to land are the legal unit, women generally have rights to land through their status either as daughters or as wives, especially if the custom is for a bride to live with her husband's family.

Two events create land pressures on families in the Kyrgyz Republic: daughters-in-law who join households and children who are born after land distribution. Both require that additional people be cared for without any provision of additional land. With no access to credit, a very limited land market, and no rural industry, family economic well-being decreases with each new child or daughter-in-law. Women who return to their families after divorce, often bringing children with them, create enormous land pressure on their families.[25]

In 1990, resettlement land in Zimbabwe was allocated to households as a unit, to some extent because the area for resettlement was limited. Data from 1997 indicates that about 75 percent of the registered land owners were male, about 20 percent of farms were held jointly, and less than 5 percent were owned by women alone, despite the fact that 80 percent of all household food security was

---

[23] The Law on the Administration of Agricultural Land (2001) (Kyrgyz Republic).

[24] *See* Giovarelli *et al., supra* n. 12.

[25] *See id.* at 11. In the Kyrgyz Republic, the State retained ownership of 25 percent of the land during the privatization process. This land was set aside so that the State would have some ability to correct errors made during the privatization process and there would be room for expansion of rural settlements. For a time, some villages used the land to assist families with children born after the distribution of land and families who had received a daughter-in-law. Now rent from the land supports local government, and some is also distributed to those who did not receive land under the initial distribution. Women rarely receive land from the land fund any more; *see* M. Childress, R. Giovarelli, R. Shimarov & K. Tilekeyev, *Rapid Appraisal of Land Reform in the Kyrgyz Republic* 22 (USAID 2003).

generated by women.[26] However, in some respects women felt that they gained increased access to land during resettlement because at least they had moved away from their husbands' extended families.[27]

3.2.1.2 Individual Titling of Land

Unfortunately, the imbalance of male and female ownership of land cannot necessarily be overcome just by individually titling land to women. Even when land is individually titled to women within their families, over time land may shift back to male control because women often do not have the ability to efficiently produce on their land. The Tigrean People's Liberation Front (TPLF) during its liberation movement in Ethiopia carried out land reform between 1975 and 1989 in Tigray, a contested area. While Tigray was under TPLF military control in early 1980, the TPLF developed a land distribution plan: All land became public property and was equitably distributed among all males above 22 years of age and females above 15 years of age who were residing in Tabia (the smallest administrative unit).[28] All use rights over land were given to individual members of the household, not to the household as a whole.[29] Children at the time had a right to a share of land, but children born after the distribution did not. Later studies found, however, that it is not land but oxen ownership that is the best measure of women's success as farmers. Thus, although women in Tigray became owners of land as a result of the land distribution, in most of the study areas, land shifted through tenancy from women-headed households to those capable of farming with traction power, oxen, or labor.[30] Both cultural taboos and a lack of resources impeded women's ability to farm using livestock, which primarily affected ownership of land held by female-headed households.

In Karnataka State, India, women have the legal right to a land title, but government programs that redistributed land generally distributed it to the male head of household. There was some indication from field research that if government

---

[26] M. Mushunje, *Women's Land Rights in Zimbabwe,* Report of Land Tenure Center 11 (U. Wisconsin–Madison 2001), available at: http://66.102.7.104/search?q=cache:9GUYz97RvSoJ:www.wisc.edu/ltc/live/bassaf0106a.pdf+mushunje+%22women%27s+land+rights+in+zimbabwe%22&hl=en.

[27] K. Izumi, *Liberalisation, Gender, and the Land Question in Sub-Saharan Africa* in *Women, Land, and Agriculture* 9, 14 (C. Sweetman, ed., Oxfam 1999).

[28] M. Berhane & M. Haile, *Impacts of the Allocation of Land to Women in Tigray Under the TPLF's Land Reform* Preface (unpublished research paper, Institute of Development Research [IDR], Addis Ababa University, Mekelle University College 1999) (copy on file with author).

[29] *See id.* at 14.

[30] *See id.* at 23.

grants of land were only given to women, men would be more willing to have land titled in women's names; otherwise, titles were always in men's names.[31]

Individual titles to land have been more successful in societies where women have cultural and societal rights to own land, as in Bulgaria or Russia. State land was distributed to individuals in Russia; in Bulgaria land was restituted to the rightful heirs to the land, regardless of gender or household status. In both cases, women are able to exercise full ownership rights because, in addition to the legal right to land, they have a socially accepted right to the land distributed to them.[32]

3.2.1.3   *Titling Land to Heads of Households Only*

In other instances, even when the law is not discriminatory, government schemes have titled land solely in the name of the male head of household. Rural households throughout India have gained ownership of land through government land allocation schemes. Since Independence in 1947, many Indian states have sought to improve both productivity and the equity of land distribution though various land reform measures. In Karnataka State, these measures have included granting permanent occupancy and ownership rights to tenants, redistributing land from owners whose holdings exceeded the ceiling limit to the landless poor, and regularizing encroachments of landless or small farmers onto government land. Karnataka has been praised among Indian states for the success of its land reform efforts,[33] but women were not targeted beneficiaries under these reforms and titles to land were almost exclusively granted in the name of the male head of household.

Karnataka has also taken up various housing schemes, which generally grant small houses and sometimes house plots to those without homes or with substandard housing. The schemes have made a largely unsuccessful effort to target women. While a policy rule states that houses or house plots must be granted in the name of the women individually or jointly with their husbands, local officials are easily dissuaded from doing so and make little effort to enforce the rule.[34]

In the case of Karnataka, women generally do not own land. Women living in households that own land often have access to it but rarely have legal rights to it. In interviews in Karnataka, many women stated that they had never heard of a woman holding land in her own name. Even so, the great majority of women

---

[31] J. Brown, K. Ananthupur & R. Giovarelli, *Women's Access and Rights to Land in Karnataka, India,* 114 Reports on Foreign Aid and Development 12 (RDI 2002).

[32] R. Giovarelli & E. Eilor, *Land Sector Analysis: Gender/Family Issues and Land Rights Study* (unpublished report, Govt. Uganda 2002) (copy on file with RDI).

[33] A. Aziz & S. Krishna, *Land Reforms in India: Karnataka Promises Kept and Missed* (Sage Pub. 1997).

[34] *See* Brown *et al., supra* n. 31, at 12.

stated that owning land was beneficial for women. The most commonly cited benefits were security in case of separation, desertion, or widowhood; an independent source of income; and greater power within the household.[35]

Under all three options—household titling, individual titling, and titling to male heads of households only—women did not necessarily gain equal rights to land; the unequal outcome was related to cultural practices and biases, lack of information, and lack of enforcement of legal rules. Legislative intervention alone cannot give women the effective right to own and control their own land if women's land ownership is not accepted and enforced culturally and socially. While distributing individual titles to land may provide the most legal protection for women, women heads of households may also need additional support. Women must have access to credit and to legal, technical, and market information, and they must be able to realize their rights to land through the courts or a community dispute resolution system.

When women have access to dispute resolution, they can often claim their legal rights. For example, in the Kyrgyz Republic, a SWISSAID- and USAID-funded legal aid project helps women resolve property disputes when they are divorcing. One client divorced her husband in 1999, having lived with him in an unregistered marriage. Their daughter stayed with her mother after the divorce. The client and her daughter—as well as other members of the family—received land shares when land was privatized, as was certified in a land certificate issued to her husband as the head of household. Her former husband refused to give up the client's share of the land. After the legal aid lawyers met with her husband and contacted the surveying and registration office, the land was split between them and her land was registered in her name. Her knowledge of her rights, and outside support for those rights, enabled her to realize them.[36]

3.2.2 Individualization of Communal Land

Individualization of land that has customarily been communal has become the major objective of land reform in many African countries where economic adjustment policies encourage market forces to determine the efficient allocation of land.[37] However, land reform programs alone are not leading to greater individualization, although they may accelerate this trend. In many cases, the State is replacing community-based institutions as both the source and the arbiter of

---

[35] *See id.* at 13.

[36] Swiss Helvetas/USAID *Legal Assistance to Rural Citizens (LARC)* (unpublished project report), available at: http://www.helvetas.kg/Files/Reports/LARC/YR_LARC_2004_E.pdf.

[37] *See* Izumi, *supra* n. 27, at 9.

rights, although some recent laws have tried to reverse this trend (Uganda and Tanzania). The notion that individualization of land is necessary for investment in communal land has been challenged by studies that found that customary communal tenure has a strong positive impact on investment as well as land values.[38]

The question arises: is individualization of communal land beneficial to women? Certainly, individualization has not resulted in a great increase in women's ability to own and control land. In fact, formal ownership of land and property has in general strengthened the control of already powerful groups and has rendered women's rights and access to resources less secure. In many cases it has led to loss of land.[39]

In precolonial Kenya, for example, women had significant access to and control over the use of land for subsistence agriculture.[40] Women "bargained" with their husbands and fathers within the context of mutual obligations and responsibilities.[41] Land was abundant and neither women nor men could alienate it. When the British introduced private ownership of land, much of the power and control over land, even under customary tenure, was vested in powerful chiefs (men). English legal norms of ownership did not take into account that male community members were obliged to provide women with temporary usufruct and that formal registration of only ownership rights would deprive women of this access.[42]

In most of Africa, men generally determine user rights for women and children. The community allocates land to male household heads and that land is passed down to male heirs.[43] Married women generally have use or cultivation rights to the land of their husbands, although difficulties arise when there is a divorce or separation.[44] Access, acquisition, holding, and use are subject to the superior right of the family, group, clan, or community. Generally there are both communal and individual rights and claims within communal systems.

---

[38] K. Deininger & G. Feder, *Land Institutions and Land Markets,* World Bank Policy Research Working Paper No. 2014, 9 (World Bank 1998).

[39] *See 1999 World Survey, supra* n. 1, at 90; *see also* S. Lastarria-Cornheil, *Impact of Privatization on Gender and Property Rights in Africa,* 25(8) World Dev. 1317 (1997); J. Dey-Abbas, *Gender Asymmetries in Intrahousehold Resource Allocation in Sub-Saharan Africa: Some Policy Implications for Land and Labor Productivity* in *Intrahousehold Resource Allocation in Developing Countries: Models, Methods, and Policy* 249–62 (L. Hadaad, J. Hoddinott & H. Alderman, eds., Johns Hopkins U. Press for Intl. Food Policy Res. Inst. 1992).

[40] G. Gopal, *Gender-Related Legal Reform and Access to Economic Resources in Eastern Africa,* World Bank Discussion Paper No. 405, 10 (World Bank 1999).

[41] *See id.* at 11.

[42] *See id.*

[43] *See* Lastarria-Cornheil, *supra* n. 39, at 1322.

[44] *See id.* at 1321.

As land has become more valuable due to cash cropping and an increase in population, women can now lose their rights to land when a family breaks down. This may occur even in communal systems of land ownership. For example, in Tanzania, widowed women who had previously been allowed to stay on their husbands' land are now being dispossessed as that land increases in value.[45] When land is individualized and made into a commodity, women may respond by not improving the value of the land for fear of losing it to a husband or male relative. There are cases in sub-Saharan Africa where women have lost control over land when they introduced irrigation and other improvements.[46]

Legislation that has not been gender-neutral but has encouraged joint titling of land to husbands and wives to ensure women's rights to land during the individualization process has been contentious in some cases. In Tanzania, the Land Commission drafted a provision requiring joint ownership of land between spouses, but the principle was deleted from the final land policy of 1995.[47] In Uganda, drafts of the Land Act of 1998 included a provision for co-ownership of land by married spouses. Parliament had agreed that customary land on which the family lived or depended for sustenance should be held in co-ownership, but this provision did not make it into the final version of the Land Act.[48]

During the transition process, when communal land rights are individualized it is important to ensure that legislation is in place that at a minimum provides that in a marital relationship, co-ownership of land and property is presumed. However, it is clear that this legal step is enormous; in many cases it will not have the acceptance of the community and will therefore not be followed. Education of policymakers and local customary leaders as to the economic value of women having secured rights to land should be a prerequisite of donor-funded registration projects. Women will also need access to some form of dispute resolution if their tentative rights are impeded.

3.3   Creating Secure Rights through Titling Projects

The focus of many donor projects is development of a land market to increase economic benefit to those who own land. In economic terms, land markets are a way to place the power over allocation of land in the hands of those most knowledgeable about the land and with the most vested interest in effective allocation

---

[45] *See* Izumi, *supra* n. 27, at 13.

[46] *See 1999 World Survey, supra* n. 1, at 91–92.

[47] *See* Izumi, *supra* n. 27, at 12.

[48] *See* Giovarelli & Eilor, *supra* n. 32, at 29.

of that land. Some donor projects see titling of land as a way to spur economic development through: (1) prompting investment; (2) increasing opportunities for credit; and (3) creating an active land market.[49]

However, these benefits of titling may not be afforded to women if they do not share formal rights in the land. While in many cases women have *access* to land, they do not have title. Rights to land imply security that is tied to an enforceable claim, while access to land is more informal and less enforceable.[50]

Bina Agarwal argues that formal land rights for women have an impact on women's welfare, efficiency, equality, and empowerment.[51] Specifically, she argues that because women spend their incomes differently from men and more generally are responsible for improving the nutritional well-being of their children, a woman's right to and control over land can determine her income-generating ability and therefore the well-being of her family.[52]

Comparative analysis of data from Nicaragua and Honduras suggests a positive correlation between women's formal property rights and their role in the household economy in terms of greater control over agricultural income, higher shares of business and labor market earnings, and the ability to receive credit more frequently.[53]

In addition, formal title to land may have an impact on women's sense of empowerment. Intrahousehold economic theory suggests that the strength of spouses' "fallback positions" is an important determinant of their ability to shape household preferences and resource allocation decisions.[54] Focus group interviews in Uganda, the Kyrgyz Republic, and India indicated that one of the key values to women of formal title to land was that they were less vulnerable to divorce or abandonment and in some cases less likely to suffer violence from their husbands.

However, as discussed above, titling of land may grant very limited rights to women within a particular social and customary context and much greater rights to men. While providing women with titles to land may not always have the intended economic effect, if titling does occur in a country, at a minimum joint

---

[49] *See generally* chapter 5 in this book.

[50] C. D. Deere & M. León, *Empowering Women, Land and Property Rights in Latin America* 3 (U. Pitt. Press 2001).

[51] Bina Agarwal, *A Field of One's Own: Gender and Land Rights in South Asia* 31 (Camb. U. Press 1994).

[52] *See* Deere & León, *supra* n. 50, at 11–12, discussing Bina Agarwal, *id.* at 31.

[53] E. Katz & J. S. Chamorro, *Gender, Land Rights, and the Household Economy in Rural Nicaragua and Honduras* (USAID BASIS/CRSP 2002).

[54] *See* Agarwal, *supra* n. 51, at 54. *See also* M. Carter & E. Katz, *Separate Spheres and the Conjugal Contract: Understanding the Impact of Gender-Based Development* in Hadaad *et al.,* eds., *supra* n. 39, at 97.

titling should be encouraged or even mandated for monogamous couples living together either in marriage or in a consensual union. Joint titling of land may at least improve the likelihood that a woman's rights to land will be more secure because she will need to give permission for sale or mortgage of the land. In India and in Uganda, women saw joint titling as a way to stop their land from being sold without their knowledge—a common practice of husbands.[55] However, for joint titling to be effective, women have to know and be able to exercise their rights to joint ownership.

There are several things to be considered in relation to joint titling of land. First, in voluntary programs, women are often not aware of their right to have their land jointly titled. Second, local governments and registration offices may impede families from registering both the man and the woman. Third, women who live in consensual union with a man but are not legally married may not have the right to joint title to their land.

A study looking at six land-titling projects in Latin America found that in Honduras, where joint titling was voluntary, only 16.7 percent of titles issued went to women. The joint titling program was weak in that women were rarely aware of their rights under the program, and the titling of land to women varied across the country according to the willingness of regional functionaries to jointly title land.[56] The application form did not provide a space for the applicant to list marital status or the name of his partner. If the partners were not married, they had to be registered as living in "consensual union," which was both costly and time-consuming.[57] Mandatory joint titling was approved in 2000.[58]

In the Lao People's Democratic Republic (Lao PDR), women from most ethnic groups benefit from a tradition of matrilineal inheritance, and the family law states that land purchased during marriage is regarded as joint property.[59] However, in practice, women's rights to land were not always recognized and there had been gender bias in titling land to men only. However, once training related to women's rights to land titles was provided to the staff of the Department of Land and to women in communities, the number of titles in the name of women and the number of joint titles both increased.[60]

In Indonesia, formal law and customary law both recognize that husband and wife are co-owners of land acquired during marriage, yet marital property is

---

[55] *See* Brown *et al., supra* n. 31, at 13; Giovarelli & Eilor, *supra* n. 32, at 22.

[56] *See* Deere & León, *supra* n. 50, at 295.

[57] *See id.* at 298.

[58] *See id.*

[59] World Bank, *Agricultural Investment Sourcebook* 411–12 (World Bank 2004), http://www-esd.worldbank.org/ais.

[60] *See id.* at 412.

almost always titled in the name of the husband. The primary concern is that most landowners are not aware that land can be jointly titled. Application forms do not indicate that land can be registered in more than one name. The registration law and accompanying regulations are silent on the issue and some registration officials were not certain that land could be titled jointly.[61]

3.3.1 Consensual Unions

Many rural women are not legally married, especially where customs and traditions predominate.[62] Legal marriage can be expensive and time-consuming and may require residence documentation that women do not have. Field research in the Kyrgyz Republic, for example, found that once the Soviet Union collapsed and legal marriage was no longer required or enforced, a majority of women in rural areas did not legally marry, although they participated in a religious ceremony.[63] In many jurisdictions, protection for women's property rights through co-ownership or joint ownership are only enforced if legal marriage can be proven. A specific legal provision that consensual unions will trigger legal protection of property rights acquired during the union (often the default marital regime) will enable many rural women to enforce their property rights who would not otherwise be able to do so.

The issue of what to do with people living in consensual union but not legally married has been taken up in many Latin American countries.[64] For example, in Peru and in Ecuador, people who live together are declared to be coproperty owners, as distinct from joint property owners. The distinction is that their marital status is not important because they both own a separate share of the property rather than owning the property together as a whole. Generally, any two people can be co-owners, and married people can also be joint owners. Co-owners can act independently on their share of the property, while joint owners must agree to an action on the whole of the property. Joint ownership requires the permission of both owners before a sale or mortgage can occur. In Colombia, co-ownership does not have to be proved, only stated as true.[65] While joint ownership may

---

[61] S. Lastarria-Cornheil, S. Agurto, J. Brown & S. E. Rosales, *Joint Titling in Nicaragua, Indonesia, and Honduras: Rapid Appraisal Synthesis* 4–5 (Land Tenure Center, U. Wisconsin–Madison 2003).

[62] *For example,* in the Cajamarca region of Peru over 60 percent of couples live in a consensual union. *See* Deere & León, *supra* n. 50, at 306.

[63] *See generally* R. Giovarelli *et al., supra* n. 12, at 20.

[64] *See generally,* C. D. Deere & M. León, *Who Owns the Land? Gender and Land-Titling Programmes in Latin America,* 1(3) J. Agrarian Change 440 (2001).

[65] *See id.* at 458.

afford greater protection than co-ownership, co-ownership provisions for consensual unions are a step in the right direction.

The Philippines has enacted a law that went even further than co-ownership for consensual unions.[66] The law states that property acquired in unions with or without marriage is covered under the national co-ownership and joint ownership laws, and the presumption is that if two people live together their land is jointly owned.[67] Even if a woman does not participate in the acquisition of property, she is deemed to have contributed jointly if she cared for and maintained the family and household.[68]

3.3.2 Joint Titling v. Co-Ownership Provisions

For legally married couples, some countries do not mandate joint titling of land and property but do provide in the civil code or other legislation for common ownership of property. Generally, common ownership provisions state that land earned or received by spouses during their marriage will be considered their common property, whether or not it is registered as such. Property that belonged to a spouse before marriage or property acquired as a gift or inherited during marriage constitutes separate property.[69]

---

[66] Family Code of the Philippines (Executive Order No. 209, July 6, 1987, as amended by Executive Order No. 227, July 17, 1987), arts. 147–48.

> Article 147: When a man and a woman who are capacitated to marry each other, live exclusively with each other as husband and wife without the benefit of marriage or under a void marriage, their wages and salaries shall be owned by them in equal shares and the property acquired by both of them through their work or industry shall be governed by the rules on co-ownership. In the absence of proof to the contrary, properties acquired while they lived together shall be presumed to have been obtained by their joint efforts, work or industry, and shall be owned by them in equal shares. For purposes of this Article, a party who did not participate in the acquisition by the other party of any property shall be deemed to have contributed jointly in the acquisition thereof if the former's efforts consisted in the care and maintenance of the family and of the household.
>
> Neither party can encumber or dispose by acts *inter vivos* of his or her share in the property acquired during cohabitation and owned in common, without the consent of the other, until after the termination of their cohabitation.

[67] M. Judd & J. Dulnuan, *Women's Legal and Customary Access to Land in the Philippines* 12 (World Bank 2001).

[68] *See id.*

[69] R. Giovarelli, *Women and Land* in *Legal Impediments to Effective Rural Land Relations in Eastern Europe and Central Asia,* World Bank Technical Paper No. 436, 253 and 260 (R. Prosterman & T. Hanstad, eds., World Bank 1999).

However, a provision in the civil code or marriage code allowing common ownership of land should not be thought to obviate the need for a requirement for joint titling in the registration legislation. Once land is registered as jointly owned, the woman's rights to the land are clear to all. With common ownership provisions, however, land can be registered in the name of the male only and if ownership were contested, a court or other body would have to decide whether the spouse has a right to a portion of the land under the law. Moreover, common ownership provisions are subject to customary and traditional interpretations of inter-household ownership.

While there is a common ownership provision in the Kyrgyz Civil Code, it does not take into account customary law, which considers the marital house and land as the premortem inheritance of sons.[70] Given this custom, the judicial interpretation of the law is that the house and land are the separate property of male heads of household. Therefore, if the intent of the couple or the law is that women and men will share the marital property equally in case of divorce, women are in a much better legal position if their land is registered as jointly owned.

3.4 Markets

Initial privatization of land is one way for women to receive individual rights to land. Once privatization is completed, however, women may acquire land rights through purchase, inheritance, labor, or other investment in improving the resource, adverse possession, prescription, or leasing. This section will look at women's involvement in market purchases and donor programs that seek to facilitate the market for them.

Before looking at postprivatization markets, however, a note about market-assisted or "community-based" land reform: Recently, some traditional approaches to privatization have been modified to reflect new thinking about market-assisted land reform, also known as community-based land reform, which attempts to get land to the poor through market mechanisms.[71] Generally, community-based land reform makes money available to the poor to purchase land so as to counteract the land and credit market shortcomings.

Because experience with these programs is limited, best practices have not yet been established and information has not yet been disaggregated by gender.[72] Where households, as opposed to individuals, are provided grants to acquire land through voluntary negotiations (in Brazil, for example), the issues discussed

---

[70] *See* Giovarelli *et al., supra* n. 12, at 14.

[71] *See* Deininger & Feder, *supra* n. 38, at 27.

[72] World Bank, *Land Policy and Administration, Module IX: Land Administration, Policy, and Markets-Overview* (World Bank 2003).

above related to household distribution of land would apply: generally in a patriarchal society, when land is distributed to households, the male head of household has more actual rights to it than the female family members, especially if the family unit breaks down.[73]

Two other issues related to gender bias should be monitored in community-based land reform programs:

First, are women able to effectively participate as community members? Community organizations, NGOs, or other implementing agencies help beneficiaries identify land available, negotiate a price, reach a preliminary agreement with the seller, and submit a proposal for approval to a local coordinating entity (for example, the district municipality or development committee). Are women involved in these community organizations or NGOs? Are women's NGOs included? What cultural or informal rules might limit women's involvement in this process? How can these be overcome?

Second, what are the cultural or traditional biases against women owning or purchasing land? How do these affect women's rights to land, and what might be done to improve women's access? Cultural bias against women's participation in a land market is discussed in more detail below.

3.4.1 Existing Formal and Informal Markets

While informal and formal land markets are critical to economic growth and efficient use of land, the customs and attitudes of society toward the purchase and sale of land by women can have a significant effect on their involvement in the land market.

In Uganda and other parts of Africa, village men in particular are often opposed to women purchasing land during marriage because they see it as an indication that they want a divorce. Only when men are educated about the economic benefit possible if their wives purchase land do they allow their wives to do so in some instances.[74]

In a 100-person household survey in Uganda (see Table 3–1) there was a difference in attitude toward the rights of women to purchase land depending on the marital status of the woman.[75] Fewer men (46.5 percent of respondents) and women (69.5 percent of respondents) thought married women should have the right to purchase land than thought widows or single women should be able to do so.

---

[73] *See generally* M. Fafchamps & A. Quisumbing, *Control and Ownership of Assets Within Rural Ethiopian Households,* Food Consumption & Nutrition Division Discussion Paper No. 120 (Intl. Food Policy Res. Inst. 2001).

[74] *See* Giovarelli & Eilor, *supra* n. 32, at 34.

[75] *See id.* at 26.

TABLE 3–1
Attitudes Toward Female Ownership of Land

Female Marital Status	Men's Attitudes Toward Female Ownership	Women's Attitudes Toward Female Ownership
Widows	68.2%	98.2%
Single women	67.4%	96.5%
Married women	46.5%	69.5%

Source: R. Giovarelli & E. Eilor, *Land Sector Analysis: Gender/Family Issues and Land Rights Study* (unpublished report, Govt. Uganda 2002).

In Mpigi district, a peri-urban area in Uganda, women interviewed in one household survey stated that, although women can acquire freehold land wherever it is available and most women want to own their own land, the deciding factors for them are usually availability of money to purchase land and the attitudes of others. Women rarely have control over any of their own money. Fear of social pressure from their husbands and male community leaders has also led some women to buy land and register it in the names of either their children or male relatives.[76]

In the State of Karnataka in India, like all other Indian citizens women have the legal right to own land. However, due to their lack of independent financial resources and to traditional gender roles, women rarely purchase land, either independently or jointly with their husbands, and household land is most commonly titled only in the name of the male head of household.[77] In Chile, because women participated in the land market only when they had resources at their disposal, only 8 percent of women had acquired their farms through purchase compared to 25 percent of the men.[78]

Since land ownership is economically empowering for women, women's land ownership can be threatening to men or to the societal value of the family as a unit. For example, under Muslim personal law in the Philippines, a woman must have her husband's consent to acquire any property by gift, except from her relatives.[79]

---

[76] *See id.* at 19.

[77] *See* Brown *et al., supra* n. 31, at 15

[78] *See* Deere & León, *supra* n. 50, at 315.

[79] *See* Judd & Dulnua, *supra* n. 67, at 29.

In many countries, it may be easier for women to lease than to purchase land, and land market programs should not focus exclusively on ownership. Leasing land is less psychologically threatening than purchasing it and requires fewer resources for entry. Of course, it should be noted that leasing is less psychologically threatening for the very reason that it does *not* create long-term secure property rights in the borrower/lessee. In Burkina Faso, for example, the increased and changing market value of land has had the surprising effect of creating avenues outside of traditional channels for women to lease land long-term, anonymously.[80] Male landholders who have excess land are more willing to lease to them because women cannot claim permanent rights to land. Husbands generally support this borrowing of land by their wives, and women are therefore better able to cultivate land independently, even though they do not own it.[81]

3.4.2   Land Market Liberalization

For women to be benefactors of programs that encourage their participation in land markets, an explicit policy favoring their participation is usually needed. Otherwise, women are unlikely to have the resources to purchase land because in many traditional societies men have primary control over resources. The rural poor are often unable to take advantage of the market because they lack three essential ingredients: (1) information about new laws and programs; (2) money to purchase land; and (3) access to credit.[82]

Women may have limited access to money, credit, and information because of both poverty and their status in the family and culture. Traditional expectations about their role in society can be a serious impediment to their entry into the land market.[83] Women who are able to purchase agricultural land usually live in urban areas and are employed or in peri-urban areas where they grow food for the urban market.[84] In both cases, they are able to accumulate their own resources. Women traders do participate actively in urban real estate markets in some countries, including much of West Africa.

Land market liberalization is facilitated by land registration, but as this chapter has discussed, women are often not registered as land owners within a family

---

[80] *See* Kevane & Gray, *supra* n. 4, at 14.

[81] *See id.* at 14.

[82] *See* the *1999 World Survey, supra* n. 1, at 92.

[83] *See id.*

[84] *See id.*; *see also* Lastarria-Cornheil, *supra* n. 39, at 1329.

unit. Without a registered right to land, women cannot use the land as collateral and their approval may not even be required for a land transaction initiated by their husbands.

Women may be more likely to purchase land collectively: Pooled resources can make it easier for women to acquire credit using social collateral or to purchase land outright. One NGO in Andhra Pradesh in South India used government poverty alleviation schemes, which granted money or land to the landless, to collectively acquire land through purchase or lease. The purchased land was divided into individual plots for the group members but then cultivated collectively to take advantage of the group's pooled resources.[85] Other examples of women acting jointly to overcome their disadvantage in the market can be found in other parts of India and in Bangladesh.[86]

3.5 Household Allocation of Land

For women, there are two separate questions related to land rights: First, does a woman have the right to use, control, own, sell, lease, bequeath, or gift land within a marriage, a consensual union, or her natal family? Second, do women who are divorced, widowed, or abandoned, or who are second wives have the right to use, control, own, sell, lease, bequeath, or gift land?

Women's rights to land are almost always related to their relationship to a family. Legal reform efforts designed to enhance women's land rights seldom consider the intrahousehold distribution of land, yet it potentially has a great impact on women. This section looks at some of the barriers to women's rights to land in terms of their family relationships.

3.5.1 Lack of Control over Land within the Marriage

Within a marriage, rural women generally have access to the use of land, but in many cases husbands can sell the land without the permission of their wives, choose what crops they grow, and control money from the harvests. In such instances, use rights are insecure even within the marriage.

In Uganda, the Land Bill of 1998 originally included a provision for which urban women fought hard. This was the "consent clause," which was intended by women to stop the sale of any household land unless the spouse gave written

---

[85] *See* the *1999 World Survey, supra* n. 1, at 93; *see also* Bina Agarwal, *Gender, Environment, and Poverty Interlinks: Regional Variations and Temporal Shifts in Rural India 1971–1991,* 25 World Development 23 (1997).

[86] *See* the *1999 World Survey, supra* n. 1, at 93.

permission for the sale. However, the consent clause, as it was enacted in the Land Act, states that:

- No one can transfer land without the prior written consent of the spouse if: (1) the spouse ordinarily resides on this land, and (2) the spouse derives sustenance from this land.
- Transfer includes: sale, exchange, transfer, pledge, mortgage, lease or *inter vivos* gift—or enter [sic] into a contract for these purposes.[87]

The consent clause can be read to apply only to land that is *both* residential and used for sustenance, not to plots of land farther from the house. Many landowners have several plots of land, most of them at some distance from the house. This interpretation, while legally viable, is not sufficient for women's needs and does not provide the equal rights promised under the constitution. In a land market survey in Uganda, respondents stated that the formal written consent required under section 40 of the Land Act is rarely obtained. Most respondents were not sure if the consent requirement covered all the land plots of a household, just the plot on which the family actually lived, or plots that were used for family sustenance.[88]

In the Philippines, the statutory obligation for consent is much broader. The written consent of both spouses is required for transactions in agricultural land distributed to agrarian reform beneficiaries, regardless of whether the land is registered in the name of both spouses or only one of them, if the land was obtained during the marriage or cohabitation.[89] A transaction involving other property of the marriage or cohabitation also requires the consent of both parties. In *Jader-Manalo v. Camaisa,* the Supreme Court ruled that for the contract to sell property to be effective, both husband and wife must concur in writing.[90]

In other countries, the problem of control over land within the marriage is related to control over decision-making related to the wife's land. In Tigray, married women are supposed to have their own land, but the land is usually controlled

---

[87] Land Act of Uganda, §40 (July 2, 1998).

[88] R. Mwebaza & R. Gaynor, *Land Sector Analysis: Land Markets, Land Consolidation, and Land Readjustment Component* 13 (unpublished report, Govt. Uganda 2002) (copy on file with RDI).

[89] *See* Judd & Dulnua, *supra* n. 67, at 13.

[90] Republic of the Philippines, Supreme Court Manila, First Division, *Jader-Manalo v. Camaisa,* G.R. No. 147978, January 23, 2002. *See also Sumbad v. Court of Appeals,* G.R. No. 106060, June 21, 1999, where the court found that in the case of a deed of donation, a common-law marriage is equal to a formal marriage, but there must be proof that the couple lived together continuously.

by a senior male in the household, and many women cannot even identify which part of the household land belongs to them.[91]

In Zimbabwe, women who were interviewed stated that their husbands would not allow them to plant anything but maize on the land given to them, and that they do all of the work but cannot do any of the planning related to crop growing.[92]

There may be little the law can do about women's control over land within the family except as it relates to transfer of the land outside of the family. Written consent should be required for any transfer of household land, no matter to whom the land is registered. There can be difficulty with such a provision, however, in terms of market efficiency in some contexts. Where polygamy exists and marriages and land are unregistered, keeping track of whose consent is required can be difficult for banks or potential buyers. Bankers in Uganda complained about the consent requirements imposed by section 40 of the Land Act. They reported that it was impossible for them to verify that all the required consents had been obtained prior to granting a loan using land as collateral.[93]

In countries where there is both polygamy and a lack of registration of both land and marriages, one possibility is to provide that a sale or mortgage is valid even if it is later contested for lack of consent, if the purchaser or mortgagee made a reasonable effort to obtain consent. Reasonable effort should be defined so as to create a balance between the needs of the bank or seller for efficiency and a woman's rights to land. Admittedly, such a balance would not be easy to establish and would be contextual. Where a lack of balance is found, the offending party (the seller or mortgagor) should have to provide land or equivalent compensation to the offended party (the wife who did not provide consent). Of course, while this may be an adequate legal solution, it is not likely that women will sue for this remedy, and therefore it may provide more security for banks and purchasers than it does for women.

3.5.2 Divorce

Three main issues affect women's rights to land upon divorce, abandonment, or ending of an unregistered union: First, divorce is still stigmatized in many countries, especially those where family is the highest value and takes precedence over individual rights. In some countries divorce is not allowed, and in others, division of property is based on the guilt of the parties.[94] Second, women often move to

---

[91] *See* Berhane & Haile, *supra* n. 28, at 40.

[92] *See* Mushunje, *supra* n. 26, at 11.

[93] *See* Mwebaza & Gaynor, *supra* n. 88, at 13.

[94] *See* Judd & Dulnua, *supra* n. 67, at 11.

their husbands' family houses upon marriage and are reluctant to claim their land upon divorce because it is part of their husbands' family land or is in their husbands' villages. Third, women often lack information about their right to land from the marital household.[95]

The legal solution that is most often promoted to protect women's property rights upon divorce or abandonment is to provide for co-ownership in the law. While co-ownership is an important goal, such a legal rule alone will have a limited impact on women's rights to property if custom and tradition do not support it. "Where customary or traditional property rights and gender relations are strong, they are likely to dominate the distribution of rights within and around the landscape."[96] It is critical to recognize local practices when designing policy.

However, because legal rules provide room for change within a culture, they can be valuable. For example, the Tigrean land reform mandated joint registration of property in marriage or, in the case of nonformalized unions, registration in the woman's name. A recent study has indicated that men have become conscious of women's rights to their land and for this reason have been more cautious about beating them and about initiating divorce. However, the rate of divorce has increased in recent years because women are leaving relationships that are violent or where the husband does not contribute to the family. Women stated that the land reform has made them independent. A woman has the right upon divorce to take both the property she brought to the marriage as dowry and her half of the marital land. Property obtained after marriage is divided equally. Women stated that if they owned land and property upon divorce, they could not be forced to stay with men.[97]

While they are not a panacea, without legal rules supporting women upon divorce, women have little choice to leave a violent or abusive relationship. In Uganda, women move to their husbands' villages upon marriage; when they are separated, divorced, or abandoned, they generally lose all their rights to their land, their children, and their house. No law protects them. No woman interviewed had voluntarily chosen to leave her husband because economically it is not a viable option. Yet a significant number of women are divorced or separated through no choice of their own. Of the women interviewed in one household study, all of whom were randomly chosen, 9.6 percent were single or divorced.[98]

In Karnataka State, India, separated or divorced Hindu women are often socially stigmatized and rarely receive maintenance. Hindu, Muslim, and

---

[95] *See* Berhane & Haile, *supra* n. 28, at 37.

[96] *See* Meinzen-Dick *et al., supra* n. 6, at 1310.

[97] *See* Berhane & Hale, *supra* n. 28, at 38.

[98] *See* Giovarelli & Eilor, *supra* n. 32, at 21.

Christian law all allow for maintenance upon divorce, but none allow a woman the right to any of her husband's ancestral or separate property. Co-ownership of marital land is not a concept supported by law.[99] Women most often must support themselves, unless they have adult sons who can assist them. Separated women are not usually supported by their exhusbands, inlaws, birth parents, or communities. Such women nearly always lose access to land that they used to work on and typically do not receive any maintenance from their husbands; nor is any of the dowry that was paid on their behalf returned. They can no longer have access to land held by their inlaws or husbands and must leave their husbands' villages. Separated and divorced women rarely go back to their birth families' homes because they are considered shamed, so they do not regain access to their fathers' land either. This is especially true if a woman's brother and his family are living in the family home. Many women said it would be socially awkward to go back to their birth families and there would not be enough land, money, or room to do so. The only land found to be retained by separated women was house plot land received from government schemes that had been titled in their own names.[100]

In cultures where women traditionally move to their husbands' homes or villages, divorce can be economically very difficult for women. Women may be too ashamed or too poor to enforce their legal rights. General legislation regarding divorce may be positive for women, though at the same time regulations for its implementation may thwart women's access to court. For example, in Kyrgyzstan, the person who applies for property division (almost always the woman) must pay the state fee. If property is worth 500 to 10,000 soms, the plaintiff must pay 5 percent of the value of the property; if the property is valued at over 10,000 soms, the plaintiff must pay 10 percent of the value.[101] Article 102 of the Civil Code provides that the court can waive payment, and poor women often do pay less than the stated percentages, but they must pay something, and usually any amount is too much. Moreover, the amount must be paid in advance in order for the judicial procedure to commence. The full burden for payment falls on the person requesting the property division and is not later reimbursed by the opposing party.[102]

Those working on land law reform in developing countries do not generally analyze the rules for division of property upon divorce. However, the legal framework surrounding divorce and division of property can have a major impact on

---

[99] *See* Brown *et al., supra* n. 31, at 8.

[100] *See id.* at 35.

[101] Law on State Duties (2000), art. 4 (Kyrgyz Republic). Judges in the Kyrgyz Republic identified this regulation as a major impediment to women's access to court for property division.

[102] *See* Giovarelli *et al., supra* n. 12, at 21.

women's right to land and on women's status within the family. While in many countries domestic violence is endemic, women often cannot leave violent situations because they lack control over resources and are economically dependent on their husbands and their husbands' families. Land reform should review legislation affecting division of property upon divorce and encourage equitable distribution of property.

3.5.3 Bride Price and Dowry

The customs of bride price and dowry (the exchange of wealth upon marriage) are often related to women's ability to own land. In India and the Kyrgyz Republic, because dowry is seen as the daughter's premortem inheritance, she does not have a right to inherit land from her natal family. However, in the Kyrgyz Republic, women do have control over their dowry throughout their married life, and it remains with them upon divorce or death of the spouse.[103]

In the State of Karnataka in India, the bride's family pays the dowry to the groom and his family, who control it throughout the marriage. Dowry is not returned upon divorce. The girl's family is essentially purchasing someone to take care of their daughter but not providing her with any economic power of her own. Interviewees stated that they would often sell land or livestock to pay dowry and wedding costs. Indeed, out of 400 households that responded to a questionnaire, the reason most commonly cited for selling land was to pay for dowry and wedding costs.[104]

In Uganda, women often gave "bride price" as the reason why women do not or should not own land. Here, the husband's family pays the wife's family for the bride. Payment of bride price simultaneously indicates respect and love for the bride and deems her the property of her husband. Upon divorce, women's families are often expected to return the bride price and women are sent away with no marital property or wealth. In interviews, men stated that women cannot own land because "property cannot own property."[105]

It is probably unrealistic to legislate against dowry and bride price. For example, in India dowry has been outlawed since the 1961 passage of the Dowry Prohibition Act. Nonetheless, not only is dowry still practiced, the incidence and requirements are increasing rather than decreasing. Since dowry and bride price continue to be practiced, in countries where women do not have rights to land or other major assets because of this exchange of money, it would significantly improve the position of rural women if they at least had a clear, easily asserted

---

[103] *See id.* at 23.

[104] *See* Brown *et al., supra* n. 31, at 19.

[105] *See* Giovarelli & Eilor, *supra* n. 32, at 18.

legal right to a portion of all marital property, including anything given for dowry or bride price. In this case, co-ownership legislation should perhaps provide that *all* property acquired during marriage is co-owned, with the possible exception of inherited property. The usual exceptions in western culture for separate property may not be appropriate in cultures where women's ownership rights to property are weak. If a portion of all marital property is not politically or culturally acceptable, at a minimum all gifts and cash received in conjunction with marriage could be deemed by the law to be jointly owned by the married couple, no matter who was given the cash or gift.

3.5.4 Polygamy

Many societies do not outlaw polygamy, and even when a country does legally prohibit it, if polygamy is customary or traditional, the prohibition is generally ineffective. However, in many countries polygamy seriously affects women's rights to property and is the source of much tension and anxiety over land rights. Polygamy complicates legislation requiring written consent of spouses for disposition of property. It complicates provisions on inheritance and co-ownership of land. Legislating around it is difficult, but to ignore formal or informal polygamy is to inadequately protect women's property rights. The situation is made even more difficult by the fact that many men refuse to acknowledge or discuss polygamy, and women are often hesitant to raise the issue.

While written law prohibits it in the Kyrgyz Republic, under customary law a *mullah* can perform and register the marriage of a second wife. More and more men have a second wife, and the arrangement is generally kept secret. However, in field research women did talk about being concerned about losing their husbands and their rights to their husbands' income if their husbands took second wives. Women state that husbands generally favor second wives, so while their husbands are living, the first wife's income and security are threatened. Because women who are second wives have no legal rights to any of the men's income or property, these women are also very vulnerable. First wives, meanwhile, are vulnerable to having to divide their property among heirs of their husbands.

A 1993 study on land disputes in Uganda found that in Kabale and Mbale Districts, land shortages, rising populations, and polygamy (allocation of land to multiple children and multiple wives) led to a predominance of intrafamilial land disputes.[106] Men choose fields for their new wives, often at the expense of their previous wives. Children's inheritance may depend on their mother's status at the

---

[106] J. Kigula, *Land Disputes in Uganda: An Overview of the Types of Land Disputes and Dispute Settlement,* Research & Policy Development Project Paper, No. 3 (unpublished, Makerere Institute of Social Research, Uganda, and the Land Tenure Center, U. Wisconsin–Madison 1993).

time of their father's death. In some sub-Saharan African countries, the eldest son of the most senior wife is likely to receive the largest share of the property.[107] As the heir he is responsible for administration of the estate, including allocation of the land among siblings. He usually is not very well disposed to the children of other wives.[108]

The law should not make broad proclamations about the relative worth of marriages (such as: the first is the most important, or marriages with children are superior). However, the law can make determinations about property ownership. One possible rule would be that upon the husband taking a second wife, all property belonging to the first marriage or consensual union would be partitioned so that the husband had only his share to distribute to his new wife and their children.

Of course, the law is a very cumbersome tool for dealing with complicated family relationships; if it does not make sense within a particular context, it will not be followed. Customary polygamy rules need to be thoroughly understood before property division legislation or titling legislation is drafted.

3.5.5 Inheritance, *Inter Vivos* Transfers, and Gifts

There are two main ways that women might inherit land and thus ownership rights in it: as a daughter from a parent, or as a wife from a husband. To emphasize the importance of inheritance for women, in a study done in Peru, Chile, Nicaragua, and Mexico, it was found that the primary way women farmer landowners had acquired their land was through inheritance (39 percent). Though men were three times as likely as women to have inherited land, inheritance was still the principal way that women became landowners.[109]

Generally law recognizes succession by both will and operation of law. Succession by will occurs when the deceased has written a will that complies with all legal requirements for validity and that orders distribution of property. Usually the testator may bequeath all or part of her property to any person—even people who are not heirs by law—although there are often obligatory shares for children or spouses. Intestate succession by operation of law occurs when there is no will or when a will does not cover the whole estate.[110]

In rural communities in developing countries, very few people write wills, so rules related to intestate succession become important. Legal intestacy rules

---

[107] T. Hilhorst, *Women's Land Rights: Current Developments in Sub-Saharan Africa* in *Evolving Land Rights, Policy and Tenure in Africa* 181, 186 (C. Toulmin & J. Quan, eds., DFID/IIED/NRI 2000).

[108] *See id.* at 186.

[109] *See* Deere & León, *supra* n. 50, at 314–18.

[110] *See generally* G. Nelson, W. Stoebuck, & D. Whitman, *The Law of Property* (West Group Pub. 2002).

usually provide that, as a first priority, children receive a certain share of the deceased's property, as does the spouse. In some countries the shares of the children and spouse are equal, and in others the shares are unequal or are not divided at all, because one child alone inherits parental property. Many pluralistic legal systems allow the marriage to determine the inheritance regime that applies. For example, if a person marries as a Muslim in India, the inheritance rules are different from those applying to a person who marries as a Hindu.[111]

Customary law also plays a major role in the inheritance rules of the community; in some countries where the intestacy rules have been written with little input from local communities, the law on intestate succession is completely ignored because it is unknown.[112] Customary rules do not necessarily provide directly for a spouse or for all the children, and in some cases customary rules exclude women from inheriting land as daughters or widows. In other areas, daughters can inherit only if there are no sons or if they are single, divorced, or widowed and have returned home. Women may continue to have access to land but without ownership. If custom dictates that a woman move to her husband's village upon marriage, her ability to inherit as a widow may be impeded.

Customary law can also make it difficult for women to inherit land even if the written law favors such inheritance. In Zimbabwe, while formal law provides for equality between men and women, customary law views women as juveniles. Therefore, in *Magaya v. Magaya*,[113] the Zimbabwe Supreme Court ruled that because under customary law women are juveniles, a woman could not inherit her father's property even though she was named in his will.

In Botswana, the formal law itself is contradictory in its treatment of women's property rights. The Married Persons Property Act (MPPA) provides for women to marry in community property or out of community property.[114] However,

---

[111] *See* Agarwal, *supra* n. 51, at 198–232.

[112] *See for example,* Giovarelli *et al., supra* n. 12, on customary and legal inheritance in the Kyrgyz Republic.

[113] [1999] ICHRL 14 (February 16, 1999). The Supreme Court ruled 5–0 that customary law had precedence over the Constitution. Venia Magaya, 58, sued her half-brother for ownership of her deceased father's land after her brother evicted her from the home. Under the Zimbabwean Constitution and international human rights treaties, Magaya had a right to the land. However, the court ruled that women should not be able to inherit land "because of the considerations in African society," basing its decision on art. 23 of the Constitution of Zimbabwe, which prohibits discrimination in the application of African customary law.

[114] If married in community property, all property is pooled and shared upon divorce. If married out of community property, essentially each spouse retains the property he or she owned before marriage and property acquired after marriage is treated as individual property unless the parties clearly intended to have joint ownership (usually evidenced by a written contract). Ministry of Lands, Housing, and the Environment of Botswana, *Review of Botswana National Land Policy, Final Report* 80 (January 31, 2003).

the Dissolution of Marriage of Persons Subject to Customary Law Act, the Succession Act, and the Common Law and Customary Law Act provide that married persons subject to customary law may be dealt with in accordance with customary law unless they execute a contract excluding the application of customary law; make a will; or otherwise demonstrate their intention to be dealt with in accordance with common law.[115] Under customary law, men are generally favored over women in terms of land rights. Much of the common law only applies when customary law does not.

Land law reformers need to study policies related to intrahousehold transfers of land like inheritance before advising on land-related legislation. Inheritance rules and practices have a major impact on women's rights to ownership of land and their poverty status. As with many issues related to the family, inheritance customs are deeply embedded in society. If a policy goal is to assist women-headed households and deal with women's poverty, establishing widows' rights to land as a policy priority would be very beneficial. A national discussion of inheritance rules and a willingness to provide money to work on inheritance policy would raise the status of the discussion of women's rights to land in developing countries.

3.5.6 Widows

In many countries, whether there are children is often important under customary law in determining whether or not women will have access to land upon the death of their spouses. Without children, women who have moved to their husbands' villages are often expected to return to their fathers. Women may not inherit land from their spouses because the land belongs to their husbands' families.

In Tigray, Ethiopia, a widowed woman is ensured access to the family land, especially if she has children from her marriage. However, widowed women are dependent on their adult sons for the use of the land.[116]

In Karnataka, India, under customary law only a widow who had young children was likely to inherit land. If a widowed woman did not have children (whether adult or young), she not only did not inherit land, she often completely lost access to the land of her husband and inlaws. Most Hindu women in this position did not regain access to their birth families' land either. These widows supported themselves by agricultural labor when they could get it and sometimes supplemented this income with government pensions of approximately 100 rupees per month (close to US$2.00).[117]

---

[115] *See id.* at 161.

[116] *See* Berhane & Haile, *supra* n. 28, at 41.

[117] *See* Brown, *et al., supra* n. 31, at 26.

During field research in Karnataka, widows with young children who had not inherited any of their husbands' land were interviewed. In these cases, the husband's family took over his land and assets and the widow was unable to get access after his death. These widows also worked as agricultural laborers, and they sometimes had to leave their children with relatives, or even at orphanages, to find work in the city.[118]

While males within the family generally take control over land upon the death of a male head of household, inheritance is sometimes the only possible chance for women to own land at all. In Burkina Faso, the only women who have direct control over land are widows. But even this situation is uncommon, and the deceased's children or brothers usually take over the land.[119]

In Uganda, under the Succession Act, widows and widowers are treated similarly, although customary law favors widowers. Under the formal intestate law, spouses have the right only to occupy, not own, their houses and the land immediately adjoining the holdings, even if they farmed land at a distance from their houses during the marriage.[120] This right to occupy is quite limited. Widows and widowers must farm the land and cannot cut down trees, erect or change buildings, or use the land for other purposes.[121] They have no right to sell the land. For other property, including other plots of land, spouses have the right only to a 15 percent share. One place where there may be room to change legislation in Uganda related to women's rights to land may be in the area of inheritance. However, for all the attention focused on Uganda's land law, the inheritance rules have remained unchanged and unchallenged.

In spite of these already limited legal rules, a serious problem in Uganda is property-grabbing by the husband's family. In one study, out of 204 widows, 29 percent said that property was taken from them at the time of their husbands' death.[122] Widow-headed households are overrepresented by far among the poor at 13 percent of the poorest quartile of the Ugandan population.[123] The widow's land is divided among her male relatives, many of whom may have helped raise the bride price at the time of her marriage.[124]

---

[118] *See id.* at 26.

[119] *See* Kevane & Gray, *supra* n. 4, at 8.

[120] Succession Act of Uganda, sched. 2, para. 1 (1964, as amended in 1972).

[121] *See id.* sched. 2, para. 7.

[122] L. Z. Gilborn, R. Nyonyintono, R. Kabumbuli, & G. Jagwe-Wadda, *Making a Difference for Children Affected by AIDS: Baseline Findings from Operations Research in Uganda* 1 (Pop. Council Inc. 2001), http://www.popcouncil.org/pdfs/horizons/orphansbsln.pdf.

[123] S. Appleton, *Women-Headed Households and Household Welfare: An Empirical Deconstruction for Uganda,* 24 World Development 1811, 1819 (1996).

[124] *See* Giovarelli & Eilor, *supra* n. 32, at 10.

Women in Uganda want a change in the law governing widows' inheritance rights in land. Even women from the most remote areas want legal changes. A survey of two districts in Uganda found that women are most concerned about widows and orphans because they are the most vulnerable members of society. Women were less likely to want rights of ownership within their marriages as long as they have access to land, but they were almost unanimous that widows should have the right to own the land they had farmed during their marriages.[125]

In the Kyrgyz Republic, customary law provides that the youngest son inherits the house and land of the family and is responsible for taking care of his parents. Although statutory law provides that property should be divided between the surviving spouse and children, most women are not in favor of the law because they do not feel they would be as well taken care of. Because the youngest son inherits the land and house, he is obligated to provide for his mother. Without such an inheritance rule, none of the children may feel obligated or have an incentive to care for their parents. Moreover, the plots of land in the Kyrgyz Republic are very small and not economically viable if they are apportioned among large families. Written inheritance law was not followed in any of the Kyrgyz villages where interviews were done. Women also stated that they receive dowry as their premortem inheritance that they have control over, and many felt that the right to inherit land was not necessary.[126] The issue of social and customary obligation as it relates to land rights should be further studied.[127]

3.5.7 Daughters

Under customary law in many countries, inheritance of land by daughters is directly related to marital residence and to the customary means of distributing wealth. Women who leave their homes and join their husbands' families often lose any right to inherit their parents' land.[128] Ironically, they also do not generally have the right to inherit their husbands' land because it belongs to their husbands' families. For many women this double bind effectively eliminates inheritance as a means of acquiring land. Frequently, however, daughters in

---

[125] *See id.* at 26.

[126] *See* Giovarelli *et al., supra* n. 12, at 23.

[127] Where there is no state social safety net for the elderly, a woman may benefit more from being cared for by her son than by directly owning land, especially given customary prohibitions against women performing certain duties.

[128] On the other hand, women in matrilineal societies are often in a very powerful position in relation to land rights. *See generally* R. Strickland, *To Have and To Hold, Women's Property and Inheritance Rights in the Context of HIV/AIDS in Sub-Saharan Africa,* ICRW Working Paper (ICRW June 2004).

patrilocal societies are not concerned about inheriting family land because they no longer live in their families' villages. Almost all the women interviewed during field research in the Kyrgyz Republic and India stated that they would not request land from their families even if they were legally entitled to a share.

In traditional African communal tenure systems, land was used mainly for cultivation and grazing and was not owned by individuals. Women moved to their husbands' clan and their land. Daughters did not need to inherit the property of their parents to protect them except when they were unmarried or were divorced and had returned home, at which time an arrangement was negotiated with their parents' clan so that they would have access to land.[129]

In Uganda, under the Succession Act, children currently have the right to share 75 percent of their parents' land equally among themselves. However, few daughters inherit land in this patrilocal society, and those who do usually retain only the use of the land while they are living with their family and do not have the right to sell it.[130]

In India, the Hindu Succession Act provides that daughters can inherit the property of their parents. As a simplistic description, Hindu personal law as followed in most of India (except in West Bengal, where a different school of Hindu law is followed) divides property into two classes: separate (usually self-acquired) property and joint family (ancestral) property. Separate property, which includes land the deceased purchased or received from the government, devolves in the first instance in equal shares to the deceased's sons, daughters, and surviving spouse and, if the deceased is a man, to his mother.[131]

The devolution of joint family property is more complicated. Traditionally, only males gained a share of the joint family property at birth (owners of such joint family property shares are known as "coparceners"). Some states, however, have passed amendments to the Hindu Succession Act to permit daughters, like sons, to become coparceners and receive a share of the undivided joint family property (including land) at birth. This is the case in Karnataka, Andhra Pradesh, Tamil Nadu, and Maharashtra.

However, field research in the State of Karnataka indicated that daughters generally did not exercise their right to inherit land from their natal families; nor did they exercise their present ownership right to the joint family land as coparceners. The only exception was when a woman came from a family that had only daughters. Daughters gave two common reasons for not asserting their rights under the Succession Act: (1) their families had paid or would pay very high dowries and

---

[129] *See* Gopal, *supra* n. 40, at 21.

[130] *See* Giovarelli & Eilor, *supra* n. 32, at 10.

[131] Hindu Succession Act of India (1956) (as amended) §§8 and 15.

other expenses to get them married; or (2) their families had limited land and they felt uncomfortable asking to take a share of that small parcel of land away from their brothers. From their perspective, these women received their share of the family property through their dowry and wedding expenses, even though dowry was given not to them but to the groom and his family.[132] Males control the dowry and may use it as capital for setting up business or buying land, which is then put in the male's name.[133] Parents responded similarly that their responsibilities to their daughters were met by marrying them off.[134]

3.6 Women's Knowledge of and Ability to Enforce Land Rights

While countries need to enact gender-sensitive legislation (family law, civil law, and the law on registration), more importantly women need to know their rights and be able to access and use them once they have them.[135] Women need "legal land literacy"— knowledge of land rights and obligations and the ability to apply the rights. Ideally, both individuals and communities would achieve an operating level of land right literacy.

Women need to be knowledgeable about land laws and procedures. They also need to understand the complexity of land issues, the relationship between different laws and practices, the options available, and the limitations of the legislation and means of implementation. Knowledge of both formal and informal systems for exercising land rights is critical in most parts of the world: What are the real rights and obligations associated with land? How can those rights be exercised to their fullest? What happens if the obligations of the holder of land rights are not fulfilled? What are the consequences of noncompliance with the written or the customary law? In addition to understanding land rights and obligations, to be land-literate means understanding how to apply that knowledge in practice.

To be sustainable and successful, land literacy must be mainstreamed into society. Not just women but also local leaders, farmers, judges, and land professionals must all understand the law and its implications and how to use and follow it. The rule of law is more likely to have value if there are many people who understand land law and use and protect their rights under the law.

---

[132] S. Arun, *Does Land Ownership Make a Difference? Women's Roles in Agriculture in Kerala, India* in *Women, Land, and Agriculture* 19, 20 (Caroline Sweetman, ed., Oxfam 1999); and Brown *et al., supra* n. 31, at 30.

[133] *See* Arun, *supra* n. 132, at 22.

[134] *See* Brown *et al., supra* n. 31, at 34.

[135] *See* the *1999 World Survey, supra* n. 1, at 92.

Major legal changes will not be effective without a sustained effort to implement the changes and to sensitize the public to and gain their support for the changes. While workshops, training material, and mass media campaigns are able to alert the public to new laws, they do little to effect a change in attitude or action unless they are augmented by the efforts of local people who both understand and support the legal changes. Combining a mass media effort with the sustained presence of knowledgeable people at the village level will have a strong lasting effect.

Several different levels of legal literacy and education are necessary if change is to occur. Those to be educated include:

- Policymakers and local customary leaders, about the economic value of women having secure rights to land;
- Husbands, about the economic benefit possible if their wives purchase or have rights to land;
- Women, about dispute resolution if rights to land are impeded;
- The public, about new laws and programs; and
- Women, about their right to land from the marital household.

The Lao PDR is an example showing how legal literacy can have an impact on women's right to land. In 1995, the government of the Lao PDR, working with the Australian Agency for International Development (AusAID) and the World Bank, created a gender-sensitive implementation procedure for land titling with the LWU as a partner. The LWU trained the Department of Land staff and field teams and provided community education related to women's rights to land titles in villages where titling occurs. As a result, there has been an increase in the number of titles in the name of women and an increase in the number of joint titles.[136]

3.7 Conclusion and Recommendations

In most of the developing world, women's sphere of operation is the household. To overcome gender biases in property systems, donors must look at legislation and programs that will reach the household level. This means addressing not only property law and contract law but also family law. In many transitional economies, while all other codes have been updated, family codes have not been; nor have donors supported the law reform process.

Overcoming gender bias requires an understanding of customary law and traditions, and of what is possible and what is not. Rural women understand where to focus change. In Uganda, for example, rural women are not pushing for co-

---

[136] World Bank, *supra* n. 59, at 412.

ownership of land, although they want it. They are pushing instead for rights for widows, an achievable goal within their social context. Rural women must be part of the discussion of how to overcome gender bias.

Finally, overcoming gender bias will require that male leaders, both within the country and within donor organizations, make a commitment to change that includes speaking out publicly against gender bias and making its elimination a priority. Information campaigns and education must include men as well as women and must focus on issues that specifically affect women.

It is too easy to dismiss equality for men and women in a property rights system as either impossible to achieve or as a second, less important, step. In fact, if gender bias is to be overcome, it must be a priority from the beginning, when registration systems are designed, when legislation is being written, and when assessments are being done.

The following sections list recommendations for overcoming gender biases.

3.7.1 General Recommendations

- Focus funds and expertise on family law in projects concerned with land rights, reviewing the family code, the inheritance rules, and civil legislation in terms of women's rights to land both within a marriage or consensual union and should the family break down.
- Where feasible, encourage passage of co-ownership rules in civil legislation.
- As part of any program related to property rights, educate women regarding their legal rights to land, and educate men about the value of women's ownership and control over land.
- Provide credit to poor, unmarried (single, divorced, widowed) women to purchase land and inputs.
- Ensure that women receive extension services to assist them with land ownership and in dealing with customary taboos against women performing certain farming tasks.
- Encourage women farmers to form self-help groups and community action groups.
- Study the effects over time of legal innovations that address women's rights to land in various countries and contexts.

3.7.2 Creating New Rights to Land

- Mandate joint titling or distribute individual titles to women in the privatization stage. As a part of the process, provide women with access to credit, legal, technical, and market information and to a mechanism to enforce their rights.

3.7.3 Securing Rights through Titling Projects

- At a minimum, pass legislation that provides that in a marital relationship, co-ownership of land and property is the presumption for land acquired during the marriage. Titling projects should not proceed without first addressing the legal issues of women's rights to land.
- Provide women with a mechanism to enforce land rights.
- Encourage registration as co-owned for land acquired after a couple begins living together in a consensual union.
- Ensure that registration legislation includes specific direction about registration of married couples and those living in consensual unions. Ensure that registration officials and bureaucrats understand and implement these directions.

3.7.4 Markets

- Educate men about the economic benefit possible if their wives purchase land, and provide resources and information to women in a market-assisted land program.
- Understand the customs of the society and how they affect women's ability to purchase land.
- Draft legislation that requires that both husband and wife consent to a transaction involving land acquired during the marriage or cohabitation, whether or not the land is registered in the name of both or of only one spouse.
- In countries where there is polygamy and neither land nor marriage is registered, draft a consent provision that (1) requires the consent of both husband and wife to transfers of land, (2) states that a sale or mortgage is valid even if later contested for lack of consent, if the purchaser or mortgagee made a reasonable effort to obtain consent, and (3) in the latter case, requires the offending party (the seller or mortgagor) to provide land or equivalent compensation to the offended party (the wife who did not provide her consent).

3.7.5 Household Allocation of Land

- During the land reform process, review legislation affecting division of property upon divorce and encourage amendments to ensure the equitable distribution of property.
- Educate women regarding their rights to property upon divorce and provide inexpensive dispute resolution.
- Adopt legislation that provides that all gifts and cash received in conjunction with a marriage be deemed to be jointly owned by both spouses, regardless of to whom the cash or gift was specifically given.

- Review regulations associated with access to the courts; for cases of division of property, provide that court costs will be shared by both parties and paid after the property has been divided.
- Where polygamy is practiced, even if it is illegal, draft legislation stating that where the husband takes a second wife, all property belonging to the first marriage or consensual union would be partitioned, and the husband would only have his share to distribute to his new wife and any children.
- Establish widows' rights to land as a priority policy issue to be considered when property system legislation is drafted. A national discussion of inheritance rules and a willingness to provide money to work on inheritance policy would raise the status of the discussion of women's rights to land.
- Educate men and women about the relationship between dowry, bride price, and property ownership, and encourage a new look at distribution of property within the family in light of a changing property system.

CHAPTER 4

A Framework for Land Market Law
with the Poor in Mind

Leonard Rolfes, Jr. *

4.1 Introduction

An estimated 1.2 billion people across the globe live on less than $1 per day. An additional 1.7 billion people live on less than $2 per day. And still more millions are considered poor in places like the former Soviet Union, using the poverty guidelines as set by those countries. Over half of these estimated 3 billion people reside in the countryside and depend significantly upon agriculture for their livelihoods.

This dependence upon agriculture means that access to land is vital to the rural poor. For most of them, land is the main means of generating income, accumulating wealth, and transferring that wealth between generations.[1] Land access also can give value to household assets that cannot be used effectively except on the land, provide cheap food, and serve important insurance functions. Moreover, when women in particular control access to land, "child welfare in terms of nutrition, health, and education is improved."[2]

Looking at the land question in a less positive light, a World Bank study of India identified landlessness as the greatest predictor of poverty, even more than scheduled castes or literacy.[3]

---

* Leonard Rolfes, Jr. is Senior Attorney at the Rural Development Institute (RDI) in Seattle, Washington. Information about the Institute can be found at http://www.rdiland.org. The views expressed in this chapter are the views of the author and do not necessarily represent the views of RDI.

[1] World Bank & Klaus Deininger, *Land Policies for Growth and Poverty Reduction,* World Bank Policy and Poverty Reduction Report xix–xx (World Bank & Oxf. U. Press 2003).

[2] Alain de Janvry, Jean-Philippe Platteau, Gustavo Gordillo & Elisabeth Sadoulet, *Access to Land and Land Policy Reforms,* in *Access to Land, Rural Poverty, and Public Action* 2, 5 (Alain de Janvry, Jean-Philippe Platteau, Gustavo Gordillo & Elisabeth Sadoulet, eds., Oxf. U. Press 2001).

[3] World Bank, *India: Achievements and Challenges in Reducing Poverty* xiv, 12 (World Bank 1997).

This chapter explores the role that markets and the law can play in helping the rural poor gain access to the land they need to lessen their harsh economic predicament. In particular, it discusses the requirements for a legal framework that will provide legal definition, and hopefully legal power, to market mechanisms that facilitate access to land. Part two of the chapter discusses the extent to which land markets do in fact improve land access for the rural poor. The third part, the heart of the chapter, lists topics that play a role in markets and land access for the poor and presents the legal issues that pertain to each, grouped into three broad categories: those that relate primarily to tenure security; those that relate primarily to improving market efficiency; and those that relate primarily to special initiatives that may help the poor gain access to land. The fourth part discusses methods of bringing customary traditions and informal practices regarding land into the formal legal system. The fifth part offers brief concluding thoughts.

This chapter is premised on the theory that law reform has an important role to play in the ability of land markets to bring economic benefits to poor people. But law reform by itself is not a panacea for poverty: If law reform is to be a useful poverty-reducing tool, the social and economic issues that cause or aggravate poverty must also be addressed. To that end, law reform provides an important complement to needed economic and social reform, serving as a valuable tool to implement reforms and improve their efficacy.

4.2   Impact of the Land Market on the Rural Poor

Land changes hands in a market setting in two main ways: temporary transfer of use rights, primarily through leasing; and permanent transfer of ownership or owner-like rights through purchase-and-sale. A threshold policy question that necessarily guides the content of land market law is whether leasing and purchase-and-sale are effective in improving the access of poor peoples to land. This question is briefly explored here.

It is generally accepted that lease markets can enhance land access for the poor.[4] Leasing, unlike sales, does not require significant up-front cash or credit, and the large amount of land potentially available for leasing, variability in farm size, payment terms, different lease lengths, and other flexible conditions provide significant opportunities for lease deals that bring benefits to tenants as well as

---

[4] Jean-Marie Baland, Frederic Gaspart, Frank Place & Jean-Philippe Platteau, *The Distributive Impact of Land Markets in Central Uganda*, Working Paper, 30 (Centre de Recherche en Economie du Développement [CRED], Dept. Econs., U. Namur 2000); Pedro Olinto, Benjamin Davis & Klaus Deininger, *Did the Poor Benefit from Land Market Liberalization in Mexico? Panel-Data Evidence of the Impact of the Ejido Reforms* 29–30 (World Bank 1999); and World Bank & Deininger, *supra* n. 1, at 84–86.

landowners. Leasing is also often cited as an entry point into the agricultural ladder "in which a landless individual progresses from agricultural worker, to sharecropper, fixed-rent tenant, and ultimately landowner."[5]

Experience in Pakistan provides empirical proof that poor people can gain access to land through the lease market. In one study, 64 percent of the landless people surveyed rented land on either a sharecropped or fixed-rent basis. The same study cautioned, however, that access through leasing declines as agriculture becomes more capital-intensive. As capital plays a larger and larger role, landlords seek to rent in more land themselves or seek out tenants who have capital assets to contribute to the production process.[6]

Meanwhile, the preponderance of the empirical evidence suggests that in developing countries land sales markets have not significantly facilitated access of the rural poor to land. Studies in rural India do indicate that sales markets have helped small and marginal farmers acquire ownership rights to land—though this may not be true for the absolute poorest[7]—but evidence from Honduras and Chile suggests that sales markets do not facilitate access, while in Paraguay markets may contribute to a reduction in access.[8] An important factor contributing to these disappointing results is weak access to capital, which has "a major depressing effect on the ability of poor households to use even liberalized land markets to improve their access to land."[9] Moreover, the sales market in certain contexts has served as a mechanism for the poor to lose land through distress sales and seizure of mortgaged land.[10] Some also argue that the sales market will increase land concentration, with "land speculators and oligarchs" buying up agricultural land to the detriment of average rural people. These concerns have been expressed in regions as disparate as Central America,[11] the former Soviet Union, and Ethiopia.[12]

---

[5] Elisabeth Sadoulet, Rinku Murgai & Alain de Janvry, *Access to Land via Rental Markets,* in de Janvry *et al.,* eds., *supra* n. 2, at 210.

[6] *See id.* at 217–18.

[7] Robin Mearns, *Access to Land in Rural India: Policy Issues and Options,* World Bank Policy Research Working Paper No. 2123, 22 (World Bank 1999).

[8] Michael R. Carter & Ramón Salgado, *Land Market Liberalization and the Agrarian Question in Latin America* in de Janvry, *et al.,* eds., *supra* n. 2, at 263 and 273.

[9] Michael R. Carter, *Designing Land and Property Rights Reform for Poverty Alleviation and Food Security,* Land Reform: Land Settlement & Cooperatives 44, 53 (2003/2).

[10] *See* Baland *et al., supra* n. 4, at 2–3; and Rashid Faruqee & Kevin Carey, *Land Markets in South Asia: What Have We Learned?* World Bank Policy Research Working Paper No. 1754, 9 (World Bank 1997).

[11] *See* Carter & Salgado, *supra* n. 8, at 256.

[12] Berhanu Nega, Berhana Adenew & Samuel G. Sellasie, paper presented at the World Bank Regional Workshop on Land Issues in Africa & the Middle East, *Country Case Study: Ethiopia* 24 (Kampala, Uganda, April 29–May 2, 2002) (copy on file with RDI).

The World Bank's 2003 research report, *Land Policies for Growth and Poverty Reduction,*[13] describes several intertwined factors that together undermine the possibility of the land sales market working well for the poor. They include:

- Imperfections in financial and other markets;
- Policy distortions, such as subsidies, that increase the returns to land, and thus are capitalized as higher land prices. Intentionally or not, these distortions tend to favor wealthier and well-connected interests, thus increasing their power vis-à-vis the poor;[14]
- Land speculation, particularly in countries where there are few other repositories for wealth;
- Limited access to outside credit for land purchases; and
- Transaction costs.[15]

In summary, the empirical evidence is fairly positive that lease markets offer the rural poor an opportunity to access land, but sales markets in general do not. Thus a difficult policy question arises: What approach to sales markets is appropriate to enhance access of the rural poor to land? One possibility is to do nothing; another is to oppose sales market development outright. But because in practice land sales will go on anyway, crafting a responsible policy approach acknowledging this reality is preferable to pretending that sales markets do not exist or opposing market development outright.

To this end, the third part of this chapter suggests policy approaches that will help poor people access land through market purchases to the extent possible. Legal rules can strengthen property rights and make markets more efficient when they are clear and transparent and they reduce transaction costs. Specific interventions, such as preferential purchase rights and public outreach, can be directly targeted at helping the poor operate in a market environment. It is important to consider the proposals made below in light of customary traditions and informal practices (see section 4.4), and to combine them in a program that makes the most sense for the country in question.

---

[13] World Bank, *Land Policies for Growth and Poverty Reduction,* World Bank Policy Research Report (World Bank 2003).

[14] A highly visible example of such a policy distortion can be found in the United States, where many farm subsidies are paid based on gross output; thus the bigger the producer the more subsidy money. As a result, 10 percent of the farms received 61 percent of the subsidies in 2000, with the subsidies being "a chief source of operating capital for large operators to expand their holdings, often by buying out their smaller neighbors." Elizabeth Becker, *Far From Dead, Subsidies Fuel Big Farms,* N.Y. Times A1 (May 14, 2001).

[15] *See* World Bank & Deininger, *supra* n. 1, at 94.

4.3   A Framework for Land Market Law with the Poor in Mind

This section presents the wide range of topics that, taken together, comprise the legal framework for a land market. Each topic is explored in depth to determine what legal rules related to it can best improve land access for the poor. The recommended legal rules are not absolutes, of course—they must be shaped to the context of the country in question—but hopefully they will be a useful practical roadmap for making land markets work for the poor.

The topics here are grouped into three policy categories: establishing adequate tenure security; making the market a more efficient place to acquire land rights; and pursuing strategies to help the poor access land in a market environment. Those topics that fall into more than one policy category are discussed under the category where they play their most significant role.

When considering the needs of the legal framework for a land market that helps the poor, it should be kept in mind that, in addition to land-specific rules, general legal rules significantly affect the ability of the land market to work as intended. The rule of law, contract law, and conflict resolution are among the areas usually guided by general legal rules that impact land markets. To illustrate the importance of these rules: Suppose a farmer wishes to purchase a land parcel from his neighbor to expand his farm. If the contract law governing the creation and termination of rights and obligations is inadequate or unclear, the farmer must expend more resources in both time and money to ensure that his land purchase is legally valid and the contract terms are effective and enforceable. This extra expense and inconvenience could lead the farmer to decide not to enter into the deal at all. Thus, he loses an opportunity to increase his income and standard of living, the seller loses a chance to receive sales proceeds to use in other business or personal endeavors, and the economy suffers from a missed development opportunity.

4.3.1   Establishing Adequate Land Tenure Security

Security of tenure is a precondition for a working land market. Rights to land must be publicly recognized, enforceable, and not arbitrarily violated. Adequate land tenure security will benefit all land market participants, including the poor, who have fewer resources to acquire and defend land rights in insecure tenure environments. The importance of tenure security to the ability of the poor to access land is shown by the case of Ethiopia. Ethiopia has historically been plagued by tenure insecurity, with endless litigation over land rights and eviction of peasants from their landholdings. One study of Ethiopian agriculture suggests that tenure insecurity is the chief obstacle to improving the productivity of poor farmers, mainly sharecroppers.[16]

---

[16] *See* Nega *et al., supra* n. 12, at 11.

As discussed below, tenure security can be bolstered through improvements in the rule of law; recognition of general property rights; effective conflict resolution systems; careful definition and limits on the state's power to take private land; and effective documentation of land rights.

4.3.1.1 The Rule of Law

Legal rules related to land markets will not be effective if the legal system as a whole is not a reliable and effective instrument for acquiring and protecting rights. This is what the rule of law provides.[17]

The rule of law can be defined as an approach to governance and the ordering of relationships between parties in which formal law (1) supplies the guiding rules for allocating resources, resolving conflicts, and rendering justice; and (2) is generally adhered to and can be relied upon by the population to produce predictable outcomes. Laws in a rule-of-law system should be public knowledge, clear in meaning and applicable to everyone.[18] The power of the rule of law comes from the fundamental belief the citizenry places in the fairness and effectiveness of the law, which leads most people to respect and follow it and to demand that others do the same. The legal system must have credibility in the eyes of the population. Does the law address their needs and problems? Can people rely on law when conducting business? Do they look to the law for guidance in the event of a problem? Do they believe that, in a contentious situation, the law will usually be applied in a fair and reasonable manner despite disparities in the relative economic, political, or social power of those affected?

The rule of law has received significant attention over the past decade for good reason. Societies in which the rule of law is an operational principle have led the way in broad-based economic development. Conversely, where the rule of law does not function well, other systems will fill the vacuum. Sometimes these systems perform reasonably well, but too often they are inefficient, impose excessive burdens on weaker actors such as the poor, or are geared to serving well-connected interests. Societies where the rule of law is weak suffer from rent-seeking by bureaucrats, other forms of corruption, and low public confidence in government and other institutions. Plunder of the public treasury, extortion of small business, and private "enforcement" of disputes are tangible signs that the rule of law in a particular setting is weak.

Developing an operational rule-of-law system must come from within a country. Leaders must submit to being ruled by the law. The societal mindset about the

---

[17] In addition to its importance for tenure security, the rule of law is important to improving market efficiency (*see infra* section 4.3.2) and implementing measures specifically targeted to help the poor gain access to land (*see infra* section 4.3.3).

[18] Thomas Carothers, *The Rule of Law Revival,* 77 For. Aff. 95(12), 1 (March/April 1998).

utility of law and the good it can bring may need changing. Though such changes do not happen overnight, they are necessary if the legal framework is to become operational for any purpose, including improving land access for the poor.

The following principles and approaches should be explored in attempts to improve the rule-of-law environment:

- The law must be fair. A major characteristic of fairness is that the law should apply equally to all, regardless of their public connections or private power.[19] Fair laws usually come out of participatory democratic processes because there the range of interests represented and the attendant publicity make it harder to favor elites and special interests at the expense of others in the society.
- The law must effectively address people's economic and social needs. Laws that do not do this will not be followed. This requires legislation that is not only proactive but that legalizes what people in practice are already doing for themselves.[20] In Sri Lanka, for example, the government has issued permits recognizing encroachments onto state-owned forest land by some 600,000 poor people.[21] If this had not been done the people would have still possessed the forest land in practice but would have used it extralegally.

  Similarly, there is often a disconnect between what law drafters and policymakers want the law to do and what the law can do. Law can take the lead in pulling society forward, but if it leaps too far ahead, it will fail.
- Strengthening law-related institutions is important to make them more "competent, efficient, and accountable."[22] Government officials should be professional and customer-oriented, receive adequate salaries to minimize temptation to engage in corrupt activities, and be held accountable for their actions.
- Criminal prosecutions, high-value civil court judgments, and other visible examples of the law's triumph over the powerful and the corrupt can bolster the average person's belief that the law can render a correct and just result.

---

[19] Tim Hanstad, *Introduction to Agricultural Land Law Reform* in *Legal Impediments to Effective Rural Land Relations in Eastern Europe and Central Asia: A Comparative Perspective,* World Bank Technical Paper No. 436, 1, 8 (Roy Prosterman & Tim Hanstad, eds., World Bank 1999).

[20] Hernando de Soto, *The Mystery of Capital: Why Capitalism Triumphs in the West and Fails Everywhere Else* 161–62 (Basic Books 2000).

[21] R. M. K. Ratnayake, paper presented to World Bank Regional Workshop on Land Issues in Asia, *Country Case Study: Sri Lanka* 11 (Phnom Penh, Cambodia, June 3–6, 2002) (copy on file with RDI).

[22] *See* Carothers, *supra* n. 18, at 3.

Building a rule-of-law environment is an ongoing process measured by incremental improvements. Countries seeking to apply rule-of-law principles should not insist that rule-of-law reform be complete and deem progress short of completion as not worthwhile or an outright failure. In fact, no country has achieved a complete rule-of-law environment, but incremental improvements to achieve rule-of-law principles are valuable and will help make legal rights affecting the poor more usable and enforceable.

4.3.1.2 Recognition of General Property Rights

Land is a particularly important form of property for economic, social, and cultural reasons, and has unique features as a fixed object. Some special rules are therefore needed to address its importance and unique nature. At the same time, land is but one type of property: among other types are movable property (such as vehicles), businesses, information, and intellectual property. The legal attributes of all forms of property, including land, can be articulated to a significant degree by the same set of general rules: Only the special features of each type of property require unique treatment. Even in countries with land codes, property rights to land are defined in large part by the general legal framework.

In the general legal framework, the major set of rules necessary to identify and protect land rights must be based on the fundamental recognition of property rights. This legal recognition is often stated in civil codes or constitutions as the right of property owners, at their discretion, to perform any actions with respect to the property that are not contrary to a law or other legal act (such as a valid contract) and that do not violate the legal rights and interests of other persons.[23] Common rights to property also are often recognized in the legal framework, as they are in the Mozambique Civil Code.[24] This general legal recognition of property rights as applied to the holder of a land right would allow the holder:

- To possess the land in accordance with the right; rights that give their holder a fuller sense of ownership would also be more secure;[25]
- To use the land right as the holder sees fit, subject to reasonable state regulation;

---

[23] For example, the Civil Code of the Russian Federation, art. 209, §2 (Nov. 30, 1994).

[24] Maria de Conceição de Quadros, paper presented at the World Bank Regional Workshop on Land Issues in Africa & the Middle East, *Country Case Study: Mozambique* 8 (Kampala, Uganda, Apr. 29–May 2, 2002) (copy on file with RDI).

[25] *See* Nega *et al., supra* n. 12, at 19.

- To harvest the crops on the land or to take any other income or profit from it; and
- To sell or lease the land.

A second important legal concept needed in the broader legal framework relates to the general inviolability of the property right: Property rights cannot be simply annulled or taken away, by either the state or other private parties. The law should provide for termination of a property right only through a freely concluded contract, to meet financial (or perhaps criminal) liabilities, or pursuant to the state's power to take a property right for social needs.[26]

4.3.1.3 Conflict Resolution

A poor farmer who acquires land rights through the market must be able to enforce these rights. Otherwise, the farmer's confidence in the security of his rights will be low, and he will not make the best use of his land. For the most part, land disputes are addressed by general conflict resolution systems, though land-specific systems also exist.

The legal framework for a conflict resolution system, whether general or land-specific, should incorporate the following components so as to meet the needs of the population in general, including the poor, who access land through market mechanisms:

- The legal authority of the conflict resolution system should be defined, including its power to interpret law, make factual and legal determinations, issue rulings and judgments, and enforce compliance with court orders.
- The legal framework should identify the different venues of conflict resolution, most notably the judicial system with its different classifications of courts. The law should also refer to administrative, arbitration, and mediation forums. For each of these venues legal authority must be defined.
- The conflict resolution system must deliver fair rulings in line with legal principles. Two measures can help. First, judges, arbitrators, and other decision makers should have adequate professional training, receive adequate salaries, and be subject to dismissal for corrupt practices. Second, the system should be thoroughly transparent; public court proceedings and published court rulings both serve this goal.
- The ordinary person must have access to the system. Access requires physically convenient conflict resolution venues, reasonable fees to access the

---

[26] Zoning and land use regulation would not fall under this general inviolability principle: they require special treatment in the context of land law itself.

system, and a system that is navigable in most cases without the need for expensive legal counsel.
- The system should hear conflicts, deliver rulings, process appeals, and ensure timely and efficient compliance with rulings.
- Alternative dispute resolution models, such as third-party mediation and arbitration, can play an important role in promoting access and efficiency. These models are often cheaper to utilize and can be speedier in resolving a dispute than going to court.
- In some countries traditional customary forms of conflict resolution have a valuable role to play. In Mozambique, for example, land conflicts are brought before customary institutions and judicial and community tribunals; formal law recognizes their legitimacy.[27] In villages in the Kyrgyz Republic, elders act as mediators to settle land-related disputes.[28]

On a practical level, which dispute resolution options are most likely to give the poor meaningful access to justice? It will be those options that are physically accessible, do not demand high fees, and deliver legally sound rulings in a timely manner. Customary forms of conflict resolution and mediation and arbitration are most likely to meet these criteria. By contrast, dispute resolution through courts is frequently time-consuming, expensive, and intimidating, while administrative rulings may not be legally sound, especially when the State is one of the parties to the dispute (though this latter problem may be tempered by a right to appeal adverse administrative decisions).

4.3.1.4   State Seizure of Private Land Rights

The ability of governments to acquire private land for public purposes against the will of the landowner is a necessary state power, though at the same time it is a significant infringement on private land rights. Too often governments seize land for reasons that cannot be justified; the poor and relatively uninformed are typically the ones who suffer as a result.[29] Moreover, land that can be confiscated easily and cheaply by the State will never achieve the full value as a marketable capital asset that it would achieve in an environment where tenure is more secure.

---

[27] *See* de Quadros, *supra* n. 24, at 7.

[28] World Bank, *Legal Rights to Land for Rural Residents in Kyrgyzstan* 1 (unpublished report, World Bank 2003) (copy on file with RDI).

[29] For example, the U.S. State of Mississippi threatened to use its sovereign power to forcibly acquire private land for a truck manufacturing plant. As one of the aggrieved landowners put it, "There's 15 of our families right around here, and none of them want to live anywhere else. But then the state comes in and pushes us around and tells us they're going to turn our land over to a private company. It's not right." David Firestone, *Black Families Resist Mississippi Land Push,* N.Y. Times A20 (September 10, 2001).

A legal framework for land markets that promotes land access for the poor should address two major issues related to state seizure of private land rights:

1. Reasons for which the State has legal power to terminate private land rights should be carefully defined and limited.[30] The primary reason should be to serve specified important public needs, such as transportation corridors and educational facilities. Other possible reasons might be as punishment for criminal acts and for urgent public necessity in emergency situations, such as a war (which should be rare). Seizing land for violation of land use rules and for economic planning, as provided for in Ukraine's Land Code,[31] is not acceptable. Seizure for reallocation to private parties is generally not acceptable, since the power would most likely be used to benefit powerful private interests, though an exception could be made to accommodate land reform mechanisms in certain situations.

2. The law should establish a process for the State to take private land that is based on the following principles:

   • The State must pay the landowner full market-based compensation at the time of the taking, or earlier.
   • The State should exhaustively explore ways to meet the need without taking land before proceeding with the taking option.
   • The private land right should be terminated only through a judicial procedure determination that the stated need for the taking is of sufficient public importance and that the compensation is sufficient.
   • The process should provide sufficient notification to the private parties concerned and permit them to fully participate in hearings and other procedural steps.

4.3.1.5 Documenting Land Rights

For a land right to be valid, other people must recognize it as legitimate. This might be as simple as neighboring land users acknowledging each other's land rights in a manner they all agree on. Such informal systems do bring benefits to poor people, as can be seen in the active market in untitled land in Uganda.[32]

---

[30] Unfortunately, in 2005, the United States Supreme Court essentially eliminated this limitation from the U.S. Constitution in its controversial ruling in *Kelo v. City of New London* 125 S. Ct. 2655 (2005).

[31] Land Code of Ukraine, arts. 143 and 151 (Nov. 15, 2001).

[32] R. Mwebaza & R. Gaynor, *Land Sector Analysis: Land Market, Land Consolidation, and Land Readjustment Component* 16 (unpublished report, Govt. Uganda 2002) (copy on file with RDI).

However, the greatest economic power of a land right—its power to create capital—is based on the right being recognized by the world at large, not just locally, in such a way as to manifest its capital-creating attributes.

Having land rights recognized by the world at large requires that they be formally documented in a way that allows outsiders to access the information. This is not easy to achieve, and there are pitfalls. If people who either hold or wish to acquire land rights view the costs of participating in the formal system to be higher than the costs of a less-formal method of recognizing rights, the formal system will fail. Also, if the formal system mandates results that bear no relationship to the reality of how rights are formed in fact, the well-connected can usurp the rights of the poor, and the formal system will cause positive harm.

To minimize chances for failure, the following ideas should be incorporated into the process for formalizing property rights:

- The system must convert into formal property the land rights that exist in practice, though they may not be provable by chains of title or other conventional means.[33]
- Invariably, there will be multiple claims to the same land parcel or other land disputes. These claims and disputes must be settled through a process and in a manner that the affected parties will accept as legitimate and utilize. This could involve setting up a specialized mechanism or using an approach rooted in customary norms.
- The system must be low in cost, administratively easy to navigate, and physically accessible to poor people.
- The system should move toward a common language to characterize land rights, though this will be achievable only over time.
- The system must recognize and formalize pre-existing rights.

The two prevalent formal systems for documenting land rights in developed countries are title registration (Europe, Australia, and most of Canada) and deed registration (United States).[34] While country strategies to document land rights may seek to establish one of these systems (probably title registration), how this is done will be different for each country.

---

[33] *See* de Soto, *supra* n. 20, at 156–57 and 171–73.

[34] Leonard Rolfes Jr., paper presented at the World Bank Regional Workshop on Land Issues in Central & Eastern Europe, *Making the Legal Basis for Private Land Rights Operational and Effective* 30 (Budapest, Hungary, Apr. 3–6, 2002).

4.3.2 Increasing Land Market Efficiency

Increasing the efficiency of land markets by reducing economic barriers and making it easier for people to carry out market transactions in land should make land markets more useful for poor people. The alternative—inefficient markets with high transaction costs and cloudy rules—seems unlikely to help the poor. Typically such conditions work to the advantage of the wealthy, the influential, and the sophisticated market participant.

This section offers legal rules to serve the efficiency goal in six areas: general rights and obligations, land purchase and sale, land lease, land mortgage, transaction costs, and land transfer by inheritance.

4.3.2.1 General Legal Rules Creating Rights and Obligations

Land markets are about willing parties agreeing to take on certain obligations in exchange for certain rights. For example, the lessor of a land parcel freely *obligates* himself to permit the lessee to use the land for a certain period; in exchange the lessor *gains the right* to receive rent. The lessee, on the other hand, freely *obligates* himself to pay the lessor the rental amount, in exchange for which the lessee *gains the right* to use the land parcel for a fixed period. Since almost any other type of property (car, television) could replace land in this simple example, it is clear that many requirements of a land transaction can be guided by legal rules applying to property in general, and do not require land-specific rules. Most jurisdictions recognize this, therefore it is important to examine general legal rights and obligations to ensure they are adequate for application to the land market.

Three components of the general legal framework on rights and obligations arising out of transactions warrant mention:

First, the legal framework should recognize the principle of *freedom of contract*. Under this principle, a person chooses whether to enter into a contract and with whom. The two parties are also free to establish rights and obligations in the contract by mutual agreement, as long as they are not contrary to law.

Second, the legal framework should include provisions on obligations, such as the basic definition of an obligation (a requirement by one person to perform a specified action, such as transferring land ownership, for the benefit of another person), remedies for failing to fulfill the obligation (such as enforcement of the obligation or monetary damages), and termination of the obligation (such as through its fulfillment or settlement if fulfillment is not possible).

Third, the legal framework should contain guidance on how to conclude a contract, such as rules on when an offer to conclude a contract arises, how it may be accepted, forms a contract can take (oral or in writing), and when contracts are deemed concluded. Similarly, the legal framework should identify transactions that will be considered invalid in whole or in part, such as those concluded under the influence of fraud, coercion, or threat. These provisions are of particular importance for the poor who have conflicts with domineering or unscrupulous interests seeking to restrict their access and rights to land.

4.3.2.2   Land Purchase and Sale

As discussed in section 4.3.1, the poor have difficulty gaining access to land through purchase and sale. To minimize this difficulty, this section proposes some relatively simple legal rules that should make land purchase and sale understandable to and usable by poor people while minimizing opportunities for coercion and fraud during the process.

Straightforward land purchase-sale transactions that are free of coercion and fraud should follow the following legal principles:

- Citizens must have a clear right to purchase land at freely negotiated prices. As a corollary, sales concluded under conditions of fraud or duress are void.
- The right of purchase must not be conditioned on special qualifications such as education or experience in agriculture. The poor can decide for themselves whether they are capable of using the land effectively.
- The law should specify the essential requirements of a purchase-sale contract: identification of the parties, description of the land, statement of the purchase price, and terms of payment, all of which must be in writing.
- The government should not participate in setting the price or concluding the contract unless it is a direct buyer or seller. This principle should be directly stated in the law to avoid any ambiguity that could be used as an excuse for intervention.
- Model sales contract forms should be drafted to facilitate transactions and protect rights, though their use should not be required.
- There must be legal recognition of a land transfer. This would usually be accomplished by a registration system maintained by a state agency, though the type of legal recognition afforded by the system may vary.

4.3.2.3   Land Lease

As noted previously, leasing is the market mechanism that offers the greatest near-term potential for increasing the access of the poor to land. As with purchase, lease rules work best for the poor when they are relatively simple to follow, contain only those features that are truly necessary to promulgate a lease transaction, and limit the participation of bureaucracies.

A legal framework for leasing that reflects such ideas should:

- Define what a lease is. A succinct definition is "the provision of a land parcel by its owner to a lessee for use for a fixed time period in exchange for payment."
- Recognize the right of private parties to conclude lease agreements at freely negotiated prices.
- State the elements required in a rental agreement: identification of the parties; description of the land parcel to be leased; start and termination dates for the term of the lease; amount, form, and timing of rental payments; and the possessory rights the lessee is receiving.
- Outline the conditions under which the lessor has the right to enter the leased land, for example, to inspect the property periodically. Such conditions could be included in the lease agreement, but statutory guidance may be warranted to prevent lessors from excessively interfering with lessees' possessory rights.
- Outline the obligations of lessor and lessee for the upkeep of the land. Again, these obligations could be stated in the lease agreement, but statutory guidance may be warranted to protect the weaker party, whether lessee or lessor.
- State whether all leases must be concluded in writing to be legally valid. Medium and long-term leases should be in writing, but in many situations requiring written contracts for short-term leases will not deliver a substantial benefit.
- Permit the lessee to sublease the land parcel if the lessor agrees. Subleasing adds flexibility, especially if primary leases are for long periods. Depending upon the situation, such as if the State is the primary lessor, the law could make subleasing the default right of the lessee unless the lessor objects, rather than requiring the lessor's consent in advance.
- Provide the grounds and procedure for termination of a lease agreement before its term is completed. The grounds should be specific and exclusive, such as failure to pay the agreed rent and violation of obligations relating to upkeep of the land. The procedure should require the lessor to notify the lessee of the violation and provide an opportunity for the lessee to remedy the violation before eviction proceedings commence.
- Identify circumstances that require registration of the lease agreement. A typical circumstance would be a lease of three years or longer.[35]

---

[35] Food and Agriculture Organization, *Good Practice Guidelines for Agricultural Leasing Arrangements,* FAO Land Tenure Studies 2, 7.25 (FAO 2001).

Finally, many countries have regulated the landlord-tenant relationship in an attempt to improve the lot of mostly poor tenants. The regulations have included the prohibition on sharecropping, establishing rent controls, and converting tenancy into near-permanent land use rights. By and large such measures have not worked as intended, and in some cases they have instead lessened access to land by the poor. In India, "estimates indicate that the introduction of tenancy legislation . . . was associated with the eviction of more than 100 million tenants, which caused the rural poor to lose access to about 30 percent of the total operated area."[36] Landlords will stop leasing land, conclude informal leases, and implement other measures to avoid becoming subject to tenancy regulations.

Moreover, landlord resistance notwithstanding, tenancy reform is very difficult to implement. Only in a few settings, such as in West Bengal, India, between 1978 and 1984, has implementation been effective and landlord resistance overcome to the extent that tenancy regulation did help the poor. The West Bengal reforms, known as Operation Barga, consisted of registering sharecropper rights; converting these rights into permanent, inheritable rights; and helping sharecroppers access production inputs and institutional credit in order to reduce their economic dependency on the landlords.[37]

In addition, tenancy regulation may be useful to address targeted social or equity issues. In Egypt, tenancy controls enacted in the 1950s provided tenants with security of tenure and the legal right to pass their tenancy rights to their heirs. When these controls were repealed in the 1990s, one result was that many landlords began refusing to continue renting land to women-headed households, presumably for religious or cultural reasons, even though "women had been the effective tenants for years and had met their obligations."[38]

Overall, regulating the landlord-tenant relationship has not been a good approach to improving access of the poor to land, though in some settings it still may deliver benefits.

4.3.2.4   Land Mortgage

In many market economies, the institution of mortgage has provided ordinary people with a phenomenal ability to acquire land. For example, in 1999 nearly 69 million U.S. households owned their own homes. The vast majority of these households

---

[36] *See* World Bank & Deininger, *supra* n. 1, at 116–17.

[37] Uday Shankar Saha & Mandira Saha, *Case Study. Regulating the Sharecropping System: Operation Barga* in de Janvry *et al.,* eds., *supra* n. 2, at 232–33.

[38] Ray Bush, *More Losers Than Winners in Egypt's Countryside: The Impact of Changes in Land Tenure,* in *Counter-Revolution in Egypt's Countryside: Land and Farmers in the Era of Economic Reform* 185, 195 (Ray Bush, ed., Zed Books Ltd. 2002).

were able to buy their homes only through loans secured by mortgages on the homes and associated land; they would not have been able to do so otherwise.[39]

However, can mortgage significantly expand land access for poor people in developing countries? There is little evidence to suggest that these people have been able to purchase land with borrowed money secured by mortgages on the land, but financing is needed to buy land, and the ability to mortgage land has made financing possible in many countries. There is little downside to creating a legal basis for mortgage lending; over the medium to long term, mortgages may end up being useful in helping the poor access land.

The legal framework for mortgages should include the following components:

- Definition of mortgage: "A lien against property that is granted to secure an obligation (such as a debt) and that is extinguished upon payment or performance according to stipulated terms."[40]
- Priority of the lender's (mortgagee's) claim to the mortgaged land over all other creditors. Any exceptions to this rule should be of overriding social interest.
- Identification of the essential items in a mortgage agreement: description of the land rights being mortgaged, information on the value of the land, description of the obligation being secured, conditions for discharge of the mortgage obligation (repayment of the loan), and conditions that if violated (for example, default) permit the mortgagee to accelerate the debt repayment and commence foreclosure.
- Description of the conditions under which the mortgaged land can be foreclosed on, and the procedure for foreclosure.
- Confirmation of the legal right to borrow money to purchase land by using the land purchased as security for the loan.

Many jurisdictions seek to protect borrowers (mortgagors) from bank predation by, for example, implementing long statutory grace periods for defaulting landowners to come into compliance with the mortgage agreement, restricting bank ownership of land, or requiring banks that acquire land by foreclosure to dispose of it quickly. The desirability of such measures must be weighed against the fact that they drive up the cost of capital for the poor and may lead banks to decide not to make mortgage loans at all.

4.3.2.5 *Transaction Costs*

High or needless transaction costs can act as a serious impediment to the poor being able to use the market to access land. If transaction costs are too high the

---

[39] *See* Rolfes, *supra* n. 34, at 17.

[40] *Black's Law Dictionary* 457 (Bryan A. Garner, ed., 2d pocket ed., West Group 2001).

poor will simply not do market deals, or will carry them out informally, with all the risks and uncertainty that this entails. Drafters must be very cognizant of land transaction costs when they design laws that affect land markets and should attempt to minimize these costs or shift responsibility for their payment to a more able party (usually the State) if at all possible.

The following list of common transaction costs discusses how they can be lessened in order to benefit the poor:

- *Surveying and mapping fees.* Because surveying and mapping fees often are so high that they amount to a significant fraction of land parcel values, they can impede land transactions. Several measures can help alleviate this problem. First, the law should not require overly precise mapping and survey standards for agricultural land because the costs of excess precision outweigh the benefits. Second, if a land parcel has already been platted, the law should not require updated surveys when the land is transferred unless the boundary lines have been adjusted. Third, initial platting of land parcels intended for use by the poor could be paid for by the State; even if platting fees are objectively small, they still may be prohibitive for the poor.
- *Appraisal fees.* Appraisers can provide a useful service by giving a professional assessment of a land parcel's market price, but sometimes their fees are too high for the poor to pay. The legal framework could leave the need for an appraisal up to the parties, rather than requiring appraisals in all market situations.
- *Notary fees.* Because these fees are often regulated by law, the law could lower or eliminate them for transactions with, say, small land parcels that are likely to be purchased or sold by the poor. Also, the benefits that notaries provide to the transaction process could be reviewed with an eye to eliminating their role if their contribution is not worth the cost.
- *Registration fees.* Fees for registration should be kept as low as possible so as not to discourage use of the registration system. Perhaps registration fees could be exempted for transactions involving small parcels of agricultural land. Still, lowering registration fees should be weighed against the need for registration systems to generate user fees. There is empirical evidence that registration systems in developing countries can survive off user fees,[41] but it is unlikely that this is true in rural areas.
- *Excise taxes on land sales.* Requiring the parties to a land sales transaction to pay a tax in order to conclude the deal is a direct disincentive to market

---

[41] Klaus Deininger & Gershon Feder, paper presented at World Bank Regional Workshop on Land Issues in Asia, *Land Institutions and Policy: Key Messages of the Policy Research Report* 15 (Phnom Penh, Cambodia, June 3–6, 2002) (copy on file with RDI).

deals, and to reporting the true sales price. Although such taxes are common in many developed economies, they clearly are problematic in developing countries where the land market is underdeveloped or accurate land valuation is an issue. There, the law should not insist on excise taxes on land sales. The State's need for revenue will be much better met over the longer term by facilitating market transactions that encourage investment in land and then taxing the resulting economic growth by other methods (income tax, sales tax on goods and services, and so on, and so forth).

- *Administrative costs.* Every contact with the state bureaucracy in the process of carrying out a land transaction imposes costs while creating opportunities for rent-seeking. For example, in Ukraine citizens may purchase agricultural land only if they have agricultural education or experience.[42] Enforcing this rule necessarily entails that, for every transaction, a state regulator must verify that the purchaser or lessee meets the qualifications. The law can do a great deal to eliminate such costs. Every proposed administrative intervention into a land deal must be put to a severe need test and cost-benefit analysis. Only if the test is passed should an intervention be called for by law.

4.3.2.6 Transferring Land Rights by Inheritance

Though inheritance is not a market transaction, it cannot be ignored because in many settings it is the most common way to transfer land rights. For example, in many countries of the former Soviet Union mostly poor pensioners own more than half the private agricultural land. Proper rules for inheritance are crucial if these pensioners are to successfully pass their land to their children, many of whom are also economically insecure.

Inheritance of land is usually governed by the rules of succession that apply to property in general. The law should identify what is required for a legally sufficient will and the priority of beneficiaries in case a person dies without a will. The law may also require that certain people be designated beneficiaries, such as a spouse or minor children.

Inheritance law is an area where formal and customary law often diverge. In Sri Lanka, a variety of informal inheritance practices are still used.[43] Drafting inheritance legislation requires special attention to reconciling the formal law with customary norms.

---

[42] Land Code of Ukraine, *supra* n. 31, at art. 130.

[43] *See* Ratnayake, *supra* n. 21, at 14–15.

4.3.3 Special Efforts to Help the Poor Within a Market Environment

This section discusses interventions into the market environment that are intended to promote land access specifically by poor people: restrictions on marketability of land rights, public education and legal aid, land taxation, homestead and garden plots, public land auctions, and land reform.

4.3.3.1 Restrictions on Marketability of Land Rights

In a completely free market a land owner may sell land to anyone without restriction and may lease it to anyone for any time period, be it six months or fifty years. In certain contexts, however, targeted restrictions on land marketability may promote access to land by the poor without causing undue harm to land values or investment incentives. As a corollary, during times of social and economic transition the poor may be especially vulnerable to losing land access. This section explores various types of market restrictions and offers guidance on the general utility of each in broadening land access or forestalling reductions in access.

- *Restricting purchase of land by foreigners.* Wealthy foreigners could theoretically buy up much of a developing country's land, thus making it unavailable or too expensive for the indigenous poor and less well-off to access. Namibia has responded to this potential threat by passing a law prohibiting foreign acquisition of commercial farm land without permission of the government.[44] While limiting the right of foreigners to purchase land would probably promote access for prospective indigenous buyers in countries where there is a foreign demand for land or significant domestic land pressure, it would do little in countries where there is no such demand. Also, limits on foreign acquisition should be weighed against the loss of foreign investment that may result.
- *Preferential rights to buy or lease land.* Some countries give preferential rights to buy or lease land to co-owners, neighbors, or lessees of the land. Romania does so as to sale, while China's Rural Land Contracting Law has a similar provision as to farmers' thirty-year use rights. A preferential purchase or lease right should provide broader access, and not unduly harm marketability, if two rules are applied: First, the preferred purchaser or lessee must meet the landowner's offer as to price and other contract terms. In other words, if a nonpreferred buyer is willing to pay a higher price than

---

[44] Hifikepunye Pohamba, paper presented at the World Bank Regional Workshop on Land Issues in Africa & the Middle East, *Namibia Country Paper: A Case Study on Land Issues* 2 (Kampala, Uganda, Apr. 29–May 2, 2002) (copy on file with RDI).

the preferred buyer, the nonpreferred buyer should acquire the land. Second, the procedure for offering the land to the preferred right holder must be quick and simple. In Romania an owner who wants to sell land notifies the local administration, which then publicizes the opportunity to preferred purchasers for forty-five days. Farmers do not consider this procedure to be overly onerous.[45]

- *Ceilings on ownership.* Upper limits on the amount of land a person or entity can own are controversial. Proponents of ceilings argue that, in countries with very little farmland relative to the number of people who need land, such as India and the Indonesian island of Java, restricting the amount of land a party may own makes the land base available to more people. Ceilings may also help prevent new consolidations of land after land reform, a role they successfully served in Japan and Korea after World War II.[46] More recently, to prevent the reconsolidation of land ownership in the hands of the collective farms, Ukraine adopted a 100-hectare ownership ceiling for agricultural land until 2010.[47]

On the other hand, there are questions about whether ceilings in fact result in expanded access and whether owners can evade ceilings through transfers to relatives and straw men.[48] Ceilings have also been cited as reducing land values, thus undermining the asset endowment of the poor. For instance, in Sri Lanka ceilings are said to have reduced land values by 50 percent.[49]

Because the evidence is not definitive about whether ceilings work to improve land access for the poor, two areas of guidance—one policy and the other legal—are offered for countries considering the use of ceilings to promote land access. First, ceilings are probably most effective when imposed to prevent further consolidation of private land into larger and larger holdings or to prevent the reversion of newly privatized land to its former controllers, as in the Ukraine example. They are less effective when used as a tool for the government to take private land above the ceiling for redistribution.

---

[45] Roy L. Prosterman & Leonard Rolfes, Jr., *Review of the Legal Basis for Agricultural Land Markets in Lithuania, Poland, and Romania,* in *Structural Change in the Farming Sectors in Central and Eastern Europe,* World Bank Technical Paper No. 465, 110, 135 (Csaba Csaki & Zvi Lerman, eds., World Bank 2000).

[46] *See* World Bank & Deininger, *supra* n. 1, at 125.

[47] Land Code of Ukraine, *supra* n. 31, at Transitional Provisions §13.

[48] Klaus Deininger, Gershon Feder, Gustavo Gordillo de Anda & Paul Munro-Farure, *Land Policy to Facilitate Growth and Poverty Reduction,* Land Reform, Land Settlement & Cooperatives 5, 12 (2003/3 spec. ed.).

[49] *See* World Bank & Deininger, *supra* n. 1, at 125.

Second, no matter what the country, some parties will try to evade the ceiling even if it does generally work. Such evasions threaten to confuse land records and at least partially defeat the intent of the ceiling. These problems might be reduced by taking three steps:

(1) When a land sale is at the stage of being legally recognized by the State, an inquiry could be made as to the purchaser's right to buy in light of the limit. This inquiry should be carried out quickly.

(2) After a land sale is legally recognized, if it is discovered that the owner's holdings exceed the limit, the sale should remain legal but the excess land could be sold at public auction, with the owner retaining the residual proceeds after auction expenses are paid.

(3) If a country institutes a ceiling regime, the law also should limit the length of land leases. Otherwise a person who seeks land in excess of the ceiling could simply conclude a long-term lease and successfully evade the law's intent.

- *Restricting land sales.* Temporary restrictions on selling land may some-times be needed to prevent the market from serving as a mechanism that reduces poor people's land rights. For example, "In some CIS countries, managers of farm enterprises took advantage of the rural population's lack of asset management experience to entice the new shareholders to sell their land shares."[50] The result was a consolidation of land "in the hands of a small number of farm bosses."[51] To avert this result, Ukraine adopted a tem-porary prohibition on agricultural land sales so that new land owners would have time to become familiar with the market and thus make good decisions for themselves regarding their land assets.[52]

- *Limits on length of leases.* As a corollary to temporary restrictions on land sales, limiting leases to no more than medium terms (such as ten years) can also preserve future access possibilities, though it may impinge upon investment. Lease term limits are particularly attractive in countries like Russia and Moldova, where the weaker party is generally the relatively impoverished new land owner who receives a pittance from a former col-lective farm for the use of land, and who may well regret locking the land into a long-term lease once land values rise. This is in contrast to more traditional developing countries, where the weaker party is usually the ten-ant and a lease term limit may be harmful to access.

---

[50] *See id.* at 123.

[51] *See id.*

[52] Land Code of Ukraine, *supra* n. 31, at Transitional Provisions §15. The prohibition on land sales is set to expire in January 2007.

4.3.3.2 Public Education and Legal Aid

A well-conceived legal framework governing land markets will be of little help to the poor if they are not educated about markets and the law. For example, since 1992 Mexican law has allowed *ejido* members to lease out or sharecrop their land to others.[53] In Oaxaca State, however, research conducted in 2002 suggests that many *ejido* members still do not know about these rights and are not taking advantage of them as *ejido* members are elsewhere in Mexico.[54] This example shows that the poor need access to *information* about land markets and their legal rights and obligations as market participants. With more and better information the poor are more likely to use their talents and labor to acquire rights to land and make wise investments in land that boost its productivity. Also, improved knowledge will better equip the poor to compete in an environment in which their needs are often not in accord with the wishes of powerful interests. Put another way, informing the poor about what their rights are, how they may be used, and what benefits they may bring is as important to an operational legal framework as the adoption of a substantive law.

Similarly, access to the advice and assistance of a lawyer or other legal specialist could help the poor to better use the market to access land resources and to protect themselves from being coerced and manipulated by unscrupulous local officials, landlords, and others.

Various models are in operation around the world for informing people about their land rights and providing legal assistance. For example, in two Russian provinces, law offices focus exclusively on helping the rural poor exercise their newfound rights to land (*see* Box 4–1). These offices publish articles in newspapers about land rights, hold town meetings, and provide direct assistance to clients, ranging from information consultations to representation in negotiations and in court. In the Kyrgyz Republic, customary practice and formal land law have been brought together by a program to educate community leaders about land law and how to advocate for their communities. These leaders attend group meetings, discuss problems, and then engage with local governmental administrators who—intentionally or not—are interfering with the exercise of private land rights (*see* Box 4–2). In Kenya, a public outreach effort educates rural people about the value of land and urges small landowners not to sell. The effort includes a series of billboards with the slogan "Selling wealth to buy poverty."[55]

---

[53] Agrarian Law of Mexico, art. 79 (Feb. 26, 1992).

[54] Jennifer Brown, *Ejidos and Comunidades in Oaxaca, Mexico: Impact of the 1992 Reforms,* Rural Development Institute Reports on Foreign Aid & Dev. #120, 23–24 (RDI Feb. 2004) (copy on file with RDI).

[55] *See* http://www.ascleiden.nl/GetPage.aspx?datastore=1&url=/publications/publicatie449081047.

Box 4–1. Legal Aid in Action: Vladimir Province, Russia

In the spring of 2001, several dozen workers at the former collective farm "Vtorovskoye"—nominally privatized in 1992 as a partnership—contacted attorneys at the Vladimir legal aid center. They had heard that members of a neighboring farm enterprise had received ownership rights to the land culti-vated by their enterprise and wondered why they had not.

Upon investigation, the legal aid center's attorneys found that in 1992 the farmland used by the former Vtorovskoye collective was scheduled to be transferred to its members in the form of land shares held in common. Furthermore, in 1994 the local district authorities had prepared land share ownership certificates for all members of former collective farms in the district and asked the managers of the reorganized farms to distribute the certificates. But the chairwoman of the Vtorovskoye partnership, who was also a prominent local official, withheld the certificates, keeping them in a safe for nearly seven years.

Even after the chairwoman's egregious action was brought to light, she resisted the petitions of the land share owners and continued to withhold the certificates. The attorneys organized meetings with the owners to discuss their options, but the meetings had to be held outside in middle of the Russian winter. Why? Because local officials barred the owners and lawyers from using the local meeting house, saying that "there was no need to disturb people . . . the less they knew, the quieter they lived."

The lawyers then represented the owners in a court action to obtain the certificates. This finally forced the chairwoman to distribute the land share certificates to their more than 250 rightful owners.

Source: Rural Dev. Inst. Eighteen-Month Report 19 (Jan. 2001–June 2002).

Countries serious about making their law more effective in improving land access for the poor should strongly consider a legal assistance program.

4.3.3.3   Land Taxation

In theory, land taxation can potentially help the poor gain access to land through the market because its direct and visible economic effects on the taxpayer make it an attractive way to manipulate behavior. However, there is a question whether land taxation is an effective tool in practice to broaden land access.

There are two main types of land taxation. The first is taxation of land transfers, with the transfer representing the taxable event. Transfer taxes are customarily levied either as a percentage of the transfer price or as a fixed amount based on a

---

Box 4–2. Legal Aid in Action: The Kyrgyz Republic

With support from the World Bank's Development Marketplace grant program, in 2002 the Land Rights Advocacy Project in the Kyrgyz Republic implemented a model of legal aid and public information designed to take advantage of the close-knit communities and able customary leaders found in Kyrgyz society. The project had two main components:

1. *A process of providing rural people with information about their legal rights to land:* Project personnel, who were themselves native to the areas in which they were working, distributed written materials and made numerous presentations to groups of villagers about their rights.

2. *Direct efforts to resolve land-related problems:* Project personnel organized village meetings where local residents and leaders could talk about land problems. If the assembled group at a meeting identified a problem, it selected someone to take the lead in achieving a positive resolution. Those chosen usually already had a customary leadership role for which they had been selected by their peers. None were government officials. Thus, the local residents trusted these leaders to work on their behalf.

After the village meeting, the project personnel conducted training and discussions with the leaders identified, answered questions, provided information, and followed the progress of complaints. Importantly, though, it was the leaders, in conjunction with the people they spoke for, that actually engaged state bureaucracies, local farm bosses, and others who were interfering with land rights.

Through the project, hundreds of problems were solved on behalf of rural, mainly poor, residents of the Kyrgyz Republic. They included overcharges for registration of land titles by the state registration authority, refusal to allocate former collective farm land to legally entitled beneficiaries, loss of access to land by a woman due to divorce, unauthorized easements, and disputes concerning use rights to pasture land.

Source: World Bank, *Legal Rights to Land for Rural Residents in Kyrgyzstan* (unpublished report, World Bank 2003) (copy on file with RDI).

government-established land valuation (which may or may not be related to market value). Hungary is an example of a country with a land transfer tax.[56]

Taxation of land transfers has been called "the ultimate 'anti-market' tax" because it drives up the price of conducting a transaction and thus discourages market activity.[57] Moreover, land transfer taxation could drive transfers into the informal sector in an effort to avoid the tax. This result would not serve the interests of the poor to obtain legally valid, widely recognized title that would give them secure property rights and expand their access to credit. For these reasons, it is unlikely that taxation of land transfers can be used effectively to help the poor gain access to land.

The second major type of land taxation, sometimes called direct taxation,[58] is a fixed amount based upon the land's market value, productivity, use classification, quality, or other factors. Under direct taxation the tax obligation is continuous (rather than arising upon the occurrence of a particular event, such as a transfer), and is usually expressed as an annual amount to be paid. Most countries employ some form of direct land taxation. In Russia, for example, tax rates on land are set for each region by federal law and are calculated in rubles per hectare based on soil quality and location.[59] Indonesia employs a flat tax on land and buildings, calculated as 0.5 percent of land value.[60]

In theory, direct land taxation could be modified in a variety of ways to help improve access through market means. Land could be taxed progressively to discourage speculation and inefficient land use; the result could be to expand opportunities for the poor to buy the land, lease or sharecrop it, or at the very least work on it for a wage. In the Philippines, for example, local governments have the ability to impose a tax on idle lands.[61] Also, eliminating taxes for the smallest holdings or for a certain time period after acquisition would give the poor an economic advantage that could enhance their access to land. In Georgia, for example, people who receive agricultural land do not have to pay taxes on it for five years, and people who own less than five hectares are exempt from land

---

[56] Richard M. Bird & Enid Slack, *Land Taxation in Practice: Selected Case Studies* 130 (unpublished report 2002) (copy on file with RDI).

[57] Richard M. Bird & Enid Slack, paper presented at the World Bank Regional Workshop on Land Issues in Central & Eastern Europe, *Land and Property Taxation: A Review* 32 (Budapest, Apr. 3–6, 2002), http://lnweb18.worldbank.org/ESSD/essdext.nsf/24Doc ByUnid/DC58024CA1B418CE85256BE20066B2C8/$FILE/enidslack_taxation_ pdfcomplet.pdf (accessed September 3, 2004).

[58] *See id.* at 31.

[59] *See id.* at 131.

[60] *See* World Bank & Deininger, *supra* n. 1, at 169.

[61] *See* Bird & Slack, *supra* n. 56, at 76.

taxation without time limit.[62] In Kenya, agricultural landholdings of less than twelve acres are not taxed.[63]

Still other ways to modify direct land taxation are to provide owners with tax-related benefits for selling land to prescribed beneficiaries or for providing defined types of access. For example, a landlord could have a portion of the land tax waived for each land lease concluded with a certified member of the target beneficiary group, with a bonus added for longer-term leases. Alternatively, a landlord could receive a tax benefit for subdividing land (perhaps informally) and leasing it in government-recommended amounts to very poor people for whom even a garden-sized parcel is helpful.

But do these approaches to modifying direct land taxation in practice help the poor access land? Experience with progressive land taxation in Argentina, Bangladesh, Jamaica, and other countries showed limited success, largely because of valuation difficulties and opposition from large landowners.[64] The efficacy of encouraging land owners to lease land to defined beneficiary groups is difficult to predict. It might also be too administratively complicated to implement effectively, and could have unintended consequences (such as excessive subsidies for large landowners) that would harm the poor.

More promising are approaches exempting new land owners from taxation for a defined time period, as in the example from Georgia, or exempting small land parcels from taxation altogether. These seem more likely to provide benefits to the poor, to be feasible to implement, and to reduce the risk of negative unintended consequences.

When designing the legal framework for any of these land taxation schemes to promote land access, the following issues should be considered:

- *Negative impact on the poor.* Any land tax proposal should be carefully assessed to ensure that it does not end up hurting the poor. India at one time instituted a significant land tax that harmed the poor and led to land consolidation.[65] In Russia today the majority of commercial agricultural land is farmed by former collective farms but is owned by poor rural people. If a land tax were introduced to promote more productive use of land, poor owners might have to sell out and thus lose an asset that offers them economic hope.

---

[62] Law of Georgia on Making Amendments and Additions to the Tax Code of Georgia, secs. 19(l) and 19(v) (December 31, 2003).

[63] *See* Bird & Slack, *supra* n. 56, at 92.

[64] *See* World Bank & Deininger, *supra* n. 1, at 169.

[65] *See id.* at 168.

- *Land appraisal.* Market appraisal of land is integral to most developed land taxation systems but can be difficult to achieve in fledgling market environments. Also, appraisal of land values carries with it an element of subjectivity that can lead to equity concerns. Some jurisdictions address these problems by using measurements of land quality "depending on the soil type, distance from major roads, and irrigation facilities" as the basis for taxation.[66]

- *Land tax administration.* The cost of obtaining information on land values, and of administering a land tax system generally, can be relatively high compared to the revenue generated. It has been argued that land taxation in developing countries "will in all likelihood be so poorly administered [that it will] produce neither equity, efficiency, nor revenue."[67] This negative outlook, expressed over thirty years ago, may be significantly tempered by using land quality assessments or modern market-based mass appraisal techniques as the basis for taxation. Still, the issue requires attention.[68]

- *Inappropriate avoidance of taxes or utilization of tax privileges.* When taxes are imposed to compel certain behavior, there is always the risk that the taxpayer will seek ways to evade payment. Similarly, when tax preferences are granted to special beneficiaries, nonbeneficiaries may concoct schemes to take advantage of the preferences.

Finally, the discussion here should be considered in light of the fact that there has been very little recent research on whether and how land taxation can be crafted to expand land access for the poor. Specialists in land taxation devote most of their attention to revenue generation and fiscal federalism issues, with a focus on urban land.[69]

4.3.3.4 Homestead and Garden Plots

Internationally, there is strong evidence of the value of homestead and garden plots to the rural poor. For example, in Indonesia *pekarangan* plots range in size from one-tenth to one-fifth of an acre, yet on this small amount of land, households can generate up to 20 percent of their income and about half their caloric

---

[66] Jonathan Skinner, *If Agricultural Land Taxation Is So Efficient, Why Is It So Rarely Used?* 5 World Bank Econ. Rev. 113, 130 (1991).

[67] Richard M. Bird, *Taxing Agricultural Land in Developing Countries* 223 (Harv. U. Press 1974).

[68] *See* Skinner, *supra* n. 66, at 125–129.

[69] *See* Bird & Slack, *supra* n. 56.

needs.[70] In Russia owners of *dacha,* household, and other small plots cultivate only about 6 percent of the agricultural land yet generate over 50 percent of the total value of the country's agricultural production.[71] These plots probably prevented millions of cases of malnutrition in Russia over the past decade. Moreover, access to very small amounts of land may sometimes be better for the poor than attempts to create full-size family farms. This is likely to be the case when a poor family relies on several disparate income sources for household support, such as direct cultivation, wage labor, entrepreneurial self-employment, and migration.[72]

Since small plots have such potential to provide significant nutritional and income benefits, their formation should be encouraged, or at least allowed. From a market perspective, eliminating both legal limits on subdivision and restrictions on the minimum size of a land plot should help facilitate access.

4.3.3.5 Auctions of Public Land

Auctioning public land is a market-based method of transferring public land that may contribute to improving land access for the poor. Land auctions have proven useful as a way to distribute state-owned land in general. For example, in 1998 the Russian province of Saratov carried out sixty-eight auctions over a six-month period, with hundreds of land parcels being privatized or leased out for long periods. The auctions were successful because transactions were concluded quickly, local governments supported them because they retained the auction proceeds, and the process was transparent.[73] Another example can be found in China, where several localities have successfully auctioned undeveloped but reclaimable arable land.[74]

To maximize the possibility that public land auctions can help give the poor access to land, the following principles should be followed:

- Land should be auctioned in relatively small parcels.
- Local, relatively land-poor residents should be given priority to participate (though there may be a "straw man" issue).
- Successful bidders should not have to pay the entire purchase price up front but may make installment payments over several years.

---

[70] Robert Mitchell & Tim Hanstad, *Small Homegarden Plots and Sustainable Livelihoods for the Poor,* Livelihood Support Programme Working Paper, 4, 8–9 (FAO 2004).

[71] *See* Rolfes, *supra* n. 34, at 26–27.

[72] *See* de Janvry *et al.,* eds., *supra* n. 2, at 6–7.

[73] *See* Rolfes, *supra* n. 34, at 22–23.

[74] Tim Hanstad & Li Ping, *Land Reform in the People's Republic of China: Auctioning Rights to Wasteland,* 19 Intl. & Comp. L. J. 545, 546–548 (1997).

4.3.3.6   Land Reform

No inquiry into increasing land access for the poor is complete without discussing the question of land reform and the prospects for further progress. Each of the main scenarios for land reform—redistribution of private land, and privatization and decollectivization of farm land held collectively—will be addressed in turn.

In the classic land reform situation, a relatively small number of private actors own a disproportionate amount of a country's land, often as absentee landlords, while a large percentage of people dependent upon agriculture are tenants or landless laborers who do not own or have owner-like rights to the land. Some have no access to land at all. This inequitable distribution pattern plagues many countries, including the Philippines, Brazil, Pakistan, and India. In Brazil, for example, in 2000 "the wealthiest 5% of the farmers owned 69% of the nation's agricultural land, while the poorest 40% owned only 1.2% of the land."[75]

Landlessness and land inequality problems have been successfully addressed in some settings through the use of land reform. Post-World War II land reforms in Japan, South Korea, and Taiwan have been widely cited as successes and credited with creating a solid foundation for economic growth.[76] More recently, in the Indian State of West Bengal effective implementation of anti-eviction and rent control protections for sharecroppers (50 percent of the crop if the landlord supplies the inputs) and redistribution of ceiling-surplus lands to poor households have been credited with "a positive impact on agricultural production, poverty alleviation, and economic growth."[77] In other settings, however, less well designed and less effectively implemented measures aimed at similar objectives have created market distortions and perverse incentives that in the long run have negatively affected access of the poor to land. For example, threats of tenants acquiring more secure property rights have resulted in mass evictions in several Latin American countries[78] and in parts of India.[79]

---

[75] World Bank, *Reaching the Rural Poor: A Renewed Strategy for Rural Development* 33 (World Bank 2003).

[76] Roy L. Prosterman & Jeffrey M. Riedinger, *Land Reform and Democratic Development* 124 (Johns Hopkins U. Press 1987).

[77] Tim Hanstad & Jennifer Brown, *Land Reform Law and Implementation in West Bengal: Lessons and Recommendations,* Rural Development Institute Reports on Foreign Aid & Development #112, 9 (RDI 2001) (copy on file with RDI).

[78] Klaus Deininger & Gershon Feder, *Land Institutions and Land Markets,* World Bank Policy Research Working Paper No. 2014, 22–23 (World Bank 1998).

[79] P. S. Appu, *Land Reforms in India* 75–79 (Vikas Publg. H. Pvt. Ltd. 1996).

The most visible land reform mechanism has been State-sponsored forced redistribution from the landed to the landless. For such an approach to work, the legal framework must provide reasonable compensation to those losing land, involve beneficiaries in implementation, and use speedy field-based adjudication mechanisms.[80] The successful examples of this approach have been few over the past twenty-five years, due to the political difficulty of implementing such a program. Most attempts have not involved any significant compensation; landowners have strongly resisted for this and other reasons. For example, in the Philippines only 3.2 percent of the households targeted under the 1970s–1980s land reform program actually received land, and only 35 percent of the land owners received compensation.[81] This does not necessarily indicate that the redistribution-with-compensation approach should be abandoned, but it does suggest that the approach can be successful only in fairly unique settings.

Another mechanism more recently introduced to address the classic situation is market-assisted land reform (MALR). In general terms, MALR seeks to energize the rural land market by addressing both supply and demand issues. On the supply side, MALR tries to eliminate policies that distort the market and distract owners of un- or underused land from making rational economic choices to sell the land. Special subsidies for large landowners are one example. If these distortions can be eliminated, so MALR theory goes, the result should be an increase in the amount of land available for purchase. On the demand side, MALR offers cash grants or other forms of financing that poor people can use to buy land on the market from a willing seller.[82] It is important that adequate supply be made available; otherwise financing of land acquisition will simply push up the land price without increasing access by the poor.[83] Ultimately, because MALR

---

[80] *See* Prosterman, *supra* n. 76, at 194.

[81] Gilberto M. Llanto & Marife M. Ballesteros, paper presented at the World Bank Regional Workshop on Land Issues in Asia, *Country Case Study: Philippines* 9 (Phnom Penh, Cambodia, June 3–6, 2002).

[82] In some contexts, such as South Africa, financial support has been given not just for land acquisition but also for general development of farm production, which seems to encourage support recipients to bid down the price of land so as to use the remaining funds for other needs.

[83] Klaus Deininger, *Making Negotiated Land Reform Work: Initial Experience from Brazil, Colombia, and South Africa,* World Bank Policy Research Working Paper No. 2040, 16 (World Bank 1999); Land Policy Group, *The Theory Behind Market-Assisted Land Reform,* http://lnweb18.worldbank.org/ESSD/ardext.nsf/11ByDocName/TopicsLandPolicyandAdministration.

requires willing sellers,[84] it is not realistic to expect the approach by itself to facilitate substantial near-term redistribution, though it likely has a role to play as one of several strategies to improve land access for the poor.

The second land reform model—privatization and decollectivization—has been underway for over a decade in most of the post-communist states of Europe and the former Soviet Union. A similar process also has been underway in Mexico, where since 1992 reforms have allowed members of *ejidos* and *comunidades* to receive certificates to possess individual land parcels.[85] These possessory rights can be leased and sometimes sold. *Ejido* members can also take the next step and privatize the *ejido's* land in full or in part.[86]

The privatization/decollectivization effort has delivered some positive results over the past decade. Well over half of the agricultural land in the former communist countries of Europe and the former Soviet Union has been privatized, with virtually the entire rural population—including the poor—receiving rights to land. In several of these countries rural families received rights to distinct plots they have been actively cultivating for years.[87] In Mexico many *ejido* and *comunidade* members have received individual land certificates for well-mapped land parcels, and legal changes now permit *ejido* members to lease or sharecrop their parcels.[88]

But the results have not all been positive. Most agricultural land in the former Soviet Union is still farmed in massive, inefficient collective farms, even though the land is privately owned. The owners do not enjoy ownership rights in any truly meaningful way. In this sense the land reforms in the former Soviet Union are only partially complete.[89] And in Mexico, field research in Oaxaca State suggests that little *ejido* land has been completely privatized.[90]

---

[84] Namibia has interesting experience with the concept of willing seller. The Agricultural (Commercial) Land Act of 1995 requires that landowners who wish to sell their land first offer it for sale to the government, which would redistribute the land to the needy. However, many willing sellers have wanted to sell to other private parties, not to the government, and have managed to do so by characterizing the transfer as a donation to a closely held corporation. As a result, over 15 percent of Namibia's commercial agricultural land is under corporate control, which could lead to access problems for poor people in the future. *See* Pohamba, *supra* n. 44, at 4–5.

[85] *See* Brown, *supra* n. 54, at 15–16.

[86] *See id.* at 20–21.

[87] *See* Rolfes, *supra* n. 34, at 21, 23, and 25.

[88] Agrarian Law of Mexico, *supra* n. 53, at art. 79; and *see* Brown, *supra* n. 54, at 23.

[89] *See* Rolfes, *supra* n. 34, at 26–29.

[90] *See* Brown, *supra* n. 54, at 21–22.

What legal measures can be used to improve the ability of the privatization/ decollectivization model to deliver benefits to poor people? First, the Mexican experience suggests that tax policy is acting as a disincentive to full privatization of *ejido* land.[91] Tax and other obstacles should therefore be identified and removed. Second, the post-Soviet experience shows that the model must deliver land rights that are closer to individual ownership than to collective ownership. Most "private" rural land in the former Soviet Union, especially Russia, is held in a unique common ownership form known as the land share. A land share represents rights to a certain amount of land on a former collective farm but does not relate to a specific physical land parcel. For example, on a typical collective farm a land share owner will have rights to a ten-hectare share somewhere on the farm's 5,000-hectare farmland base. While these shares are legally tradable, and in most cases have been leased, the sense of ownership and the accompanying interest in doing something with the land right is by and large nonexistent. While the land may be considered private in a technical sense, by and large the attributes of ownership are not present.

Replacing land shares with rights to specific land parcels is probably the best legal measure that can be taken to create firmer ownership rights and hopefully the breakup of collective farms as time goes on. Moldova and Ukraine converted most of their land shares to individual land parcels. Another option is to convert land shares from their current incarnation as common rights in an entire collective farm to common rights in single defined fields with a size of, say, not more than fifty hectares.

4.4 Bringing Customary and Informal Practices into the Legal System

The previous discussion of the framework for a land market law presupposes to a significant degree that it will be formalized: The law will be adopted by legislatures or executive authorities and implemented in large part with the participation of official government bodies. The historical and legal tradition of the countries of Eastern Europe and much of the former Soviet Union has enabled this paradigm to be applied there over the past fifteen years. However, in many other parts of the world, customary institutions or informal practices are important vehicles for making decisions regarding land use and land transfer. Virtually all the land area in Africa is administered by customary institutions, for example.[92] In Indonesia, much of the rural land is subject to communal rights held by

---

[91] *See id.* at 22.

[92] World Bank & Deininger, *supra* n. 1, at 62.

customary (*adat*) communities; these communal rights are characterized in many different ways across the Indonesian archipelago.[93]

Eventually, though, land rights will come under the umbrella of formal law in places where customary or informal practices currently predominate. Though this may take decades, it is inevitable. Thus, the question is how to make the transition to formal law in a manner that causes minimum disruption, respects rights created by customary or informal practices, preserves practices that work well, protects poor people, and delivers a formal legal regime that people will accept as legitimate and useful. The following points should be considered in attempting to make the transition:

- Customary practices work well in many places and for many purposes, one of which is to provide land access to the poor. Such practices have evolved over time to meet the particular needs of people in particular areas. Where customary practices are effective, they should be recognized by the formal law, as has been done in Malawi, Mozambique, Tanzania, and many other African countries.[94]
- While customary practices often meet particular needs, it is also true that in certain cases they do not serve the people well in general.[95] They may predominantly serve the interests of local power brokers, for example. Therefore, customary practices must be carefully examined to determine the benefits they provide before they are recognized by the formal law.
- Formal law has limited ability to change customary and informal practices by fiat. Premature changes will result in a disconnect between what the formal law is and what customary practice says about land rights. For example, in the Central Asian country of the Kyrgyz Republic the custom for ethnic Kyrgyz people, still practiced, is for property to be inherited by the youngest son, yet tradition is at odds with the country's formal inheritance law.[96] Thus, ideas described in the previous section that are not consistent with customary and informal practices generally should not be forced upon the population, even if they would seem to improve land rights. Rather, a transition scheme should be constructed that enables the population to

---

[93] Rachel Haverfield, *Hak Ulayat and the State: Land Reform in Indonesia* in *Indonesia: Law and Society* 42, 45–46 (Timothy Lindsey, ed., Federation Press 1999).

[94] World Bank & Deininger, *supra* n. 1, at 63.

[95] *See generally Searching for Land Tenure Security in Africa* (John W. Bruce & Shem E. Migot-Adholla, eds., World Bank 1994).

[96] *See* Rolfes, *supra* n. 34, at 43.

Box 4–3. Land Transfers by Custom in Uganda

In Uganda the land in most land transactions is not formally titled. For these transactions the buyer and seller typically enter into an agreement that is witnessed by local council officials or clan elders. Neither the agreement nor the transaction itself is recorded or registered in any way.[97]

Transaction participants were generally "satisfied with the way in which the market is functioning, and did not perceive the costs as being prohibitively high or the procedures as being too complex."[98] However, with "regard to transactions on titled land, there was a general perception that the costs were too high and the procedures too complicated."[99] Trying to impose formal registration procedures on customary transactions could therefore have the "unintended effect of stifling rather than stimulating land markets."[100]

Source: R. Mwebaza & R. Gaynor, *Land Sector Analysis: Land Market, Land Consolidation, and Land Readjustment Component* (unpublished report, Govt. Uganda 2002) (copy on file with RDI).

---

accept new approaches in the formal law when they are ready, retaining customary or informal practices until this occurs.

• Prematurely imposing formal legal changes to customary or informal practices can also cause positive harm, including the weakening or loss of existing rights. For example, the 2000 Côte d'Ivoire Land Law ignored customary traditions used for demarcation of land, decreeing instead "that all customary rights not transformed into full title within 10 years would revert back to the state."[101] The state's ability to actually implement this provision is limited[102] and implementation could result in many people losing longstanding customary rights to land. Another example is in Uganda (*see* Box 4–3), where premature imposition of formal registration may be stifling land markets.

---

[97] *See* Mwebaza & Gaynor, *supra* n. 32, at v.

[98] *See id.*

[99] *See id.*

[100] *See id.* at vii.

[101] World Bank & Deininger, *supra* n. 1, at 64.

[102] *See id.*

4.5 Conclusion

The ideas and recommendations discussed in this chapter relate to the legal framework for land markets that improves access of the poor to land. They fall into three major areas:

1. Establishing and protecting secure tenure in land. Proper definition of property rights, certain aspects of the rule of law, protection of private land from inappropriate seizure by the State through its takings power, and effective conflict resolution mechanisms are examples of tenure security–enhancing measures.
2. Making the market a more efficient place to acquire land rights and to decrease distortions that "game" the system to the benefit of powerful interests or make it harder for the poor to meaningfully participate in the market. Clear and concrete land purchase and lease contract rules and reducing transaction costs, are examples of increased efficiency.
3. Pursuing legal strategies to give the poor more immediate access to land through the market in ways that do not distort market decision-making, trigger perverse economic results, or incite landowners to take self-protective countermeasures that could result in net harm to the poor. Examples of such strategies are providing legal aid and information and restricting the marketability of land in certain contexts.

Adopting and implementing a good legal framework will not by itself lead to improvements for the poor in the absence of economic and social reforms. But a country that can successfully develop and adopt a legal framework that draws from the ideas presented here will have made an important step forward toward a strong market system through which over time the poor can increasingly access land and thus improve their economic lives.

CHAPTER 5

Can Land Titling and Registration Reduce Poverty?

David Bledsoe*

5.1 Introduction

Land titling and registration are tools used in developing and transitional countries for pursuing at least two distinct benefits: spurring economic development
and alleviating poverty.[1]

The pursuit of these benefits rests upon the primary condition that titling and
registration give holders of land formal rights and increase their tenure security.
It is widely assumed that rights and security create benefits in three primary
ways:

1. Increased tenure security reduces the likelihood and fear of losing the value
    of investments made in the land, which means that overall investment in the
    land is stimulated. Such investments increase production yields, economic
    returns, and household incomes. The value of the land asset increases
    accordingly.

---

* David Bledsoe is a Senior Attorney at the Rural Development Institute (RDI) in Seattle,
Washington. Information about the Institute can be found at http://www.rdiland.org. The
views expressed in this chapter are the views of the author and do not necessarily
represent the views of RDI.

[1] Australian Agency for International Development (AusAID), *Improving Access to Land
and Enhancing the Security of Land Rights: A Review of Land Titling and Land
Administration Projects,* Quality Assurance Series No. 20, xiii, 11–12 (AusAID 2000);
L. Strachan, *Assets-Based Development: The Role for Pro-Poor Land Tenure Reform*
10–11 (Discussion Paper, Canadian International Development Agency 2001); Peru
Urban Property Rights Project, 1998 (P039086), Project Appraisal Document, at 5 and 27
[hereafter, Peru Urban Property Rights]; Cambodia Land Management and Administration
Project, 2002 (P070875), Project Appraisal Document, at 2, 5, 10, 14, and 27 [hereafter,
Cambodia Land Management]; World Bank, *World Development Report 2002: Building
Institutions for Markets* 31–38 (World Bank 2002) [hereafter, World Development Report
2002]; Laos Second Land Titling Project, 2003 (P075006), Project Appraisal Report, at 2
and 36 [hereafter, Laos Appraisal Report]; Laos Second Land Titling Project, 2003
(P075006), Project Appraisal Document, at 16 [hereafter, Laos Appraisal Document];
A. Galal & O. Razzaz, *Reforming Land and Real Estate Markets,* World Bank Policy
Research Working Paper, No. 2616, 5–9 (World Bank 2001).

2. Secure formal land rights can provide a real and secure source of collateral, which increases the availability of credit to obtain funds for investment in or even purchase of land.
3. Because secure rights also make the land market more efficient and consequently function better as the means for moving land resources into the hands of those who can put them to the most productive and efficient use. Again, increases in overall economic activity and return are anticipated.[2]

Although economic growth does not necessarily alleviate poverty, there is to some extent a necessary link. Poverty alleviation is certainly linked to economic development for the poor. While alleviation of poverty is of primary interest in this chapter, at a minimum an understanding of how titling and registration are thought to spur economic development must inform that discussion. For the poor to benefit from titling and registration, they must be reached and helped by the economic benefits created by titling and registration.

To provide necessary context, the next section describes a few of the more notable titling and registration programs around the world. The third section describes how titling and registration are thought to spur economic development and then provides evidence from the literature as to whether or not this is happening. The fourth section relates titling and registration to the alleviation of poverty. Then, given the reality that land titling and registration is likely to continue to be a widely pursued development activity, the final section offers some recommendations and suggestions.

5.2   Titling and Registration Programs

To provide context for the examples used in other sections, this section summarizes a few past and current titling and registration programs around the world. No attempt has been made to create an exhaustive catalog; instead, a few of the more notable and oft-cited programs are identified and discussed.

---

[2] AusAID, *supra* n. 1, at 7–8; G. Feder & A. Nishio, *The Benefits of Land Registration and Titling: Economic and Social Perspectives,* 15(1) Land Use Policy 25, 26–28 (1999); S. Pagiola, *Economic Analysis of Rural Land Administration Projects,* Land Policy & Admin. Thematic Team, 3–9 (World Bank 1999); T. Hanstad, *Designing Land Registration Systems for Developing Countries,* 13 Am. U. Intl. L. Rev. 647, 657–64 (1998); G. Feder & D. Feeny, *Land Tenure and Property Rights: Theory and Implications for Development Policy,* 5(1) World Bank Econ. Rev. 135, 139–143 (1991); H. Binswanger, K. Deininger & G. Feder, *Power, Distortion, Revolt, and Reform in Agricultural Land Relations,* in *Handbook of Development Economics,* vol. III, 2719–21 (J. Behrman & T. N. Srinivasan, eds., Elsevier Science 1995).

5.2.1 East Asia

The land systems in East Asian developing economies are varied but can be grouped into several categories by a few common characteristics. China and Vietnam, for example, can be grouped together because of the heavy state involvement in land allocation and tenure formalization, and the Philippines and Indonesia because of their customary tenure patterns, historical periods of occupations, and relatively inegalitarian distribution patterns. Lao People's Democratic Republic (Lao PDR) and Cambodia can be paired because of their nascent rights regimes, lack of tenure security, and land use patterns. Thailand stands alone by virtue of its longer history of private legal property rights.[3]

In Thailand, beginning with phase I in 1985 and then spanning two additional phases and eighteen years, a mass titling effort was made to clarify existing but undocumented (and sometimes confused) land rights and to transform old titles into new ones. By the closeout of phase III in 2002, about 11.5 million titles had been issued.[4] An oft-cited 1988 study of portions of the first phase, using data collected in 1984 and 1985, looks at credit and borrowing patterns of Thai farmers in selected villages within four of Thailand's seventy-six provinces.[5]

In Cambodia, a seven-year World Bank loan–funded land management and administration project is the first phase of the government's longer-term Land Administration, Management and Distribution Program. Now in its third year, the current phase consists primarily of a ten-province titling pilot that will issue and register about 1 million title; in conjunction with this systematic titling, a sporadic program will issue first-time titles on demand in a number of other provinces. The pilot also has institutional development, public awareness and participation, dispute resolution, land management, and land policy and regulatory components.[6]

In the Lao PDR, where there are an estimated 850,000 rural and urban land holdings, phase I of a titling and registration effort, which began in 1997, focused primarily on the regulatory framework and property valuation. It is projected that the program, now in its second phase, will have issued 600,000 titles by its 2009 close. Additional phase II components are land policy and regulatory

---

[3] M. Childress, *East Asia and Pacific Region: Regional Study on Land Administration, Securitization, and Markets* 1–5 (World Bank 2003).

[4] The Thailand Fourth Land Titling Project, 1999 (P069035), Project Information Document 1–3 [hereafter, Thailand Information Document]; Thailand Land Titling (03) Project, 1994 (P004803), Project Implementation Completion Report 2–8 [hereafter, Thailand Completion Report].

[5] *See* G. Feder, T. Onchan, Y. Chalamwong & C. Hongladarom, *Land Policies and Farm Productivity in Thailand* (Johns Hopkins U. Press 1988).

[6] *See* Cambodia Land Management, *supra* n. 1, at 32–37.

development, land administration capacity building, and training and public education and participation.[7]

5.2.2 Former Soviet Union

Since the breakup of the Soviet Union, there has been a big push to move land formally owned by the State into private hands. This individualization of state land has required massive demarcation and titling efforts. In many cases, setting up a registration system followed or is following these titling efforts. The titling and registration systems and accompanying legislation had to be developed from scratch because under the Soviet regime there were no individual rights to land.[8]

The Kyrgyz Republic's current World Bank loan–funded land and real estate registration project follows a land component within an earlier agriculture support services project that had issued land certificates to most Kyrgyz land rights holders. The current project, which was closed out in 2005, created 50 local land registration offices and also had systematic title registration, creation of registration zones and index maps, and public awareness campaigns and training components.[9]

In Moldova during a six-year USAID-funded national land titling and registration program about 2.4 million land titles were prepared for about 783,000 individual owners. Many of the titles were registered in local land registries. Together, they represent privatization of 901 collective farms that participated in the program.[10] During a five-year World Bank loan-funded cadastre project that ran from 1999 through 2003, an estimated 330,000 urban properties and 200,000 rural properties were titled and registered. The project also had an institutional capacity-building component.[11]

In Armenia, both USAID bilateral funding and a World Bank loan have gone to support land titling and registration in the past six years. The USAID project was directed to improvements to a nationwide title registration system, recommendations for real estate broker and appraiser legislation, proposed changes to laws affecting real estate and rights to real estate, assistance to new and existing

---

[7] *See* Laos Appraisal Report, *supra* n. 1, at 2–3, 7–9, and 43–49.

[8] *See generally*, R. Giovarelli & D. Bledsoe, *Land Reform in Eastern Europe: Western CIS, Transcaucusus, Balkans, and EU Accession Countries*, Sustainable Dev. Dept., SD dimensions (FAO 2004/2001).

[9] The Kyrgyz Republic Land and Real Estate Registration Project, 2000 (P049719), Project Appraisal Document, at 26–32 [hereafter, Kyrgyz Republic Appraisal Document].

[10] S. Dobrilovic & R. Mitchell, *Project to Develop Land and Real Estate Markets in Moldova: End of Contract Report* 3–6 and 9–15 (USAID/Booz Allen & Hamilton 2000).

[11] The Moldova First Cadastre Project, 1998 (P035771), Staff Appraisal Report, at 9–11 [hereafter, Moldova Appraisal Report].

private real estate entities, and a public information campaign.[12] The project was funded by World Bank loans. It ended in 2004, after helping to create 47 land registration centers, to survey 2.5 million privately owned parcels, and to set up about 1.25 million property records. Most of these records were entered into the new registry by 2005.[13]

In Ukraine, a modest USAID land demarcation and titling program has been issuing titles since 2001. Through mid-2004, about 750,000 State Acts (titles) had been issued for agricultural land and about 12,000 for nonagricultural parcels, though no title registry yet exists. This project also had significant legal and regulatory, public education, and legal aid components.[14] A World Bank loan–funded land titling and cadastre development project that began in mid-2003 has the goal of issuing up to 4 million State Acts; it also has legal reform, public awareness, training, surveying, title registry, and farm restructuring components.[15]

Tajikistan's six-year farm privatization support program, funded by World Bank loans, sought to formalize long-term inheritable land use rights to individuals on ten collective farms. Land was transferred to 5,782 farm families by way of land use certificates that defined boundaries and that were registered in a central database. Some other nonproject farms have since used the project's methods to extend formalized use rights to other farm households. A second World Bank loan–funded farm privatization project is now under consideration.[16]

5.2.3 Latin America

Latin American land reform and titling and registration efforts have a longer history; they reflect a milieu of unequal land distribution, large agricultural laborer populations, insecure smallholder property rights, and interjections of conflicting indigenous rights. Abundant in land but with large populations of landless poor,

---

[12] United States Agency for International Development, *Armenia: Real Estate Market Reform and Title Registration* 1–2 (USAID 2001), available at: http://www.usaid.gov/am/activitypages/ronco.html.

[13] The Armenia Title Registration Project, 1998 (P057560), Project Implementation Completion Report, at 4–10 [hereafter, Armenia Completion Report].

[14] S. Dobrilovic, *Ukraine Land Titling Initiative: Monthly Report for April 2004* 1–11 (Chemonics Intl. 2004).

[15] Ukraine Rural Land Titling and Cadastre Development Project, 2003 (P035777), Project Appraisal Document, at 41–49 [hereafter, Ukraine Appraisal Document].

[16] Tajikistan Farm Privatization Support Project, 1999 (P049718), Project Appraisal Document, at 31–41 [hereafter, Tajikistan Appraisal Document]; Land Registration and Cadastre System for Sustainable Agriculture Project (LRCSP), 2005 (P089566), Project Information Document, at 1–5 [hereafter Tajikistan Information Document].

most Latin American countries have seen both urban and agricultural land programs.[17]

In Honduras there have been several land administration and titling and registration projects over the years. From 1997 through 2003, a World Bank loan–funded rural land management project registered 72,000 urban and 77,000 rural properties as part of its land administration component, which was supported by natural resources management, uplands producer, and biodiversity conservation components.[18] A World Bank loan–funded US$17 million pilot project, originally slated for completion in 2004 but now extended to late 2006, is designed to help 1,600 farm households purchase land to establish agricultural enterprises. Funds are being made available to private financial institutions to make loans for land purchases. The project also covers legal services, project administration, other technical assistance, and subproject grants to new rights holders.[19] A newer World Bank loan-funded project begun in 2004 is expected to run for twelve years in three four-year phases. In the first phase (2004–2008), it is planned that 745,000 land parcels will be surveyed and registered. This phase will also have policy and regulatory and institutional capacity-building components.[20]

A long-running land use rationalization project in Paraguay, funded by World Bank loans with bilateral assistance from USAID and Japan, aimed to improve the government's land and resources information base and management capabilities. The project included creation of a rural cadastre in several regions, development of geographic information system (GIS) capacities, and evaluation of the existing land titling system.[21] This work has been complicated by the fact that many existing property rights were of less than fee simple scope because the land distribution and formalization effort that began in 1963 restricted the alienability of much of the land. The project also granted some land rights to holders whom many consider inappropriate. An Inter-American Development Bank loan has approved funding for a more extensive cadastre and property registry program.

---

[17] R. Lopez & A. Valdez, *Fighting Rural Poverty in Latin America: New Evidence and Policy* in *Rural Poverty in Latin America* 19–24 (R. Lopez & A. Valdez, eds., Macmillan Press, Ltd. 2000); and C. D. Deere & M. León, *Empowering Women: Land and Property Rights in Latin America* 292 (U. Pitt. Press 2001).

[18] JSDF–Developing Central American Small Farmers Links to Specialty Coffee Market (Rural Land Management Project), 1997 (P007398). Project Implementation Completion Report, at 3–9 [hereafter, Honduras Land Administration].

[19] Honduras Access to Land Pilot Project, 2000 (P073035), Project Appraisal Document, at 24–26 [hereafter, Honduras Access to Land].

[20] Honduras Land Administration Project, 2004 (P055991), Project Appraisal Document, at 32–39 [hereafter, Honduras Land Administration Appraisal].

[21] Paraguay Land Use Rationalization Project, 1992 (P007911), Project Description, http://web.worldbank.org/external/projects/main?pagePK=104231&piPK=73230&theSitePK=40941&menuPK=228424&Projectid=P007911 [hereafter, Paraguay Project Description].

The work will increase the legal security of ownership titles and will modernize the registration and cadastral systems. This project will continue through 2006.[22]

In Nicaragua, World Bank loans have funded several land-related programs over the past eleven years. The Agricultural Technology and Land Management Project, which ran from 1993 to 2000, included a component to improve Nicaragua's national land cadastre, titling, and registration systems; the relatively limited land-titling task issued 50,000 titles. The current Land Administration Project, running from 2003 into 2007, aims to reform the land-related policy and legal framework, facilitate institutional decentralization and strengthening, strengthen property rights administration, issue titles and facilitate resolution of attendant disputes, and demarcate protected areas and indigenous lands. It is hoped that over 57,000 titles will be issued within three demonstration departments and several other locales.[23]

In Peru, an urban property rights titling and registration project, which was funded by World Bank loans and closed in 2004, was targeted at predominantly poor settlements in larger urban areas. One component supported legal, regulatory, and institutional reforms to sustain and deepen existing market reforms; another sought to strengthen and expand the two national urban property rights organizations. The third component, which issued about 800,000 titles, converted urban property in informal settlements to formal and secure property rights.

5.2.4 Africa

At the risk of oversimplification, African titling and registration have raised a series of paradoxes that make them difficult to negotiate. The list is long: individualization and common use; informal tenure regimes and formalization of tenure; commercial and community land uses; urban and rural settlements; traditional cattle grazers and traditional small-plot croppers; customary dispute resolution and violent outbreaks over resources.[24] In some cases, titling and

---

[22] Inter-American Development Bank, *Paraguay Cadastre and Property Registry Program Loan Proposal* 1–13 (IADB 2002).

[23] Nicaragua Land Administration Project, 2002 (P056018), Project Appraisal Document, at 3, 5, 14–15, and 57–69 [hereafter, Nicaragua Appraisal Document].

[24] J. W. Bruce, *Country Profiles of Land Tenure: Africa 1996*, Land Tenure Center Research Paper No. 130 (Land Tenure Center, U. Wisconsin–Madison 1998); M. Rwabahungu, *Tenurial Reforms in West and Central Africa: Legislation, Conflicts, and Social Movements*, in *Whose Land? Civil Society Perspectives on Land Reform and Rural Poverty Reduction* (K. Ghimire, ed., Int'l Fund Ag. Dev. 2001); E. Koch, J. M. Massyn & A. van Niekerk, *The Fate of Land Reform in Southern Africa: The Role of the State, the Market, and Civil Society*, in *Whose Land? Civil Society Perspectives on Land Reform and Rural Poverty Reduction* (K. Ghimire, ed., Intl. Fund Ag. Dev. 2001); *Searching for Land Tenure Security in Africa* (J. W. Bruce & S. E. Migot-Adholla, eds., Kendall/Hunt 1994); and F. Muhereza & D. Bledsoe, *Final Report—Land Sector Analysis: Common Property Resources Component* (Gov. Uganda 2002).

registration of individualized rural parcels have been condemned as inconsistent with and destructive of an otherwise functional common property tradition.[25] Titling and registration of community-held, commonly used land are seen as an attractive option by others.[26] Some call for formalization, titling, and registration of millions of residential parcels in informally settled urban areas.[27] Others hope to plan their way out of urban inundations of squatters by creating master plans that simply call for lower development densities.[28]

Current and past titling and registration projects are varied. Kenya probably stands as the most extensive and "Westernized" example of land plot individualization, titling, and registration in Africa. Beginning in the 1950s, large portions of several of Kenya's districts were individualized and formalized.[29] In Uganda, since the passage of the 1998 Land Act, the government has been considering land demarcation and titling pilots as a means of stimulating land markets, although it is anticipated that local demand will drive any subsequent titling.[30] Rwanda has recently conducted a land assessment, the conclusions of which recommend a two-tier land titling and registration system: an informal system at the local level and a more formalized system at the center that would title commercial concessions.[31] In Angola, pilot projects directed by the Food and Agriculture Organization are now demarcating and semiformally registering community common land holdings.[32]

---

[25] J. W. Bruce, *Land Tenure Issues in Project Design and Strategies for Agricultural Development in Sub-Saharan Africa* 81–84 (Land Tenure Center, U. Wisconsin–Madison 1986); J. Quan, *Land Tenure, Economic Growth and Poverty in Sub-Saharan Africa* in *Evolving Land Rights, Policy and Tenure in Africa* 35–38 (C. Toulmin & J. Quan, eds., IIED & Natural Res. Inst. 2000); J. Platteau, *Does Africa Need Land Reform?* in *Evolving Land Rights, Policy and Tenure in Africa* 66–67 (C. Toulmin & J. Quan, eds., IIED & Natural Res. Inst. 2000).

[26] United Nations Office for the Coordination of Humanitarian Affairs (UNOCHA), *Angola: Land Reform Needed,* IRIN News 1 (Apr. 26, 2002); Republic of Uganda, Land Act §5 (1998).

[27] Development Workshop, *Terra Firme: Oportunidades e Constrangimentos para uma Gestão Apropriada da Terra Urbana em Angola* (Dev. Wkshp. 2003).

[28] Republic of Angola, Territory and Planning Act (2004).

[29] *See* Bruce, *supra* n. 24, at 175–76.

[30] Republic of Uganda, *Land Sector Strategic Plan: 2001–2011* 36–38 (Rep. Uganda 2002).

[31] Republic of Rwanda, *Land Assessment Report* 36 (Natural Res. Inst. (NRI), University of Greenwich 2004).

[32] D. Bledsoe & C. Pinto, *Republic of Angola: Land Law and Policy Assessment* 13 (USAID 2002).

5.3 Titling and Registration and Economic Growth

5.3.1 Introduction

As noted, the economic development benefits sought through titling and registration are believed to come from formal rights and increased tenure security. Many assume that such rights and security prompt increased investment and corresponding production gains, and that there will be as a consequence increases in credit opportunities and borrowing. Finally, it is thought that formalized rights and increased security lead to more active and efficient land markets.[33] The remainder of this section describes these potential economic benefits in more detail and then gives evidence from the literature about achieving them.

Hard information about the costs and success or failure of titling and registration projects is surprisingly limited, repetitive, and sometimes inconclusive.[34] Some of the early studies are considered analytically unsound or statistically unsupported.[35] Certainly, the land administration portfolios of the World Bank and bilateral donors are relatively young, with most projects having started only in the 1990s. For most, it is too soon to assess long-term impacts. Most titling and registration projects are virtually without performance data to support findings of a causal, attributable relationship between tenure security and economic benefits.

Some positive evidence does exist. Relying on real but limited data, some say that titling and registration can in fact increase credit opportunities and boost capital-to-land ratios, improvements, land values, and outputs and inputs per unit of land.[36] Others note that the data show that benefits have in many cases failed to appear.[37]

---

[33] *See* AusAID, *supra* n. 1, at 7–8; Feder & Nishio, *supra* n. 2, at 26–28; Pagiola, *supra* n. 2, at 3–9; Hanstad, *supra* n. 2, at 657–64; Feder & Feeney, *supra* n. 2, at 139–43; and Binswanger *et al.*, *supra* n. 2, at 2719–21.

[34] *See* Lopez & Valdes, *supra* n. 17, at 23; Platteau, *supra* n. 24, at 56–69; H. Lemel, *Land Titling: Conceptual, Empirical, and Policy Issues,* in *Land Use Policy* 285–89 (Butterworth & Co. 1988); AusAID, *supra* n. 1, at 26 and 28–29; and A. Brasselle, F. Gaspart & J. Platteau, *Land Tenure Security and Investment Incentives: Puzzling Evidence from Burkina Faso,* 67 J. Dev. Econs. 373, 374–375 (2002).

[35] *See* Feder *et al., supra* n. 5, at 7–9.

[36] *See id.*

[37] F. Finan, E. Sadoulet & A. de Janvry, *Measuring the Poverty Reduction Potential of Land in Mexico,* CUDARE Working Papers No. 983, 2 (U. Cal, Berk. 2002); *see also* Lopez & Valdes, *supra* n. 17, at 23–24; D. W. Palmer, *Incentive-based Maintenance of Land Registration Systems* 2 (dissertation for Ph.D in philosophy, University of Florida 1996).

5.3.2   Security of Tenure and Increased Investment and Productivity

A landholder has secure tenure if there is little or no likelihood of losing physical possession of the land in the future. With titling and registration increasing tenure security, because the likelihood and fear of losing the value of investments in land is decreased, overall investment in land is thought to be stimulated. For agricultural land, the investment might take the form of more and better farm inputs and such physical improvements as irrigation, terracing, drainage, tree planting, demarcation of boundaries, and produce storage. For urban landholders, investments might fund housing and industry or other commercial activities. The investments increase production yields, economic returns, and household incomes. The value of the land asset increases accordingly.[38]

There is little direct evidence, however, of increased investment and production in countries that have had titling and registration projects. The Thai titling and registration effort is one of the few to include meaningful data collection and an econometric multivariate analysis. That analysis generally indicated that capital-to-land ratios, improvements, land values, and outputs and inputs per unit of land were higher for the titled than the untitled land.[39] Another study, using data from land registration in Thailand (1960 through 1996), projected the effect of Thai land registration on broader financial and economic growth patterns. The study concluded that registration has had a significant effect on longer-term economic growth, which occurred after an initial negative impact that lasted two years and after an extended period of recovery therefrom. Given that the longer-term positive impact reflects the theoretical expectations, it was suggested that the effects of early speculation and related land price increases and initial caution on the part of financial agents caused the initial negative impact.[40]

In the countries of the former Soviet Union, neither economic nor production effects directly linked or attributable to land titling or registration projects have yet been confirmed, partly because these programs are relatively young but also because many other economic factors are at play, including disrupted input and output markets. For example, in the Kyrgyz Republic, where land share certificates have been issued and registered for substantially all the collective farms

---

[38] *See* AusAID, *supra* n. 1, at 7–8; Feder & Nishio, *supra* n. 2, at 26–28; Pagiola, *supra* n. 2, at 3–9; Hanstad, *supra* n. 2, at 657–664; Feder & Feeny, *supra* n. 2, at 139–143; and Binswanger *et al., supra* n. 2.

[39] *See* Feder *et al., supra* n. 5, at 101–14.

[40] F. Byamugisha, *How Land Registration Affects Financial Development and Economic Growth in Thailand,* Policy Research Working Paper Series No. 2241, 19 and 22 (World Bank 1999).

reorganized by 2000, total agricultural production, crop production, and food production increased from 1994 through 2000 but dropped off in 2001.[41] No data about investment are available. Remnants of the collective farm legacy remain, however, and may restrain the titling and registration investment and production benefits that might otherwise be expected. Former collective farm bosses in some Kyrgyz oblasts have prevented or obstructed farmers and farm families from breaking off from collective farms to farm independently. It is only within the last several years that legal education and advocacy support have been provided so that these landowners know how to overcome this kind of obstruction. Continuing to increase legal literacy and legal aid would probably help in realizing titling and registration benefits.

In Moldova, total agricultural production, crop production, and food production figures have moved up and down, but the 2001 figures show a decline from 1994, 1996, and 2000 totals.[42] Here too there has been obstructionist behavior by former farm bosses that may limit the creation of private farms and the attendant investment and production increases. The titling programs have, however, had legal education and advocacy components. Efforts to achieve a certain level of legal literacy and to provide related advocacy support may over time improve the value and yields of titling and registration.

In Armenia, total agricultural and crop production has dropped steadily since 1998.[43] No investment data are available. In Ukraine, figures for total agricultural production, crop production, and food production have shown increases over the data for 1999, 2000, and 2001.[44] Some new title holders have reported that former farm bosses have made lease agreements with the title holders but have failed to pay lease payments when due, so here, too, benefits may be constrained by unfair behavior. The legal education and advocacy efforts that are getting underway in Ukraine will probably help.

Few of the Latin American programs have been systematically evaluated to confirm linkages between tenure security and economic development (investment, credit, land markets). Some recent studies of titling in Honduras and Paraguay did find beneficial effects of tenure security on investment and of land titles on increased productivity—but the studies also indicated that most of the benefits went to a small minority of farmers who were not the poorest or those

[41] R. Giovarelli, *Land and Agrarian Reform in Kyrgyz Republic Research Results* 3 (unpublished memorandum on file with RDI 2002); *see also* Food and Agricultural Organization of the United Nations, Agricultural Production Indices, http://apps.fao.org/page/collections?subset=agriculture (FAOSTAT Database, Nov. 7, 2002).

[42] *See* FAO, *id.*

[43] *See id.*

[44] *See id.*

with the least land.[45] Another recent study of tenure insecurity and investment and productivity in Nicaragua showed some positive connection between tenure insecurity and lower production levels, although there was no indication that the insecurity reduced investment.[46]

There is little or no evidence that land titling and registration of individual parcels have spurred investment or worked to increase agricultural production in Africa. Evidence from sporadic titling in Kenya and Burkina Faso shows that investment has not increased there.[47] In Uganda some forms of tenure *insecurity* may actually have spurred investment: Parcel occupiers may increase investment in perennial crops and other improvements so as to make eviction more costly because of higher mandated compensation amounts where compensation requirements are enforced.[48] One study of thirty-six Ugandan villages concluded that tree planting increased the security of rights to inherited land.[49] Improvements made or added to the land can increase tenure security by denoting permanency and owner-like status. The notion that investment might increase security must be accounted for in any analysis of African titling and registration. Not accounting for it is likely to yield results showing that increased security results in investment.[50]

In situations where titling requires that rights holders bear real costs, it may also be that the parcels that would benefit most from investment are those to be registered, at least for sporadic titling. These situations are ones of correlation rather than causality.[51]

Other findings tend to establish that some customary tenure systems in Africa, even those that provide for less than full transfer rights, provide sufficient rights and security to prompt investments in the land that work to increase tenure

---

[45] M. R. Carter & E. Zegarra, *Land Markets and the Persistence of Rural Poverty: Post-Liberalization Policy Options,* in Lopez & Valdes, eds., *supra* n. 17, at 81–82; *see also* R. Lopez & T. S. Thomas, *Rural Poverty in Paraguay: The Determinants of Farm Household Income,* in Lopez & Valdes eds., *supra* n. 17, at 252–57; and Lopez & Valdes, *supra* n. 17, at 23–24.

[46] J. Foltz, B. Larson & R. Lopez, *Land Tenure, Investment, and Agricultural Production in Nicaragua,* Dev. Disc. Papers: Cent. Am. Project Series, 17–18 (Harv. Inst. Intl. Dev. 2000).

[47] *See* Quan, *supra* n. 25, at 35–36; Brasselle, *et al., supra* n. 34, at 395–96.

[48] J. Mackinnon & R. Reinikka, *Lessons from Uganda on Strategies to Fight Poverty* 38 (Centre Study Afr. Econs. & World Bank 2000).

[49] J. Baland, F. Gaspart, F. Place & J. Platteau, *Poverty, Tenure Security, and Access to Land in Central Uganda: The Role of Market and Non-Market Processes* 27–28 and 30 (World Bank 1999).

[50] *See* Braselle *et al., supra* n. 47, at 375, 391.

[51] *See id.* at 374.

security. Land tenure security under customary systems may therefore be stronger than at first appears; what seem at first inspection to be precarious rights may in fact be stronger than suspected. Methods of measuring land tenure security may be at fault because they do not always distinguish between levels of security as they actually exist.[52] Perceptions of insecurity should be scrutinized to affirm assumptions about the effect of insecurity prior to titling and registration efforts in Africa.

Despite these African examples, it is probably useful to remember that land titling and registration—particularly in Africa—is contextual. Most of the examples given illustrate individualization and formalization of small agricultural parcels. But what might not be useful in one situation might be useful in another. For example, because of the intense urban and peri-urban informal settlements that make up and surround so many African cities, titling and registration of urban residential plots may be a sensible way to formalize investment, create assets for the urban poor, and prevent displacement and landlessness.

In summary, however: The direct evidence is lacking. It has not been extensively shown that titling and registration significantly increase investment or production.

5.3.3 Credit and Borrowing

The formal, secure land rights created by titling and registration are thought to better provide for a real and secure source of collateral. It is assumed that the collateral increases the availability and terms of credit to obtain funds for investment in land. Some see the tenure security–credit nexus as more tenuous than the connection between security and increased investment. Moreover, the credit benefit is seen as being less likely to benefit rich and poor farmers equally. This imbalance reflects the fact that the relative burden of obtaining credit is greater for the poor, and the risk of foreclosure (endangering the source of subsistence) is more likely to limit their willingness to pledge land as collateral.[53] In any case, there is little direct evidence of increased credit opportunities and borrowing in countries that have had titling and registration projects.

One exception, again, is the oft-cited 1988 study of portions of the Thailand first-phase project, which used data collected in 1984 and 1985. This study looks at credit and borrowing patterns of Thai farmers in sixty-eight villages within four of Thailand's seventy-six provinces.[54] Specifically, the study looked at

---

[52] *See id.,* at 379–81.

[53] H. Lemel, *Land Titling: Conceptual, Empirical, and Policy Issues,* in *Land Use Policy* 283–85 (Butterworth & Co. 1988).

[54] *See,* Feder *et al., supra* n. 5.

patterns of borrowing and nonborrowing by titled and untitled farmers from institutional sources, noninstitutional sources, and both. The descriptive study found inconsistent indications of whether titling might increase the incidence of borrowing. There was no significant difference between titled and untitled farmers among those that borrowed from institutional sources only or from noninstitutional sources only. Nor was there a significant difference between titled and untitled farmers in nonborrowing. Only among borrowers from both institutional and noninstitutional sources was there a difference: untitled farmers borrowed almost twice as many times. In one province, however, there were no significant differences between titled and untitled farmers in nonborrowing or in types of borrowing, but the incidence of titled farmers that borrowed only from noninstitutional sources was higher than that of untitled farmers.[55]

Looking at the distribution of loans by sources, the Thai descriptive study found no significant difference between the number of loans obtained by titled and untitled farmers from either institutional or noninstitutional sources, and, for loans obtained from institutional lenders, the mean interest rate obtained by titled and untitled farmers was virtually the same.[56]

There were, however, several findings based on the descriptive data that supported the study hypothesis that credit benefits would accrue to titled farmers. First, titled farmers obtained more medium and long-term loans from institutional lenders than did untitled farmers. Second, titled farmers obtained lower interest rates from noninstitutional lenders (for both titled and untitled farmers, medium- and long-term loans from noninstitutional lenders were very rare). Third, the amount of loan funding per unit of land was higher in most cases when titled land was used as collateral. Finally, the study authors concluded, even when identical kinds of security were provided, titled farmers received more credit funding per unit of land than untitled farmers.[57]

Because credit and borrowing are affected by many factors related to title, the Thai study also applied econometric multivariate (switching regression) analysis to the descriptive data.[58] This analysis concluded that the security of ownership inherent in having a formal title to land provided significant advantages in obtaining institutional credit.[59]

Another important conclusion drawn from the Thai study might have been worth further study at the time, and perhaps even now. The data showed that

---

[55] *See id.* at 49–57.

[56] *See id.* at 53.

[57] *See id.* at 49–56.

[58] *See id.* at 57–58.

[59] *See id.* at 67.

group guarantees to make loan payments were important when individual untitled farmers obtained loans from institutional lenders.[60] While this might help to explain why credit access and types of credit were not significantly different for titled and for untitled farmers, it might also have prompted inquiry into whether efforts to increase group guarantees might have been more cost-effective for purposes of improving credit access than titling land.

An AusAID review of its participation in land titling projects, including the Thai project, observed that the conclusions drawn from the mainly positive Thai studies have been used to support titling and registration projects elsewhere, but that this use is not necessarily valid because the conditions might be different elsewhere. For example, inflation in Thai property values in the 1980s created a high demand for titles, which worked to meet a necessary precondition for success. The review concluded that the Thai results, like all results, have limited applicability.[61] The World Bank's performance audit of the second Thai titling project echoed this cautionary note when it concluded that the Thai project impacts can be significantly attributed to circumstances that may not apply in other countries.[62] The lesson to be learned here is that, whatever the benefits sought from titling and registration, past program results from one country cannot be used alone to justify or presage the success of a proposed program in another country. The prospects for any proposed program should be assessed in light of conditions in the target country. The same accrual of benefits cannot be assumed if conditions differ.

There is little evidence that African titling and registration projects have increased opportunities to obtain credit.[63] In Kenya, some smallholders avoid applying for loans secured by their land because they are afraid of foreclosure. In Uganda, some landholders are presumed to be fearful of using secured credit for the same reason.[64] In Uganda most respondents to a survey in 2001 said they were unaware that a purchase money mortgage might conceivably finance a land purchase.[65]

For Latin America, there is virtually no evidence about the credit benefit, although a 1996 study of titling in Honduras showed some beneficial effects of tenure security on credit availability.[66]

---

[60] *See id.* at 54.

[61] *See* AusAID, *supra* n. 1, at 28–29, 53, and 110.

[62] World Bank, *Thailand Land Reform Areas Project and Second Land Titling Project Performance Audit Report* 25 (World Bank 1998).

[63] *See* Platteau, *supra* n. 25, at 59–61.

[64] *See* Mackinnon & Reinikka, *supra* n. 48, at 38.

[65] R. Mwebaza & R. Gaynor, *Final Report—Land Sector Analysis: Land Market, Land Consolidation, and Land Re-adjustment Component* 19 (Gov. Uganda 2002).

[66] *See* Carter & Zegarra, *supra* n. 45, at 82.

For the credit benefit provided by titling and registration elsewhere, the direct support is a bit more evident. The Thai data, while in no way extensive or conclusive, does show some sign of that benefit accruing. However, it remains to be seen whether other titling and registration projects have significantly increased credit and borrowing opportunities.

5.3.4 Land Markets

The secure rights that come with titling and registration are also thought to make the land market more efficient so that they function better as the means for moving land resources to those who can put them to the most productive and efficient use. Again, with more efficient land use, increases in economic activity and productivity generally are expected. As a rule, if uneconomically large holdings are titled, the land market would tend to break them up into more efficient sizes. Conversely, if uneconomically small holdings are titled, the market would tend to increase the size of parcels and concentrate ownership to some extent.[67] As with the investment, production, and credit benefits of titling and registration, the direct evidence for a security–market efficiency–economic development linkage is sparse.

For countries in the former Soviet Union that have had land titling and registration projects, there is little information on land markets or numbers of land transactions.[68] Where information is available, it does not show sudden increases in land market activity. For example, in Armenia, where by December 2001 about half the titles had been issued for the 1.3 million privately held parcels, land market activity has been slow to increase; the reasons cited are low prices, relatively high registration and notary costs, and retention of land as a subsistence resource.[69]

Information from Africa is also limited, although evidence from Kenya suggests that titling has not prompted an increase in land market transactions or in transfers that display evidence of more efficient land use.[70] Moreover, systematic individualization and formalization are not always prerequisite to the establishment of African land markets or to land investments. A recent land market study of both titled and untitled land in Uganda showed that markets in untitled land were active and vibrant despite the absence of formal titles and registration. In the

---

[67] H. Dekker, *The Invisible Line: Land Reform, Land Tenure Security, and Land Registration,* Ashgate Intl. Land Mgmt. Series 39–41 (Ashgate Pub. Ltd. 2003).

[68] Z. Lerman, *Comparative Institutional Evolution: Rural Land Reform in the ECA Region,* World Development Report Background Paper 9–11 (World Bank 2001).

[69] K. Chluba & E. Schmidt-Kallert, *Strategy for Land Consolidation and Improved Land Management in Armenia* 14–15 (FAO 2001).

[70] *See* Platteau, *supra* n. 25, at 56–58.

provinces studied, occupants of customary land had clearly established their rights over particular plots and were able to transfer the rights through sale, inheritance, gift, and exchange even without formal titles.[71] These findings reaffirm Kigula (1993), Troutt (1994), and Sebina-Zziwa *et al.* (2000), who all concluded that there was an active market in untitled land.[72] They also affirm the assertion by Migot-Adholla *et al.* (1991) that indigenous land tenure systems can be dynamic; they tend to adapt to spontaneous individualization of land rights over time, which enables farm households to acquire broader and more powerful transfer and exclusion rights over their land.[73]

In some cases, formalizing titles and transactions may have a negative effect on the land market. For example, survey respondents in Uganda who held untitled land were more satisfied with land market mechanisms than were holders of titled land. Transactions in untitled land were common and were concluded efficiently and inexpensively outside of governmental structures. By contrast, transactions in titled land are relatively complicated and expensive. Uganda survey respondents cited the imposition of extralegal payments extracted by registration officials as the primary disincentive to using the registration system, although a minority also pointed to complicated registration procedures as a disincentive.[74] The implication of these findings is that titling land and imposing formal registration procedures on transactions could have the unintended effect of stifling, rather than stimulating, land markets and investments. These kinds of systemic restraints are probably not insurmountable, however. Given sufficient political will, the implementation of anticorruption and transparency measures and of reforms directed at overly complicated procedures and poor customer service can reduce oppressive effects on land markets.

For the land market benefit, direct evidence is again lacking. It has not been shown broadly that titling and registration have significantly increased land market activity and efficient transactions. Overall, evidence supporting the ability of titling and registration to create the economic benefits intended is sparse,

---

[71] *See* Mwebaza & Gaynor, *supra* n. 65, at 12–16.

[72] J. Kigula, *Land Disputes in Uganda: An Overview of the Types of Land Disputes and the Disputes Settlement Fora* (Makere Inst. Soc. Research, Kampala, Uganda & Land Tenure Center, U. Wisconsin–Madison 1993); E. Troutt, *Rural African Land Markets and Access to Agricultural Land: The Central Region of Uganda* (Makere Inst. Soc. Research, Kampala, Uganda & Land Tenure Center, U. Wisconsin–Madison 1994); A. Sebina-Zziwa *et al., Land Act Monitoring Exercise I* (DFID & Ugandan Ministry of Water, Lands, & Env. 2000).

[73] S. E. Migot-Adholla, S. P. Hazell, B. Blorel & F. Place, *Indigenous Land Rights in Sub-Saharan Africa: A Constraint on Productivity*, 5.1 World Bank Econ. Rev. 155–75 (World Bank 1991).

[74] *See* Mwebaza & Gaynor, *supra* n. 65, at 17.

although some positive support does exist. In some cases there is evidence that titling and registration have not yielded the intended benefits. Part of the reason that supporting data is lacking stems from the relative youth of many titling and registration projects. Benefits take time to accrue. The lack of data support, however, makes it correspondingly more difficult to show a positive link between titling and registration and the alleviation of poverty.

5.4 Titling and Registration and Poverty Alleviation

5.4.1 Introduction

Many practitioners and observers are confident that titling and registration can reduce poverty. Although they mostly agree that (a) a variety of enabling preconditions must be met, (b) needed complementary components must be included, and (c) beneficiaries must be consciously targeted,[75] many say that poverty can be reduced.[76] Often titling and registration program design documents explicitly state that they are intended to directly benefit the poor.[77] Showing an even stronger intention to benefit the poor, some design documents point out a danger that titling and registration program benefits will more likely accrue to better-off landholders, and that poorer landholders may be at risk of failing to benefit.[78] Much of the design documentation sets up long horizons on project benefits,

---

[75] Both AusAID and the World Bank have conducted audits and evaluations of their titling and registration projects. Importantly, they both conclude that the intended benefits of titling and registration can only be achieved if certain assumptions and preconditions have been met and complementary components have been provided. For example, before titling can give landholders formal rights and security, the tenure laws must be appropriate, unambiguous, enforceable, and available and allow equitable and easy first registration. The title must in fact be registered in an official registry. The registry must be efficient, correct, and secure, and titling itself must be affordable and accessible. Other preconditions for success include a basic demand for titles, the presence of basic credit mechanisms and capital, the efficacy and possibility of investments, potential for income increase, land valuation capacities, reasonable transaction costs, a bar to rent seeking, availability of information, adequate institutional capacities, suitable public perceptions, perpetuation of systems, fee and revenue streams, and the inclusion of the poor. Satisfaction of all preconditions and implementation of all complementary components are central to obtaining benefits from titling and registration. *See* Pagiola, *supra* n. 2; AusAID, *supra* n. 1, at 7–8 and 76–77. *Also see* World Bank & Klaus Deininger, *Land Policies for Growth and Poverty Reduction,* World Bank Policy and Poverty Reduction Report 74–75 (World Bank & Oxf. U. Press 2003), for a general description of the kinds of complementary support necessary for benefits to be seen.

[76] *See* Pagiola, *supra* n. 2, at xix–xx, 74–75; AusAID, *supra* n. 1.

[77] *See* Ukraine Appraisal Document, *supra* n. 15, at 52; Laos Appraisal Document, *supra* n. 1, at 2, 26, and 36; and Cambodia Appraisal Document, *supra* n. 1, at 2, 5, 10, and 27.

[78] *See* Laos Appraisal Document, *supra* n. 1, at 27.

noting that no benefits may accrue during the life of the project and that thirty-year benefit windows can be expected.[79]

Poverty is measured in a variety of ways; no single indicator can usefully measure it.[80] This makes it more complicated to determine whether titling and registration alleviates poverty. When defining and measuring poverty, some concentrate on objective levels of private consumption or lack of consumption of calories or dollars. Others look at the variety of conditions that almost always accompany consumption deprivation, such as poor housing, bad health, and bad or no education.[81] Yet others include in any definition of poverty control and enjoyment of assets.[82] One poverty specialist has created an asset index as part of its endeavor to assess the poverty of microfinance targets. In this index, land is one of the primary assets and indicators of household assets.[83]

Several things seem certain, however. If land titling and registration programs are to have an impact on poverty, they must first make good on their promise of delivering economic benefits, and the benefits must reach the poor: The landed poor must receive titles, see tenure security increase, obtain more credit opportunities; increase investments, and increase production. The literature giving empirical evidence of economic benefits of titling and registration is scant. There are essentially no studies or data that link these benefits to the poor or give specific examples of how titling and registration has reduced poverty.[84] Though there are some signs that the benefits may not be reaching the poor, there are also signs that titling and registration can sometimes threaten the poor.

5.4.2 Are the Poor Benefiting?

Where most landholders are poor, the implication is that titling and registration are slow to reduce poverty. In the former Soviet Union and Eastern Europe, where many titling and registration projects are in place, the landed poor have little access to land-based credit from the financial sector, although some credit is

---

[79] *See, for example,* Cambodia Appraisal Document, *supra* n. 1, at 44.

[80] *See, for example*, R. Lok-Dessallien, *Review of Poverty Concepts and Indicators,* SEPED Series on Pov. Reduc., 2–15 (UNDP 2001); and M. H. Kahn, *Rural Poverty in Developing Countries: Issues and Policies*, IMF Working Paper WP/00/78, 3–9 (IMF 2000).

[81] International Fund for Agricultural Development (IFAD), *Rural Poverty Report 2001: The Challenge of Ending Rural Poverty* 1–3 (Oxf. U. Press 2001).

[82] International Fund for Agricultural Development (IFAD), *Rural Poverty Report 2000/2001 Fact Sheet: Assets and the Rural Poor* 1–3, http://www.ifad.org/media/pack/rpr/3.htm (IFAD 2001).

[83] Consultative Group to Assist the Poorest (CGAP), *Assessing the Relative Poverty of Microfinance Clients* 2 (CGAP 1999).

[84] *See* Finan *et al., supra* n. 37, at 2.

obtained through donor- and government-subsidized programs.[85] In many cases, even under a donor credit support program, titled land serves merely as back-up collateral or is not considered at all; primary collateral is crops, machinery, houses, and buildings.[86] The financial sector sees the land market as too risky and inefficient, and there is concern about foreclosing on people whose only asset is their land. Many banks are in any case undercapitalized so they tend not to make long-term loans.[87] In Africa, where only 5 percent of households have access to formal credit, smallholder access to credit is a major problem.[88]

To reiterate, there is simply not sufficient evidence to show that the poor are benefiting, and in some cases there are signs of the opposite. In the Kyrgyz Republic, where there was early privatization and titling and registration have been extensive, there are very few sales of small farm plots, and the sales that do occur stem from migration of the Russian population from Central Asia or are distress sales by the extreme poor.[89] Moreover, although it was expected that poor farmers would lease out their land if they could earn more money that way than they would by producing on the land, this has not occurred. With limited rural industry and few other possibilities for employment, the landed poor are locked into subsistence farming. They are loath to part with their land.

The lack of movement in Kyrgyz land has also restricted the ability of better-capitalized farmers, who might show some demand, to obtain more land and to make investments that increase production.[90] Finally, even with regard to tenure security, few land transfers occurring within a family through inheritance are registered. Rural residents trust local government and neighbors to "know" whose land is whose.[91] At least in the Kyrgyz Republic, there is little current demand by the landed poor for the benefits of titling beyond initial security of tenure.

---

[85] *See* Giovarelli & Bledsoe, *supra* n. 8; R. Giovarelli, *Mortgage in the Bulgarian Agricultural Sector,* Rural Dev. Inst. Report on Foreign Assistance & Dev. No. 104, 5 (RDI 2000); R. Giovarelli, L. Rolfes, Jr., B. Schwarzwalder, J. Duncan & D. Bledsoe, *Legal Impediments to Effective Rural Land Relations in Eastern Europe and Central Asia,* World Bank Technical Paper No. 436, 139–147 (R. Prosterman & T. Hanstad, eds., World Bank 1999) [hereafter *Legal Impediments*].

[86] *See* Giovarelli & Bledsoe, *supra* n. 85.

[87] *See* Giovarelli, *supra* n. 85, at 5; Giovarelli *et al., Legal Impediments, supra* n. 85, at 139–47.

[88] Norway Ministry of Foreign Affairs, *Agriculture—A Way out of Poverty* 41 (Norway 2002); A. Diagne & M. Zeller, *Access to Credit and its Impact on Welfare in Malawi,* International Food Policy Research Institute Research Report 116, 123–129 (IFPR 2001).

[89] M. Childress, R. Giovarelli, R. Shimarov & K. Tilekeyev, *Rapid Appraisal of Land Reform in the Kyrgyz Republic* 5 (USAID 2003).

[90] *See id.* at 48.

[91] R. Giovarelli, C. Aidarbekova, J. Duncan, K. Rasmussen & A. Tabyshalieva, *Women's Rights to Land in the Kyrgyz Republic* 23 (World Bank 2001).

As mentioned above, in Uganda, where most landholders are poor, one study showed a very active land market outside of any titling system but very little use of formal credit to finance land purchases. Land titling had not significantly influenced market information or price-setting. Respondents said that the weight of a title in setting the price of land ranked lower than soil quality, distance from roads, and general location. A right to sell land was verified primarily through neighbors and consultation with local government. Land registration records rarely played a role even in verifying boundaries.[92] In Uganda as well, it seems the landed poor have little current demand for the benefits of titling.

Titling and registration projects could probably be better designed to reach the poor. To date, most titling project preparation, design, and monitoring have lacked thorough treatment of how to target the poor and assess how the poor will or will not be affected, although the design of more recent World Bank titling and registration projects does include a social assessment that touches upon poverty. Design documents also vow to closely monitor follow-on poverty impacts.[93] Most recent World Bank titling and registration project completion documents do not thoroughly address how the project affects the poor.[94]

One other tool does merit mention. The World Bank's poverty and social impact analysis (PSIA) process looks at how interventions affect the poor and vulnerable. A PSIA is not required during the design of all interventions, but recent statements from the Bank's Social Development Department have stressed the suitability of PSIAs for land reform projects. Advocates of the PSIA process are critical of the effectiveness of some past land interventions in alleviating poverty. They are convinced that land reforms (a) have been unsuccessful in reducing poverty; (b) have caused conflicts affecting the poor; and (c) have been exclusive and discriminative. For example, a 2003 PSIA of possible land interventions in Zambia suggested that a proposed large-scale titling program would adversely affect the poor. Instead it proposed improvements to infrastructure, stronger legal and institutional arrangements to protect women's rights, improvements to dispute resolution systems, and broader recognition of customary land ownership.[95] While the PSIA approach may not be wholly suitable for use during project design, some of its tenets might be useful in better targeting the poor and in assessing project impacts on poverty.

---

[92] *See* Mwebaza & Gaynor, *supra* n. 65, at 16.

[93] *See* Honduras Land Administration Appraisal, *supra* n. 20, at 12–14.

[94] *See, for example,* Honduras Land Administration, *supra* n. 18.

[95] S. Jorgensen, *Integrating Land Policy Issues into Poverty and Social Impact Analysis and Country Strategies* 4–11 (World Bank 2003) http://lnweb18.worldbank.org/ESSD/essdext.nsf/24DocByUnid/C157A5D06EE30C7F85256CED007F97B7/$FILE/SteenLauJorgenson.pdf.

Other project sponsors are also aware of the need to better target the poor. AusAID's review of its participation in large land titling projects concluded that a case could be made that titling can support poverty reduction, but there was a need to actually make the case and better target the poor and at-risk. To make the case, AusAID called for evidence of impact, effectiveness, relevance, efficiency, and sustainability. To better target the poor, it recommended that countrywide macro indicators be created before projects are implemented and the resulting information used to design the intervention.[96]

The kinds of information yielded by the World Bank's PSIAs and AusAID's macro indicators might then be profitably used by titling and registration project designers and implementers to answer questions about how better to target the poor, thus providing the evidence that is now lacking. Do the landed poor want titles or is tenure security already provided for by customary mechanisms? If they get titles, is there demand for other benefits? Can they have access to and take advantage of credit? Increase investment? Buy and sell land? If not, are the costs of titling worthwhile? If the costs are in fact projected to be worthwhile, what kinds of supporting measures should be put in place to move the poor along to a point where they can use these benefits?

5.4.3 Are the Poor Excluded?

Sometimes the poor are excluded from titling and registration efforts and from enjoying the follow-on benefits. Of course, in one central respect titling and registration are all about exclusion. The intentionally limited and conclusive nature of land titling and registration is obviously aimed at formalizing the validity and security of the ownership of those deemed legally designated to hold it. Economic and public policy decisions have made this sort of exclusion the primary objective. But sometimes the intended exclusionary nature of titling and registration can yield results that might seem unfair. For example, systematic titling of land to former collective farm workers in the former Soviet Union is or was limited to qualifying collective farm workers and their families. That meant some who were peripherally associated with the collective farming activities ("social sphere workers," such as teachers and medical personnel) were excluded from receiving land, as were those who were not collective farm members. In these cases, the legislative drafting or project design reflects resource allocation choices to exclude some.[97]

---

[96] AusAID, *supra* n. 1, at 11–14.

[97] M. Gorton, *Agricultural Land Reform in Moldova,* INTAS Research Project, INTAS99-00753, 12 (U. Newcastle 2000); Moldova Land Code, art. 12, Allocation of Equivalent Land Shares into Private Ownership (including all amendments as of July 22, 1999).

Other forms of exclusion exist as well, and some types of titling and registration are more likely to exclude than others. For example, sporadic titling and registration may be more likely to exclude the poor than systematic titling and registration, which is generally regarded as potentially more inclusive. Systematic titling is the identification, adjudication, surveying, and formalization through the issuance of titles of all eligible parcels within a single area during a single period. A final step in systematic registration is entering the title information into a formalized registration system. Registration often, though not always, accompanies titling. Titling registration is considered sporadic when those eligible make application or otherwise trigger entry into the system for formal recognition and formalization of rights.

The World Bank and most other sponsors have expressed a preference for systematic titling and registration when the case can be made for land rights formalization. Systematic efforts are seen as best able to take advantage of economies of scale in measurement, adjudication, and conflict resolution. Similarly, the complementary components that are seen as necessary for titling to provide theoretical benefits, such as credit support measures, are better able to take advantage of those economies of scale. Systematic efforts are also inclusive; they are seen as the best path to including the poor, the indigenous, and other marginalized populations. For example, systematic programs can be targeted to areas where the poor hold land so as to give them early benefits of tenure security and economic benefits. Moreover, systematic first registration is usually subsidized, allowing poor land-rights holders to formalize their rights without incurring costs that might otherwise prevent them from participating. To best target any population during systematic registration projects, such measures as public information campaigns and accessible and swift dispute resolution are necessary. Systematic projects are also able to take advantage of economies of scale.[98]

Sporadic approaches can exclude rights holders for several reasons. First, the poor are usually bereft of the resources (time, money, information, education) needed to take advantage of opportunities or to trigger enabling events (a purchase, for example). Second, sporadic efforts are often characterized by other conditions that exclude participants from titling and registering property. For example, expensive land surveys can deter rights holders from formalizing rights, and because users usually fund sporadic titling and registration services at least in part, onerous costs can create accessibility problems. Also, procedures and requirements can be opaque and unknowable, further deterring

---

[98] K. Deininger & H. Binswanger, *The Evolution of the World Bank's Land Policy: Principles, Experience, and Future Changes,* 14(2) World Bank Research Observer 260 (World Bank 1999); Deininger, *supra* n. 76, at 56–57.

access.[99] Rent-seeking by registration officials can also keep rights holders away. Finally, the exclusionary nature of sporadic approaches is manifested by the great amount of time it takes to sporadically register most or all properties.[100] One 1998 estimate of the time to complete sporadic titling in Indonesia and to bring all eligible properties within the system at the then-current rate was ninety years.[101] Until well into that ninety-year period, most land rights holders—most of them poor—would not receive the intended benefits of titling and registration.

Cambodia provides some examples of the shortfalls of sporadic registration. There, the approach, in part and at first, had focused on residential and commercial land, excluding agricultural parcels because registration infrastructure is largely absent in rural areas. There was also a lack of trained local staff, a failure to consistently follow procedures, insufficient equipment and archiving capability at the local level, inaccurate survey plans, the entry of inaccurate or fraudulent information (to avoid transfer taxes), and corruption. That is why the Cambodian government has decided to move resources to systematic mass registration, which will take advantage of mapping economies, opportunities for widespread dispute resolution, and survey detail. The approach will promote accessibility by displaying graphic and textual documentation in the villages for thirty days, soliciting input and appeals, and resolving disputes through bodies composed of local community leaders and titling program representatives.[102] An improved sporadic titling system will be simultaneously pursued with the aims of simplicity, transparency, and accuracy.[103]

However, systematic titling and registration can also exclude certain rights-holders. During systematic efforts, holders of uncertain or irregular rights can be prevented from obtaining title.[104] Because of the costs of resolving the status of these problem parcels, they are often left unregistered and their titles left undone,

---

[99] L. Holstein, paper presented at the International Conference on Land Tenure Administration, *Towards Best Practices from World Bank Experience in Land Titling and Registration* 16–17 (U. Fla. Geomatics Program, Nov. 12–14, 1996) (copy on file with the author).

[100] *See id.* at 16.

[101] C. Grant, paper presented at the 39th Australian Surveyors Congress, *When Titling Meets Tradition* 2 (Launceston, Australia, Nov. 8–13, 1998) (copy on file with the author).

[102] M. Torhonen, paper presented at the International Conference on Spatial Information for Sustainable Development, *Systematic Registration for Cambodia: Why and How?* 1–6 (Nairobi, Kenya, Oct. 2–5, 2001) (copy on file with the author); *see* Cambodia Appraisal Document, *supra* n. 1.

[103] H. E. S. Setha, paper presented at the Regional Workshop on Land Issues in Asia, *Discussion Paper* 4–5 (Phnom Penh, Cambodia, June 4–5, 2002).

[104] *See* Holstein, *supra* n. 99, at 17.

subject to later resolution; or they are registered in the name of the State. Problem parcels are typically those subject to dispute, lacking evidence of ownership, or irregularly developed. In Georgia, up to 50 percent of residential plots have gone unregistered in some places because of encroachments and irregularities.[105] In Albania, up to 30 percent of the parcels in some areas are registered in the name of the State because of unresolved issues.[106] In both cases, the very people who have clouded title, who are consequently in the most need of resolution and formalization, are excluded from the process. It is again the poorer rights holders who are most likely to lack the resources to clear those rights.

Women and other disenfranchised groups—often the poorest of the poor—are at times inappropriately and inequitably excluded from tenure security and the consequent benefits provided by titling and registration. For example, a study of data and anecdotal evidence from titling efforts in Honduras, Colombia, Mexico, Peru, Ecuador, and Chile shows that women do not receive land rights under many titling and registration projects.[107] Reasons for their exclusion include:

- Legislation that does not provide for joint titling of land to couples (even when the law conflicts with constitutional or civil code provisions that establish women's rights to property)
- Land legislation that purports to be gender-neutral and does not expressly provide for establishing and protecting women's land rights when men are the customary heads of household
- Legislation that makes it voluntary to jointly title land (in conjunction with titling and registration procedures that do not facilitate joint titling, and sometimes with default marital regimes that presume separate property)
- An impetus born of the individualization of land rights that creates a tendency to restrict title to only one person per household
- Requirements that consensual but not legally formalized unions be officially registered before joint titling can occur
- Requirements that titling program participants have the civil capacity that is awarded upon registration to vote
- Land titling publicity programs that target only men's attention and interest groups and associations

---

[105] J. Salukvadze, *Comparative Analyses of Land Administration Systems: with Special Reference to Armenia, Moldova, Latvia and Kyrgyzstan* 37 (2002), comments on paper by Gavin Adlington (copy on file with author).

[106] R. Gaynor & D. Bledsoe, *Evaluation of the Albania Land Market Project* 5 (USAID/ARD 2000).

[107] *See* Deere & León, *supra* n. 17, at 188, 294–300.

- Unwillingness of functionaries (because of a desire for expediency) to comply with program requirements to confirm marital or union status
- Institutional inertia in pushing for recognition of joint titling as the norm and in creating an environment of gender awareness and sensitivity.

These exclusionary circumstances are in part the result of several hurdles faced by women. First, (usually inaccurate) gendered perspectives about divisions in agricultural labor create an environment where women are not taken seriously as agriculturalists. Second, their low independent income prompts some to question women's ability to pay for land or make mortgage payments. Third, women are frequently unaware of their rights to titled land.[108] These hurdles, along with the specific reasons for their exclusion from earlier titling and registration projects, are signs that particularized targeting of women would be useful during titling and registration projects.[109]

However, there are some legal tools that can be used to prevent exclusion of the poor. For example, laws have been passed to preserve land rights for a limited period, or to permit later cure of the clouded rights that create problem parcels. The English title registration system, set forth in large part by the Land Registration Act (1925), permits possessory and qualified titles to be registered.[110]

Possessory title allows registration "as is"—all existing defects continue in the registered title, but subsequent interests (arising after a transaction, for example) must be registered. This could lower the costs of cleaning up title for registration; prevent claimants from being permanently excluded by leaving latent, unexercised rights in place, and reduce the number of problem parcels registered in the name of the State. Title is subject to all latent rights existing at the time of registration, but after fifteen years without challenge, the possessory title becomes absolute.[111]

Qualified titles are those registered with broad exceptions evident on the face of the certificate of title. A qualified title can only be converted to an absolute title if the defect is cured or evidence that the defect has been cured in the past later comes to light.[112] The Singapore land title registration system also recognizes provisional (called "qualified") titles, similar to the English system. This

---

[108] *See id.* at 294–27.

[109] *See generally,* chapter 3 of this book, for a more extensive discussion of land titling and registration and women's rights and access to land.

[110] T. Fiflis, *English Registered Conveyancing: A Study in Effective Land Transfer,* 59 Nw. U. L. Rev. 470, 482–83 (1964).

[111] S. Simpson, *Land Law and Registration* 214–15 (Cambridge U. Press 1976).

[112] United Nations Economic Commission for Europe (UNECE), *Key Aspects of Land Registration and Cadastral Legislation, Part 1* 48 (UNECE 2000).

allows title to be issued contingent on there being no challenge to the title for that parcel over a set number of years. Singapore differs from England in that the statute of limitations for conversion of title from provisional to absolute is only five years rather than fifteen.[113]

These kinds of legal tools might be particularly suitable where it is suspected that there are many conflicting claims to the same land parcels that are unlikely to be resolved. Where poor people do not have resources to make and support a claim, these tools can provide a legal safety net that preserves rights until the claimant is able to pursue the claim. Of course, the disadvantage of possessory and qualified titles is that the protection they provide is more limited and titleholders have less certainty.[114] This lack of certainty, which would affect both titleholders and others if the property was the subject of a market transaction, would tend to generally inhibit market activity.

5.4.4 Do Titling and Registration Create Landless Poor?

Titling and registration can create landlessness in several ways. First, in rare cases, individualization and titling of otherwise commonly used lands can create landlessness when the common users no longer have access.[115] This can occur when laws permit individual users to apply for and receive title to land that is also being used by others. Second, titling and registration can create landlessness when the benefits of the process are inappropriately captured by a few or when the process is otherwise corrupted and has inequitable results.[116] Capture can occur when bribes are permitted to influence titling decisions or when titling processes require fees or other costly requirements (surveys, for example) that the current user or tenant cannot afford but that can be afforded by another party who is not due the formalized right. Third, titling and registration can create land-lessness when opportunities for increased mortgage lending result in foreclosures due to onerous or inequitable foreclosure laws.[117] Lack of notice of default and of reasonable opportunities to cure default, as well as provisions for unreasonable loan acceleration upon default, can cause landlessness by way of foreclosure. Finally, when titling and registration are not accompanied by measures that ensure adequate access to credit and markets, technical assistance, and extension

---

[113] *See* Simpson, *supra* n. 111, at 215–16.

[114] *See id.* at 216–18.

[115] *See* Bruce, *supra* n. 24, at 81–84; and Muhereza & Bledsoe, *supra* n. 24, at 12–13.

[116] *See* Quan, *supra* n. 25, at 35–36.

[117] *See* Giovarelli *et al., Legal Impediments, supra* n. 85, at 140–47.

services, some smallholders may have to sell or abandon their land, often to the advantage of better-situated landholders.[118]

However, there are some tools that can help prevent landlessness from being created in these ways. For example, to prohibit individuals from formalizing claims to land that is otherwise commonly used, registration laws can be crafted to require a showing that an individual claim of title is not encroaching on land that might otherwise be common property (forests, wetlands, and grazing lands, for example). Another solution is to preserve a right to appeal individual formalization of a land right for common property users who can show encroachment upon a long and recognizably common property resource. Similarly, titling and registration laws can be crafted to expressly foresee corrupt practices, extralegal fees, failures to convey joint title, and mortgage foreclosures that are inappropriately swift or that preclude reasonable cure.

Because the poorest landholders are often in need of subsistence resources or know the least about their rights, the law has stepped in to protect them. To protect new landowners from the perils of speculation and to prevent unwise sale of newly obtained land, some countries impose moratoriums on land sales for a period after land is originally privatized or titled. However, many moratoriums have been suspended or allowed to lapse, primarily to unfetter land markets. In Armenia, for example, a three-year moratorium that was enacted when land was privatized and distributed lapsed in February 1994.[119] In Ukraine, a six-year sales moratorium expired in 2005 although exemptions made most agricultural land subject to sale.[120] A Kyrgyz moratorium on the sale of agricultural land was put into place when land was privatized and allocated, but it was lifted in September 2001.[121] The Moldovan Land Code contained a ten-year moratorium on sales, but it was lifted in late 1996 when it was declared unconstitutional.[122] Some countries have attempted to protect new landowners from the danger of mortgage

---

[118] *See* AusAID, *supra* n. 1, at 30. Unfortunately, some countries enact laws that simply strip land rights from new rights holders. *For example,* in a measure that divested unwitting land rights holders of their right to convert land shares into demarcated parcels, the new Kazakh Land Code terminated the validity of formalized land shares if they are not either transferred as contributions into a joint stock company or production cooperative or converted into private family farm parcels, by January 2005. Land Code of Kazakhstan, art. 170 (2003).

[119] Z. Lerman & A. Mirzakhanian, *Private Agriculture in Armenia* 7 (Lexington Books 2001).

[120] Land Code of Ukraine, sec. X, art. 15 (2001).

[121] Kyrgyz Republic Law on Administration of Agricultural Land (2000); Kyrgyz Republic Regulation No. 427 on the Procedure of Purchase and Sale of Agricultural Land (Aug. 13, 2001).

[122] *See* Giovarelli *et al., Legal Impediments, supra* n. 85, at 110.

foreclosure by setting moratoriums on mortgages. For example, a 1997 Russian law prohibited mortgages on agricultural land.[123]

Many Indian States place sales moratoriums on the transfer of land obtained through land reform or other government grant. For example, the State of West Bengal has restricted alienation of land held by members of Scheduled Tribes to protect them from improvident disposition of land. The West Bengal law also prohibits the transfer of land given to the landowner by the government, except for certain mortgages.[124] Similarly, to protect landowners from inappropriate transfers, the State of Karnataka prohibits for fifteen years the transfer of surplus land granted to a landowner by the State, except for some mortgages. Also in Karnataka, whenever land tenants have been deemed "occupants" (and consequently been awarded long-term use rights and a future opportunity to own land), any transfer is prohibited, except for certain mortgages.[125]

In an attempt to provide a cure for improvident land transfers, West Bengal State in 1973 enacted the Restoration of Alienated Land Act. It says that any transfers by landowners of less than two hectares that were made after 1967 can be voided and the land returned to the original owner if it was a distress sale made necessary by a need to meet a family's basic maintenance or to support the cost of cultivation. However, there are no known examples of the act ever being used, and it expired in 1980. To get the land returned, the transferor needed to apply and then make a showing of the facts at a quasijudicial hearing. If successful, the transferor was to pay the transferee the amount the transferee paid for the land, plus 4 percent interest, plus the cost of any improvements.[126]

Such legal tools might be used to protect new land-rights holders from losing their land, but they bring disadvantages as well. By limiting or voiding land transfers, the tools tend to fetter the land market and make transactions more risky. Positive redistributional effects of the land market can be stifled and higher land prices may result.

Despite the somewhat axiomatic certainty of some, there is simply no hard evidence that land titling and registration alleviates poverty. In fact, the impacts of titling and registration on poverty, good or bad, have not been determined. Nor has there been any systematic approach to gauging those impacts, although the PSIA template might be a start. There does not seem to be a systematic way to target the poor either. Many titling and registration project documents state that poverty alleviation is a goal, but few set out how the poor are to be targeted. As to exclusion of the poor and women and the creation of landlessness, there is no

---

[123] Russian Federation Law on Mortgages, art. 63 (No. 102–FZ, July 16, 1998).

[124] West Bengal Land Reforms Act, sec. 14B (1955).

[125] Karnataka Land Reforms Act, sec. 61 (1961).

[126] West Bengal Restoration of Alienated Land Act (1973).

hard evidence of the extent of these impacts either. However, it is likely that there are exclusions and that some of the poor lose their land as or after rights have been formalized. Thus, though there are legal tools that can help prevent exclusion and landlessness, they must be exercised cautiously. They can also restrain land markets and efficient transactions.

5.5   Conclusions and Recommendations

Despite a lack of clear evidence that they deliver the intended economic benefits or directly alleviate poverty, land titling and registration will likely continue to be a widely pursued development activity.[127] The lack of evidence is not surprising. Titling and registration projects are relatively young; the benefits they might deliver can take decades to develop. It is also difficult and costly to benchmark land tenure situations, and probably even more difficult and costly to monitor results so as to gauge meaningful impacts and show causal attribution. Poverty impacts, good and bad, are among the hardest to pin down.

Titling and registration sponsors and donors have learned that titling and registration must be preceded by enabling preconditions and that the projects must be accompanied and followed by a variety of complementary components. Sponsors and donors also know that beneficiaries, including the poor, need to be targeted before they will be reliably and sustainably touched by benefits.

This section highlights several issues already mentioned and provides ideas about how to respond to them.

Issue: A small universe of comparative information on the performance and impacts of titling and registration projects informs decisions on whether to proceed with such projects and on their design and implementation. Benchmarking and impact assessment have not been standardized. Project design and implementation are often based on assumptions derived from a few projects (such as the one in Thailand), and the situation in the target country or locality may be quite different from those in the country on which the assumptions are based.

Relative few projects are used as evidence to show that titling and registration can increase tenure security, prompt investment, create credit opportunities, and enhance land markets—all of which are intended to spur economic growth and alleviate poverty. Data gathered from these few projects are lacking or incomplete. Methodologies for gathering information and assessing its meaning are inconsistent. Although observers endeavor to qualify their observations and conclusions, their information is often used to support decisions to proceed with new projects, and it is then used to actually design and implement them. Additional data on existing titling and registration programs, analyzed in a scientific way, are needed

---

[127] *See, for example,* AusAID, *supra* n. 1, at 49–55; Strachan, *supra* n. 1, at 23–24; and IFAD, *supra* n. 81, at 74–75.

both to justify proceeding with projects in other countries and to help design the projects (see recommendation on feasibility assessment and design below).

Recommendation: Donor agencies involved in titling and registration projects should collaborate on standardized approaches to monitoring and assessing them and on characterization of the data gathered. Project designers should guard against incorporating assumptions into new projects that are based on the unique circumstances within another country.

Specifically, the World Bank, the other development banks, the primary bilateral donor agencies, and a few independent experts should form a single task force charged with creating a standardized approach to benchmarking, project monitoring, and evaluation. The task force should create design and targeting guidelines that prompt designers to carefully vet assumptions based on other countries. The task force should operate pursuant to a memorandum of understanding that is sufficiently general that it prompts agreement. The task force leader should be selected on the basis of leadership, management, and consensus-building skills, rather than familiarity with titling and registration theory and practice. The task force might consider sponsoring a grant award competition that solicits approaches on the basis of a performance specification, with a significant monetary grant dedicated to the funding of the best proposal.

Issue: Poverty targeting and impact analysis are frequently not a significant part of project feasibility assessment and design.

Presuming that one of the goals is to target and benefit the poor and often excluded groups, such as women, there ought not to be much distinction between the sort of analysis done to make sure that the poor are targeted and that done to inform decisions about proceeding with a project and how it should be designed. The link between the economic benefits of titling and registration and the alleviation of poverty needs to be articulated so that targeting is meaningful and impacts can be measured. It is difficult to target the poor and to assess impacts upon them when the connections between economic development and poverty alleviation are unclear.

Recommendation: Titling and registration project performance, cost/benefit analysis, and design tools should be driven in large part by assessment of poverty targeting and poverty impact.

Those typically responsible for poverty and social impact assessments should participate in the task force charged with creating tools. There should be a real connection between the poverty targeting and impact assessment and the project design analysis. The poverty linkage should be seen less as an end-of-process ratification and more as a start-of-process data-gathering and design tool. The task force should also be charged with developing standardized approaches to poverty targeting and impact assessment.

Issue: Titling and registration can be exclusionary and can create landlessness.

Inappropriate and unforeseen exclusions can occur during both systematic and sporadic titling efforts; intentional exclusions can be severe and unforgiving. Women and other disadvantaged groups can be excluded by virtue of their status alone. In some cases, landlessness is created or abetted by titling and registration efforts.

Recommendation: Exclusions and landlessness should be a focus of poverty targeting and impact assessment. Legal and other tools should be used as needed to prevent or mitigate exclusions and creation of landlessness.

Possessory and qualified titles, moratoriums on and prohibition of transfers, common property protections, restoration of transferred land, and requirements for legal education should all be explored for appropriate use. As with any other complementary component in a larger titling and registration project, these legal tools should be refined so they can provide suitable protection but, to the extent possible, not limit investment and stifle land markets. If the chilling effect on investments and land markets is too severe, use of the tools may need to be modified. Continuing assessment will be necessary. Other causes of landlessness that may accompany titling and registration, including failure of credit markets and the lack of a social safety net, should be explored in detail during project design and implementation.

Issue: The exclusion of the poor, women, and other groups from the universe of titling and registration beneficiaries probably results in part from lack of opportunity for these groups to be heard or seen while projects are being designed.

If input and perspectives are missing, needed project sensitivities will likely be missing, or at least not be realistic about how to prevent exclusion.

Recommendation: Members of typically excluded groups should be consulted and studied with particularity when information is gathered to inform project design.

Investigative fieldwork should be done among these groups, and data-gathering techniques should be used that can obtain the needed information from them. Targeting and impact assessment efforts should solicit the information that would highlight the needs of excluded groups. A number of well-known measures can be used to promote women's participation in titling and registration, for instance, such as consciousness-raising, joint ownership and titling mandates, education of field staff, and assessment of customary realities and their relationship to the formal law. Their use during targeting efforts should be considered.[128]

---

[128] *See generally,* chapter 3 of this book for a more extensive discussion of land titling and registration and women's rights and access to land.

CHAPTER 6

Property Rights and Environmentally Sound Management of Farmland and Forests

Robert Mitchell*

This chapter provides a broad overview of environmental challenges posed by expansion and intensification of agriculture and increasing pressures upon forests. It examines the environmental impact of a number of legal tools used to influence land and natural resource use in farming and forestry systems. Though an exhaustive examination of trends and legal tools is beyond the scope of the chapter, and each of its sections has been the topic of book-length treatments, a broad overview may be helpful to explore the interplay between property rights and environmental concerns—two topics that are often discussed separately.

6.1   Introduction

The global population is estimated to reach roughly 8 billion by 2025, resulting in significant increases in the demand for food crops, meat, and forest products. Satisfying that demand will increase environmental stress on many ecosystems as the result of some combination of agricultural extensification (bringing new land under cultivation) and intensification (producing more per unit of current farm land).[1] Extensification has continued in many regions in recent decades. From 1961 through 2000, for example, area under cultivation increased 74 percent in Brazil (to 261,406 hectares) and 60 percent in China (to 548,658 hectares).[2]

While area under cultivation increases, forests shrink as the result of both demand for forest products and clearance of forests to create agricultural land and

---

* Robert Mitchell is a Senior Attorney at the Rural Development Institute (RDI) in Seattle, Washington. Information about the Institute can be found at http://www.rdiland.org. The views expressed in this chapter are the views of the author and do not necessarily represent the views of RDI.

[1] P. J. Gregory *et al., Environmental Consequences of Alternative Practices for Intensifying Crop Production,* 88 Agric., Ecosystems & Env. 279, 280–81 (2002).

[2] Food and Agriculture Organization of the United Nations, http://apps.fao.org/page/collections?subset=agriculture (accessed January 2006).

**Box 6–1. Negative Environmental Impacts Associated
with Farming and Forestry**

i. *Wildlife and natural habitat:* elimination of animal and plant species, elimination of natural habitat, desertification

ii. *Soils:* erosion, soil mining, salinization, desertification, loss of soil biota

iii. *Water:* sedimentation that reduces reservoir capacity for flood control, clogs river channels, damages fisheries, and impairs drinking water quality; water pollution caused by chemical fertilizers, pesticides, herbicides, and animal wastes.

iv. *Crop health:* crop monocultures vulnerable to pests and disease.

v. *Climate change:* regional and global changes caused by loss of CO_2 sequestration capacity, changes in rainfall through alteration of water cycle.

Source: Summarized by author from a variety of authorities.

---

rangeland. Even after accounting for reforestation, globally since 1990 there has been an estimated annual net loss of 9.4 million hectares of forest (0.22 percent annually), of which most was natural forest in the tropics.[3]

Unless managed carefully, increased farming, whether through intensification or extensification, may have a host of negative environmental impacts, including soil erosion, siltation of reservoirs, increased risk of flooding, loss of plant and animal species, soil mining, salinization of soil, water mining, water pollution, and climate change. Deforestation of whatever type may eliminate wild animal and plant species, compromise watershed quality, and reduce global capacity to sequester greenhouse gases. Box 6–1 summarizes these and other impacts.

Land and resource management policies can play an important role in preserving and facilitating sustainable use of forests, arable lands, and rangelands. In less developed countries, land and resource management policies also play a significant role in determining the extent to which the poor and other marginalized groups share in the benefits of increased agricultural production or preservation of forests and rangelands. Policies that exclude such groups from the benefits of resource use may be not only inequitable but also socially

---

[3] Food and Agriculture Organization, http://www. biodiv.org/programmes/areas/forest (accessed February 2004).

unsustainable over the long run, contributing to political destabilization.[4] For these reasons, land and natural resource management policies should not be based solely on consideration of the environmental impacts of resource use, any more than they should be based solely on questions of who benefits from resource use.

State political and administrative capacity to implement desired policies is likely to greatly influence a State's options for managing resource use. Thus, for example, a State that lacks the political or administrative capacity to accomplish agricultural intensification in ways that allow poor and marginalized groups to benefit may be justified in adopting a policy of agricultural extensification that more easily allows poor and marginalized groups to benefit, even though extensification may increase the risk of environmental harms. Though political and administrative capacity are not fixed in the long term, they may significantly constrain options in the short and medium term.

States attempt to implement land and resource use policies through a variety of mechanisms, including subsidies and tax incentives for resource users, public education programs, and construction of physical infrastructure to aid irrigation or control flooding. They may also adopt and implement legislation to advance land and resource use policy. Rather than examine the panoply of mechanisms for influencing resource use, this chapter attempts to review the land and resource conservation merits of certain legal interventions, with an emphasis on the role of property rights.

Although many factors contribute to the effectiveness or noneffectiveness of laws applied to influence resource management, one important factor is the capacity of state and local institutions to implement such laws. Whereas a law may effectively advance some goals, it may be less effective, irrelevant, or even counterproductive in achieving other goals. For example, while the form of land tenure may influence resource use and management practices that maximize and sustain onsite benefits of farming, land tenure may often be much less important for minimizing externalities of farming that affect the wider public, such as the downstream effects of erosion control or the costs associated with climate forcing and loss of species.

This chapter is organized in three parts. The next section briefly reviews potential environmental and social harms associated with farming and use of forests. Due to space limitations, it does not separately treat land and resource issues related to livestock raising, despite its often overriding importance. The next section argues for classifying laws for managing land and resource use into three categories related to the capacity of individuals, groups, and the State to enforce the law. The final section gives examples of laws for regulating land and resource use.

---

[4] R. L. Prosterman & J. M. Reidinger, *Land Reform and Economic Development* 7, 10 (Johns Hopkins U. Press 1987).

6.2 Framing the Issues

Changes to the natural environment are caused by many processes, including natural processes (not human-induced) that occur over long cycles. While it is easy to overestimate the impact of human activity on the environment,[5] nevertheless, human use of land and natural resources is responsible for profound environmental changes, especially at the local level. Two such uses are farming and use of forests.[6]

6.2.1 Farming

Negative environmental impacts directly associated with farming may be either onsite or offsite (externalities). The primary negative onsite impacts are reduction of quality of soils and loss of soils through erosion, but may also include loss of plant and animal species. While loss of soil and reduction of soil quality undoubtedly represent losses to the larger society, they are most profoundly felt by farmers who have an ongoing relationship with the land; they are therefore properly regarded as private costs of farming. Significant potential negative externalities associated with farming are downstream flooding caused by reduced reservoir capacity; reductions in water quality because of sedimentation deposits; water pollution caused by run-off of chemical fertilizers, pesticides, and animal wastes; and loss of species caused by, for example, cropping decisions and improper use of chemicals and pesticides. Negative offsite impacts affect the larger community and are therefore properly regarded as public costs of farming.

In developing countries, where most families earn their living from agriculture and where a sizable proportion of families are economically vulnerable, land and resource policies inevitably have significant impact on the poor and other marginalized groups.[7] Ideally, land and resource policies that seek to safeguard the environment should also seek to safeguard and expand opportunities for the poor

---

[5] M. Leach, R. Mearns & I. Scoones, *Environmental Entitlements: Dynamics and Institutions in Community-Based Natural Resource Management*, 27(2) World Dev. 225, 230–32 (1999).

[6] The chapter discusses farming and forests separately. In some ways this may be an unnatural organization of the discussion, since farm policy can greatly affect the rate at which forests are converted to farmland or rangeland, and the national policies of some countries even encourage deforestation in order to expand land under cultivation or pasture. However, division of the discussion between farming and forests may be useful in isolating issues, considerations, and legal tools that are unique to conservation of farmland on the one hand or of forests and forest land on the other. It is important in each case to consider whether a given policy or legal tool is likely to impact both farms and forests.

[7] *See generally,* World Bank & Klaus Deininger, *Land Policies for Growth and Poverty Reduction,* World Bank Policy & Poverty Reduction Report (World Bank & Oxf. U. Press 2003).

to participate in the benefits of farming. Indeed, policies that neglect the interests of the poor can exacerbate pressures on the environment. As Parnwell asks with reference to poor farmers in northeast Thailand:

> [H]ow do you convince the head of a poverty-stricken household that he should not grow cassava on the small patch of upland that he works, perhaps illegally, and which provides his only source of cash income? How can you persuade him that he should invest more manpower and capital in improving his single hectare of riceland which is flooded every other year, when half of his family spends most of the year working in Bangkok?[8]

In addition to direct negative impacts from farming, agricultural extensification often replaces natural forests and wetlands with farms and rangelands. Extensification may have important negative environmental consequences, including loss of biodiversity and climate change. Even where extensification does not directly replace forests, if lands brought under cultivation are located near forests, farming households may negatively impact forest health by removing trees for use as fuel or building material and may impact wildlife populations through increased use of biocides and increased hunting.[9] The relationship between agricultural extensification and loss of natural forests is one of the most important areas where land policy impacts the environment.

The potential public costs of agricultural land policies therefore include both offsite and onsite environmental degradation and may directly affect the well-being of poor and marginalized groups that are denied access to land and resources. In the case of farming, the challenge is to find legal tools that advance state policies that simultaneously (1) promote ecologically sustainable farming by minimizing onsite and offsite environmental costs; and (2) ensure that the poor participate through equitable access to land resources. These public costs and the legal tools that may help address them are explored in more detail in the last part of this chapter.

6.2.2 Forests

Forests are logged to supply timber and paper and are cleared for agricultural extensification and grazing. Loss of forests can contribute to local flooding, regional and global climate change, and loss of animal and plant species dependent on natural forest. Survival of wild animal species is threatened by

---

[8] M. J. G. Parnwell, *Rural Poverty, Development and the Environment: The Case of North-East Thailand,* 15(1) J. Biogeography 199, 207 (1988).

[9] *See, for example,* G. Ledec, *Effects of Kenya's Bura Irrigation Settlement Project on Biological Diversity and Other Conservation Concerns,* 1(3) Cons. Biol. 247, 250–55 (Oct. 1987).

overhunting, especially by local populations. Animal and plant species may also be threatened by replacement of natural forest with monoculture tree crops.

Many forests serve important social functions, providing homes and an economic base for forest-dwelling communities and supplying fuel wood and other products to households in villages near the forest. Forest resources, including nontimber products, can be especially important to the household economy of the rural poor. Overharvesting of both timber and nontimber products can stress the health of forests.

The challenge is to find policies that (1) promote sustainable use of forests; (2) promote preservation of watersheds and water quality; (3) promote preservation of animal and plant species in forests; and (4) balance those needs against the needs of human populations that depend upon forest resources. We are interested in identifying legal tools that can help implement such policies. These challenges are explored in more detail in the last part of this chapter.

6.3 Property Rights: The Importance of Enforceability

Rules allow States, groups, and individuals to influence and to predict how others will behave—what they will do or refrain from doing in particular situations. For this discussion we examine both the *rules* that prohibit or authorize human action and the *processes and institutions* through which the rules are interpreted and enforced. But it is surely obvious that in deciding how to behave, individuals consider not only the law but also their own unique social, political, economic, and physical environment.[10]

We are here concerned primarily with rules that take the form of formal laws (including, for example, regulations and decrees) promulgated by States and state institutions, as well as contractual arrangements through which the State invites enterprises and groups to manage publicly owned natural resources. This focus on formal laws is not intended to underestimate the importance of informal laws and institutions, which may be embedded in longstanding custom or may evolve spontaneously in response to temporary or local circumstances. Such mechanisms are often more important than formal laws and can be more appropriate to local needs. One challenge of modern lawmaking is to find ways to accommodate such mechanisms, where they are effective and accepted as legitimate by local people, within the framework of national law.

Policy enforceability is relatively neglected in writings on land and natural resource policy. A refreshing exception is an article by Firmin-Sellers that

---

[10] A. Seidman & R. B. Seidman, *Beyond Contested Elections: The Processes of Bill Creation and Fulfillment of Democracy's Promises to the Third World,* 34 Harv. J. Legis. 1, 29 (1997).

examines the "political" history of property rights in customary law and formal law systems in Ghana.[11] The article argues that property rights systems must be defended through the coercive force of ruling institutions as well as a commitment by the ruling institution not to abuse its power to violate the rights.

The likelihood that a law will be implemented and enforced should be a threshold consideration as it is drafted and adopted. One useful approach to looking at legal tools may therefore be to categorize them according to who is likely to be best positioned to implement the rule in practice. From a review of the literature, it appears that legal arrangements related to control and use of land and resources may be classified into four broad classes: (1) those that vest or strengthen control rights in individuals; (2) those that empower communities, associations, and other local groups to assert group control rights; (3) those that reserve control rights to the State or create restrictions on private and group control rights to protect individual, group, and broader societal interests; and (4) those that rely upon coalitions of states and international nongovernmental organizations to protect resources perceived to have international importance. These categories often overlap; they are neither rigid nor exclusive.

Control rights asserted by individuals and groups often benefit from state sanction or the sanction of international conventions. But individuals and groups may also take steps to compel others to respect the control rights they are asserting, confident that, if necessary, the broader community or state stands willing to support their self-help measures.

If prevailing social mores legitimize particular property rights regimes, people will observe them more readily, thus lowering establishment and enforcement costs.[12] While informal laws and customs may be more important than formal law in many places (including many economically developed countries), inconsistency between formal and informal law may cause individuals to perceive some risk that the State may act to undermine informal law. Policymakers who can bring the formal law into harmony with informal law or custom, or who can increase the legitimacy of informal law, can thereby strengthen reliance on and leverage existing adherence to informal law.

States can legitimize informal laws and customs in a variety of ways. For example, the State may empower customary tribunals to resolve particular types of property disputes, or state tribunals may observe procedures that sanction consideration of customary rules and practices in resolving disputes.

---

[11] K. Firmin-Sellers, *The Politics of Property Rights,* 89(4) Am. Political Sci. Rev. 867 (1995).

[12] C. G. Stevenson, *Common Property Economics: A General Theory and Land Use Applications* 73 (Camb. U. Press 1991).

TABLE 6–1
Control Right Assertion and Resource Use

Primary Level Where Control Rights Are Asserted	Associated Characteristics of Resource Use	Example of Resource Use
Individual	Management of inputs important, small- to medium-scale resource	Sedentary farming
Group	Many users, limiting overuse important, large-scale resource	Use of water, forest, or rangeland
State	Costs borne by broader society, large-scale resource	Prevention of flooding or water pollution
Coalitions of states, international nongovernmental organizations	Costs borne by global community, large-scale or unique resource	Preservation of rare species and habitats

Source: Adopted and summarized by author from various authorities.

But formal law may operate at the local level even in the absence of effective local state institutions. There are no doubt limits to what formal laws can accomplish in the face of local norms and customs that directly conflict with those laws.[13] However, to the extent a formal law is consistent with the interests of a local group that has enough knowledge and opportunity to assert application of the law in support of those interests the law may strengthen the group's ability to assert its claims and may allow outsiders—such as local NGOs—to make assertions on behalf of the group. In this way, formal law may create expectations and influence the balance of power among local actors. While formal law is unlikely to be decisive unless state institutions support its implementation, even in the absence of such institutions formal law can influence the bargaining that occurs locally among groups and individuals.

In the case of legal tools for regulating land and resource use, factors relevant to the analysis include the scale of resource exploitation, whether the resource is exploited by individuals or groups (and the size of the groups), and whether exploitation of the resource by one group imposes costs (externalities) on other groups or the larger society. Table 6–1 lists modes of enforcement and

---

[13] *See* Leach, *supra* n. 5, at 238.

characteristics of resource use associated with each factor. These are explored in the following sections.

6.3.1 Individual Assertion of Control Rights and Individual Management

Legal tools that vest rights of control and management in individuals are likely to be more effective in promoting resource use in which individual management of inputs is important. Sedentary farming is a prime example. The theory is that farmers who control their own land individually—in the sense that they are able to control the use of and benefit stream from the land and prevent strangers from interfering with their control—are more likely to conserve the land as a valuable, profit-producing resource. Building on Demsetz,[14] Ellickson describes three ways in which individual management of one's own land is more efficient than group management of shared land with respect to actions that are primarily local to the land, such as cultivating tomatoes:

> First, self-control by one person . . . is much simpler than the multiperson coordination entailed in intragroup monitoring. . . . Second, individual ownership not only greatly reduces the number of instances in which people have to be watched, but makes that task simpler when it must be performed. A key advantage of individual land ownership is that detecting the presence of a trespasser is much less demanding than evaluating the conduct of a person who is privileged to be where he is. . . . For this reason, managers are paid more than night watchmen. Third, . . . an individual landowner is much more highly motivated than a group member to police boundaries or to carry out any other sort of monitoring function. A sole owner bears the entirety of any loss stemming from his slack oversight, whereas a group member bears only a fraction.[15]

More will be said in the last part of this chapter about the evidence to support the proposition that enhancing and protecting individual control of land can improve land conservation practices.

Examples of legal tools that substantially rely on individual assertion of control rights are (1) state privatization of farm land, (2) state titling of farm land, (3) state redistribution of farm land, and (4) state allocation of forests to individuals for caretaking, including allocation by contract. In each case, creation of an individual "property right" in the resource gives the individual the legal authority to manage the resource and exclude others from exploiting it.

---

[14] H. Demsetz, *Toward a Theory of Property Rights,* 57 Am. Econ. Rev. 347 (1967).

[15] R. C. Ellickson, *Property in Land,* 102 Yale L. J. 1315, 1327–28 (1993).

Tools that rely upon individual assertion of control rights are likely to be less effective in discouraging negative externalities associated with resource use, such as offsite flooding and the contamination of waterways by farming. However, tools that promote onsite productivity may incidentally have beneficial offsite effects. To the extent that legal tools ignore the needs of the landless and other impoverished and marginalized groups, however, they will not only be less equitable but are also likely to be less effective over the long term, as is examined further in the last part of this chapter.

6.3.2   Group Assertion of Control Rights and Group Management

Legal tools that rely upon group assertion of control rights are likely to be more useful in promoting protection of common resources that are important to a number of users and for which preventing overuse is more important than management of inputs; forests and rangelands often satisfy these criteria. Group management may be an especially beneficial alternative to individualization when it is difficult to divide the resource (for example, a groundwater aquifer), where the society has traditionally managed the resource as common property, or where the resource provides a safety net to the poor.[16]

Group assertion of control rights and management of resources may be the only viable alternative where state administrative capacity is not adequate at the local level, where groups actively resist state administration of local resources, or where an identified and relatively cohesive group is the primary or exclusive user of a particular resource.

Examples of legal tools that substantially rely upon group assertion of control rights are (1) state recognition of group tenure to common resources (through group titling or otherwise); (2) state empowerment of a group (community, association, tribe) to benefit from a resource and exclude outsiders (including through management contracts); (3) state mandate of empowerment of vulnerable subgroups by mandate to share in the benefits of common resources; and (4) state-sanctioned water user associations to manage catchment area or portion to reduce negative off-site effects of farming.

While tools that rely upon group assertion of control rights may suffice to conserve the resource, they may be relatively ineffective in discouraging negative offsite effects borne by outsiders, such as downstream water users. However, the existence of the group institution may provide a useful point of contact for affected outsiders who wish to negotiate with group members about such offsite effects.

---

[16] *See* Stevenson, *supra* n. 12, at 4.

6.3.3 State Restrictions on Control Rights and State Management

Legal tools that provide for state restriction of individual and group control rights or that vest control rights in the State are more likely to be necessary with respect to environmental and other impacts that affect the interests of the society as a whole. Examples of such impacts are offsite effects of agricultural intensification (e.g., flooding and water pollution), effects related to resources used by more than one group (e.g., grazing lands used by different groups of migrating herders), and effects related to resources for which members of a group do not benefit sufficiently from preservation of the resource (e.g., preservation of large wildlife).

Examples of legal tools that substantially rely upon state restriction of private control rights or assertion of state control rights are (1) designation of protected forests, wildlife preserves, wetlands, and other natural habitat to be monitored and managed by the State; (2) regulation of water catchment areas used by many individuals and groups; (3) licensing groups to use common resources and assisting such groups through state enforcement of penalties against encroaching outsiders; and (4) zoning to preserve agricultural land.

6.3.4 International Instruments

According to one recent estimate, more than 1,000 international instruments either focus completely on the environment or have at least one important provision concerned with the environment.[17] A recent study by the Food and Agriculture Organization (FAO) gives a good overview of the more significant instruments related to land, environment, and protection of vulnerable populations.[18] International instruments are unlikely to address with any specificity the structure of national laws on land and resource use, particularly the mechanisms through which states apply and enforce such laws. Nevertheless, they are likely to be useful in highlighting the need for participating States to assess the ecological impacts of national policies and set goals for reducing negative impacts through national legislation, public education, and government policy. International instruments may also put pressure on national governments to enact legislation to conserve land and resources in ways that protect vulnerable populations. Table 6–2 lists representative international instruments related to land and resource use.

---

[17] E. B. Weiss, *Understanding Compliance with International Environmental Agreements: The Baker's Dozen Myths,* 32 U. Rich. L. Rev. 1555 (1999).

[18] Food and Agriculture Organization, *Law and Sustainable Development Since Rio: Legal Trends in Agriculture and Natural Resource Management,* FAO Legislative Study No. 73 (FAO 2002) [hereafter, *FAO Legal Trends*].

TABLE 6–2

**International Instruments Related to Land and Resource
Use and the Environment**

Year	Instrument	Notable Provisions
2002	Stockholm Convention on Persistent Organic Pollutants	Elimination or restriction of production, use, and release of chemicals that can affect human health throughout the globe, regardless of the location of their use
1997	Kyoto Protocol to the UN Framework Convention on Climate Change	Commitment of signatories to reduce six greenhouse gas emissions by 2012 to 95 percent of 1990 levels; permits use of "emissions trading" through which the buyer uses the allowances to comply with greenhouse gas emission reduction obligations under the protocol and the seller uses proceeds to finance domestic emission reduction projects and carbon sequestration projects, including projects in developing countries
1996	Rome Declaration of the World Food Summit (and Plan of Action)	Importance of legal and other mechanisms to advance land reform, recognize and protect property and water, enhance access to resources by women and the poor, and promote conservation and sustainable use of natural resources
1996	UN Convention to Combat Desertification	Importance of combating desertification and mitigating effects of drought, through, *inter alia,* conservation and regeneration of vegetation cover
1994	UN Framework Convention on Climate Change	Importance of stabilizing concentration of greenhouse gases in the atmosphere, through, *inter alia,* use of afforestation and improved forest management to offset greenhouse gas emissions
1993	Convention on Biological Diversity	Protecting customary use of biological resources in accordance with traditional cultural practices (art. 10(c))

TABLE 6–2 (*Continued*)

Year	Instrument	Notable Provisions
1992	Agenda 21 (Rio)	Need for clear title and land rights for individuals and communities; equitable access for rural women, small farmers, the rural landless, and indigenous people, and prevention of fragmentation (ch. 14). Importance of private property rights and rights of indigenous people to sustainable management of resources (ch. 10); importance of property rights of women, pastoral groups, and nomadic groups to combating desertification (ch. 12); need to preserve forests and rehabilitate degraded forests (ch. 11)
1983	International Tropical Timber Agreement (revised 1997)	Promotion of timber trade based on sustainable exploitation of tropical forests
1975	Convention on International Trade in Endangered Species of Wild Fauna and Flora	Promote preservation of endangered species through restrictions on trade, including trade in tree species that are important for preservation of wild habitat
1971	Convention on Wetlands (Ramsar Convention)	Preservation of wetlands of international importance through designation, national monitoring, and taking wetlands into account in national land use planning
1968	African Convention on the Conservation of Nature and Natural Resources (revised 2003)	Preservation of rare and representative ecosystems and species through creation of nature reserves and national parks

Source: Based on chapters on "Land" and "Forestry," in Food and Agriculture Organization, *Law and Sustainable Development Since Rio: Legal Trends in Agriculture and Natural Resource Management,* FAO Legislative Study No. 73 (FAO 2002); and on text of the instruments listed.

The Convention on Biological Diversity, which entered into force in December 1993 and has been ratified by 158 states (and acceded to, accepted, or approved by 29 more states), is perhaps representative. The convention obligates signatory States to develop a national biodiversity strategy and action plan and to file a report every four years on efforts to implement treaty commitments. With respect to land and natural resource use, the convention invites States to establish protected areas and to prepare impact statements as a method of minimizing adverse impacts of development projects that may negatively affect biodiversity. States are left to decide whether they have the capability to implement these provisions, and whether implementation is possible or appropriate.[19] Although Article 8(j) of the convention provides that practices of indigenous peoples should be respected and protected, this is made "subject to" the signatory State's national legislation—a very broad qualification.[20] Lack of consensus on how to measure performance under the convention has been identified as a major shortcoming.[21]

Another representative instrument is the Convention on Wetlands, signed in Ramsar, Iran, in 1971 and commonly referred to as the Ramsar Convention. As of the end of 2005 there were 141 contracting parties. Signatory States must designate and protect at least one wetland, consider wetland conservation in national land use planning, and provide training in wetland management. Although comprehensive data are not readily available, many States have designated multiple sites as protected wetlands, including more than six million hectares in Brazil and more than two million hectares in China. However, countries are not strictly obligated to protect all important wetlands, as confirmed by a recent study in Mexico that found thirty-four sites that qualify as wetlands of international importance that were not on the protected list.[22]

The 1997 Kyoto Protocol to the United Nations Framework Convention on Climate Change is another example of an instrument intended to apply broadly to protect a world resource. The instrument encourages signatory States to purchase emission allowances from other signatories that have satisfied protocol obligations to reduce greenhouse emissions. The selling signatory may use the proceeds to finance further reductions, through such means as restoring or

---

[19] J. C. Kunich, *Fiddling Around While the Hotspots Burn Out,* 14 Geo. Intl. Envtl. L. Rev. 179, 187 (2001).

[20] G. F. Maggio, *Recognizing the Vital Role of Local Communities in International Legal Instruments for Conserving Biodiversity,* 16 UCLA J. Envtl. L. & Policy 179, 211 (1997).

[21] P. G. le Prestre, *The CBD at Ten: the Long Road to Effectiveness*, 3(5) J. Intl. Wildlife L. & Policy 269, 278–279 (2002).

[22] A. Perez-Arteaga, K. J. Gaston & M. Kershaw, *Undesignated Sites in Mexico Qualifying as Wetlands of International Importance,* 107 Biological Conservation 47, 49 (2002).

replanting natural forests to sequester greenhouse gases. As of July 2001, such projects may be carried out in developing countries.[23] Guidelines are now being drafted to ensure that reforestation is done in ways that do not harm biodiversity.

6.4 Policies, Legal Tools, and Environmental Impacts

Which type of resource management will be most effective—individual, group, or state—will be influenced by many factors, including the scale of the resource; the identity and interests of resource users (including those with informal use claims); the capacity of users and state institutions to manage the resource; the capacity and willingness of users and the State to finance the infrastructure necessary to preserve the resource; and the types of externalities associated with use of the resource. The issues are often complicated because different actors use different means to gain control of resources, their exploitation strategies can impact the environment in different ways, and resources are used by nonhomogenous groups even in local settings.[24] Table 6–3 summarizes resource management options and environmental externalities for five resource types. Boxes appear around the more common management options, but no option is excluded.

Local environments may be dominated by a particular land use, such as farming, or be characterized by a mix of different land uses. Because of space limitations, the following sections separately address two principal land uses—farming and forests—although both uses may occur within the same local environment.

6.4.1 Farming

The primary focus of this section is land conservation in established rather than in nonestablished farming systems. In the latter, which may appear when forests and marginal lands are converted to farming, the granting of secure tenure to settlers who claim forest land may actually undermine conservation efforts. The relationship between farming and loss of natural forest is further explored at the end of this section.

In established farming systems, environmental impacts of farming related to land use are appropriately considered at the level of the watershed. Land use within watersheds is associated with six characteristic environmental effects: (1) soil erosion at the land-use site; (2) harmful sedimentation offsite; (3) pollution of water by chemicals; (4) changes in total water yield in streams;

---

[23] C. E. di Leva, *The Conservation of Nature and Natural Resources Through Legal and Market-Based Instruments,* 11 Rev. European Community & Intl. Envtl. L. 84, 91 (2002).

[24] *See* Leach, *supra* n. 5, at 229–30.

TABLE 6–3

Resource Management Options and Environmental Externalities

Management Option	Resource				
	Water	Arable	Forest	Rangeland	Wildlife
Zoning		Zoning to preserve arable land	Zoning to preserve forest		
State management	State water management	State arable land	State-managed forest (co-managed)	State-managed rangeland (co-managed)	State wildlife preserve (co-managed)
Group management	Water user association	Group arable land	Group-managed forest	Group-managed rangeland	Group wildlife preserve
Individual management		Individual arable land	Individual forest	Individual rangeland	Individual wildlife preserve
Externalities associated with improper management of resource	Soil erosion Siltation Water pollution Water mining	Soil erosion Siltation Water pollution Water mining Climate forcing Loss of species	Soil erosion Siltation Flooding Loss of species Climate forcing	Desertification Loss of species	Loss of species

Source: Adapted and summarized by author from various authorities.

(5) changes in distribution or timing of water delivery in streams; and (6) changes in the groundwater table.[25] To this we should add a seventh effect: reduced biodiversity, both onsite and offsite, resulting, for example, from cropping decisions or improper management of biocides. Box 6–2 describes several issues related to watershed management.

Two excellent ways to reduce soil erosion are maintenance of undisturbed forest on sloping land and terracing of arable land to create level or near-level ground.[26] Although reducing erosion benefits the individual farmer, it also has important offsite benefits. Erosion control directly reduces sedimentation, which is much less costly than attempting to remove sediment after it is deposited downstream. Good soil and water conservation measures can also help reduce runoff of harmful agrochemicals into surface waters (though such measures may increase transport of chemicals to groundwater by allowing more time for water to carry the chemicals into the soil).[27]

Biodiversity on cultivated land may be enhanced through decisions related to crop selection, cropping patterns, and application of biocides. In Mexico, production of coffee in shaded polycultural farms, which are generally small-scale farms, has been found to sustain a significantly larger variety of insects, reptiles, birds, and midsize mammals than unshaded monocrop farms.[28]

The following sections examine legal tools related to control of soil erosion at the farm level and control of externalities related to erosion, water use, and loss of biodiversity.

6.4.1.1   Strengthening Possessory Rights of Individuals

Much has been written about the land conservation benefits of strengthening the possessory land rights of individuals. Rights to land that are secure, long-term, and exclusive can promote land conservation in two principal ways: (1) by providing the land possessor with assurance that he or she will benefit from investments in land improvements through increased yields and increased value at time of lease or sale of the land; and (2) by providing financial institutions with assurance that the purported owner has secure, verifiable rights to land and that the institution's interests will be protected if it accepts the land as collateral for loans. Owners who can demonstrate the security of their land rights may thus be

---

[25] L. S. Hamilton & A. J. Pearce, *Biophysical Aspects in Watershed Management, in Watershed Resources Management: Studies from Asia and the Pacific* 33 (K. W. Easter, J. A. Dixon & M. M. Hufschmidt, eds., Institute of Southeast Asian Studies 1991).

[26] *See id.* at 37.

[27] *See id.* at 41.

[28] P. Moguel & V. M. Toledo, *Review: Biodiversity Conservation in Traditional Coffee Systems of Mexico,* 13(1) Cons. Biol. 11, 13 (Feb. 1999).

Box 6–2. Water Use Regulation and Land Conservation

Whether farmers obtain water from rainfall, managed irrigation systems, or groundwater wells, all water sources present problems of storage and runoff. Water runoff and gravity combine to cause soil erosion and all the harms associated with sedimentation of waterways and reservoirs. Because so many impacts of water flow are offsite, individual farmers have neither the incentive nor the capacity to prevent such harms. Effective water management therefore requires organization by either local groups or the State, or local groups and the State acting together as comanagers of the resource. As downstream impacts of water use increase or become more distant from water-using farmers, the incentive and capacity of local groups to deal with the impacts diminish and the task must increasingly require state involvement.

Forest use, herding, and farming in upland catchment sections of the watershed can greatly influence the amount, timing, and quality of the waters when they reach lowland farmers and urban populations. Upland communities may have very different social and economic priorities than lowland farmers. Upland users are unlikely to bear the cost of measures to improve the quality and quantity of downstream water that primarily benefits downstream users.[29]

In lowland farming areas, water user groups can help farmers to use irrigation water more efficiently, thereby reducing water demand and runoff. Where water is scarce, user associations help to ensure that water deliveries to farmers are timely and adequate, help to resolve disputes among farmers, and provide a means for affected downstream stakeholders to negotiate resolution of offsite impacts.

States often find it advantageous to involve local organizations in watershed management because (1) local organizations are often more effective than the State at securing compliance among water users, (2) local stakeholders are knowledgeable about local needs and may be better placed to identify and promote adoption of appropriate technologies, and (3) local organizations can bear much of the cost of enforcing conservation measures.[30] Writing about farming in Ethiopia, Admassie concludes that only

---

[29] J. A. Ashby, E. B. Knapp & H. M. Ravnborg, *Involving Local Organizations in Watershed Management,* in *Agriculture and the Environment: Perspectives on Sustainable Rural Development* 118, 119 (E. Lutz, ed., World Bank 1998).

[30] *See id.* at 118.

Box 6–2 (*Continued*)

local communities can manage land systems in ways that are environmentally sustainable since farmers are unable to control offsite impacts, the State is not equipped to manage at the local level, and there are no large private landlords who have an interest in managing large systems.[31]

Source: Adopted and summarized by author from various authorities.

---

permitted to access formal credit markets to finance long-term improvements to land.[32] Such rights can be safeguarded through a variety of mechanisms, including titling and registration of ownership, recognition of long-term use rights, and formal recognition of rights of occupation.

While the literature contains some dissent from the orthodox view that secure tenure contributes to land stewardship in established farming systems, most studies that have examined the relationship conclude that secure tenure does indeed enhance stewardship. For example, Hayes and colleagues found that tenure security was positively and significantly related to the propensity to make long-term investments in wells and fences in peri-urban farms in the Gambia.[33] In a study of land improvements in farming regions of Ghana, Besley found that more secure land rights appeared to promote investment in the northern cocoa-producing region but did not have a strong effect in the southern vegetable-producing region.[34] A study of smallholders in Honduras found that owners constructed rock walls to prevent erosion, planted trees, and followed other soil conservation measures, whereas leaseholders made no such improvements.[35] There is evidence from Niger that farmers who use livestock manure as the principal technique for maintaining soil fertility are much more likely to apply scarce manure to owned land than to borrowed land.[36]

---

[31] Y. Admassie, *Twenty Years to Nowhere: Property Rights, Land Management and Conservation in Ethiopia* xxx (Red Sea Press 2000).

[32] D. Wachter, *Farmland Degradation in Developing Countries: The Role of Property Rights and an Assessment of Land Titling as a Policy Intervention,* Land Tenure Center Paper No. 145, 22–23 (U. Wis. 1992); T. Besley, *Property Rights and Investment Incentives: Theory and Evidence from Ghana,* 103(5) J. Political Econ. 903, 906–907 (1995).

[33] J. Hayes, M. Roth & L. Zepeda, *Tenure Security, Investment and Productivity in Gambian Agriculture: a Generalized Probit Analysis,* 79(2) Am. J. Agric. Econs. 369, 377 (1997).

[34] *See* Besley, *supra* n. 29, at 926 and 931.

[35] S. C. Stonich, *Dynamics of Social Processes and Environmental Destruction: A Central American Case Study,* 15 Pop. & Dev. Rev. 284, 288 (1989).

[36] S. Gavian & M. Fafchamps, *Land Tenure and Allocative Efficiency in Niger,* 78(2) Am. J. Agric. Econs. 460, 467 (1996).

While tenure security undoubtedly contributes to the willingness of farmers to make long-term investments, other factors are also likely to influence the farmer's decision to invest in improvements. For example, farmers who invest in long-term improvements may incur opportunity costs in the form of reduced time devoted to on-farm production or foregone off-farm employment between cropping seasons, the cost of hiring labor to help with construction of improvements, and, in the case of agroforestry, the cost of reduced area for annual crops while the trees are not yet producing.[37]

Of course, not all agricultural intensification is environmentally friendly. Soil conservation may be accompanied by tree-felling to increase cropped area, and monocropping may adversely impact biodiversity.[38]

6.4.1.1.1 Formal Recognition of Rights of Occupation   Perhaps the most straightforward way the State can strengthen the possessory rights of individuals is through legislation formally recognizing the control rights of land occupiers. In 1997, Mozambique adopted a new land law that provides for automatic recognition of exclusive rights to land of individual citizens who have worked on the land "in good faith" for ten years or more.[39] The rights are automatically established without any need for the State to issue a title certificate or perform registration. Although the national constitution does not permit private ownership *per se,* the rights recognized are exclusive and transferable and cannot be arbitrarily revoked by the State. The law also extends such

---

[37] E. B. Barbier, *The Farm-Level Economics of Soil Conservation: The Uplands of Java,* 66 Land Econs. 199, 199–202 (1990).

[38] *See supra* n. 28 and accompanying text. Farming techniques affect land conservation in at least two important ways: (1) They can directly influence the rate at which farmland is degraded and the extent to which negative externalities are produced. (2) They help to influence the rate at which it is economically profitable to conserve existing farmland rather than open up new farmland. New farming techniques—such as integrated nutrient management (appropriate combination of fertilizers and manures) and reduced tillage—can maximize benefits of green revolution technologies while minimizing negative environmental impacts. *See* Gregory *et al., supra* n. 1, at 283–84. In the developing world, where farmers do not have ready access to or cannot afford expensive inputs and technologies, the goal should be to combine natural processes (such as nutrient recycling, soil regeneration, and use of biopesticides) with local knowledge and skills to create farming systems that are more environmentally sustainable and that meet the needs of local producers and consumers. J. N. Pretty, J. I. L. Morison & R. E. Hine, *Reducing Food Poverty by Increasing Agricultural Sustainability in Developing Countries,* 95 Agric., Ecosystems & Envt. 217, 218–219 (2003). Because farming techniques influence the profitability of physical measures to conserve soil and water, they help to determine whether farmers will adopt conservation measures.

[39] *See* chapter titled "Land" in *FAO Legal Trends, supra* n. 18, at 233.

automatic rights to communities, as will be discussed further in the context of forests.

This approach has parallels in the doctrines of "adverse possession" in common law jurisprudence and "prescription" in civil law jurisprudence. Such laws allows a land occupier to obtain ownership of land based upon actual occupation of the land continuously for some specified number of years; it must be obvious, nonpermissive (that is, without permission of others who claim ownership of the land), and "exclusive" in the sense that the occupier has not allowed others to occupy the land. The occupier need not apply to the State for recognition of rights; these are deemed to arise automatically by operation of law.[40]

Laws formalizing rights of occupation might be justified on the basis of the arguments used to support adverse possession. Adverse possession arguably: (1) discourages land owners from ignoring their land; (2) protects against the hardship caused by removing the person who has occupied the land for a long period; (3) encourages the productive use of land by rewarding land occupiers; and (4) over time helps to reduce the number of "latent" defects to land titles, thereby making it less risky for people to buy land.[41]

One potential advantage that rules to formalize rights of occupation might have over land titling and registration programs is that the former costs much less to implement because there is no need for the State to investigate and adjudicate land claims on a mass basis: Over time, disagreements are likely to diminish as occupation remains undisturbed. If the law allows land purchasers to assert the occupancy periods of those who sold them the land (a concept known in U.S. adverse possession jurisprudence as "tacking"), land occupiers will enjoy all essential benefits of land ownership (or rights similar to ownership, as in Mozambique). Of course, financial institutions may insist that the occupier obtain documentary evidence of ownership before they will accept the land as collateral for a loan. In that respect titling and registration provide a more beneficial security of right from the standpoint of land conservation since the long-term occupier may not be able to access credit to invest in land conservation.

---

[40] The automatic formalization of occupation rights should be distinguished from laws that allow land occupiers to apply for formal recognition of title, as provided, for example, by section 94–B of the Karnataka Land Revenue Act 1964 (as amended), which authorizes the deputy commissioner to ownership title to occupiers who satisfy provisions of the section.

[41] D. K. Irving, *Should the Law Recognize the Acquisition of Title by Adverse Possession?* 2 Australian Prop. L. J. 1, 6–9 (1994). The land occupier's belief that he or she owns the land should be irrelevant so long as the occupier makes productive use of the land. *See* P. C. Olsen, *Adverse Possession in Oregon: The Belief in Ownership Requirement*, 23 Envtl. L. 1297 (1993).

Another significant issue with respect to both rules formalizing occupation rights and any land tenure law that recognizes land use as creating legitimate claims to property rights is the danger that the rule will encourage uncontrolled conversion of forests, wetlands, rangeland, and marginal lands to arable use or might encourage invasion of private land. Any law formalizing occupation rights should be drafted so as to invalidate land claims that violate zoning laws and laws protecting forests and other nonarable land from unregulated conversion. The law should also provide a mechanism through which private owners can formally object to occupation during the statutorily prescribed period and thereby defeat the vesting of occupation rights.

6.4.1.1.2 Formal Protection of Long-Term Use Rights Where the State does not allow land ownership, long-term use rights may provide similar incentives for land conservation. Evidence from China suggests that state recognition of long-term use rights to arable land gives farmers a sense of security sufficient to motivate them to invest in land. The threat of arbitrary government confiscation of property is much more likely to reduce economic investment than is the absence of judicially enforced contract rights; confiscation makes practically all long-term investments unattractive, but lack of judicial enforcement of contract rights is likely to deter only a relatively small number of contracts between total strangers.[42] Free from the threat of confiscation or encroachment, the landowner may confidently invest in improving the land, secure in the knowledge that the investment can be recouped through increased productivity or increased receipts in the case of transfer through lease or sale.

Thus Chinese farmers who individually cultivate land in villages in which the State has not periodically redistributed land among farm families report dramatically higher confidence in the security of their land rights compared to farmers living in villages where the State has conducted redistribution.[43] Deininger and Jin found that in Chinese villages where the State had adopted a policy of not redistributing land periodically, farmers are more likely to make such investments in land as digging wells or ditches, planting orchards and trees, and otherwise improving the soil.[44] They also found that an even more important predictor of

---

[42] D. C. Clarke, *Economic Development and the Rights Hypothesis: The China Problem*, 51 Am. J. Comp. L. 89, 96–97 (2003).

[43] B. Schwarzwalder, R. L. Prosterman, J. Ye, J. Riedinger & P. Li, *An Update on China's Rural Land Tenure Reforms: Analysis and Recommendations Based on a Seventeen-Province Survey*, 16 Colum. J. Asian L. 143, 181 (2002).

[44] K. Deininger & S. Jin, *The Impact of Property Rights on Households' Investment, Risk Coping, and Policy Preferences: Evidence from China*, World Bank Policy Research Paper 2931, 14–15 (World Bank 2002).

investment is the ability to transfer the land by lease and thereby recoup the value of investments, suggesting that nontransferable rights, even if secure, will have only a modest impact on investment.

However, research from Ethiopia suggests that the threat of redistribution of land does not always undermine long-term investment, particularly where farmers conclude that investment may actually reduce the risk that their land will be chosen for redistribution. Researchers there found that the threat of State redistribution of farmland does not significantly affect investment in improvements to land, and households may even invest in improvements to prevent the State from targeting their land for redistribution.[45] Benin and Pender conclude that periodic redistribution may encourage investment by allowing new households to obtain land and use excess labor and other inputs to invest in land improvements.[46] Yet Holden and Yohannis predict that redistribution may fragment land to the point that poor households cannot afford to invest in long-term improvements.[47]

As with titling and registration, most positive environmental impacts associated with securing long-term use rights relate to onsite improvements that reduce degradation of land and may incidentally reduce the negative offsite impacts of farming.

6.4.1.1.3 Titling and Registration of Ownership   Land titling and government registration of rights to land are perhaps the best-known methods for strengthening individual possessory rights to arable land. The individual owner retains the primary interest in asserting control rights and is in the best position to detect and deter encroachments.

It is often presumed that a primary purpose of titling and registration is to protect landowners from seizure or encroachment by other citizens (including neighboring landowners in the case of boundary disputes). But in many settings, particularly those where customary law institutions are not robust, an even more important protection granted through titling and registration may be that against arbitrary confiscation by the State, which has much greater power than other individuals to displace the landowner and seize the land. Although the ultimate protection against arbitrary and uncompensated expropriation of land rights is likely to rest in the constitution or laws on land taking, the act of titling and registration makes it more difficult for officials to ignore obligations to observe correct processes and pay for taking land.

---

[45] S. Benin & J. Pender, *Impacts of Land Redistribution on Land Management and Productivity in the Ethiopian Highlands,* 12 Land Degrad. & Dev. 555, 561 (2001); S. Holden & H. Yohannis, *Land Redistribution, Tenure Insecurity, and Intensity of Production: A Study of Farm Households in Southern Ethiopia,* 78(4) Land Econs. 573, 586–87 (2002).

[46] *See* Benin & Pender, *id.* at 565.

[47] *See* Holden & Yohannis, *supra* n. 45, at 587.

A second important benefit of titling and registration is to help landowners access formal credit markets to fund long-term improvements to land. Titling and registration commoditize land by allowing financial institutions to accept it as collateral for loans, including loans used to purchase the pledged land or to invest in improvements to it. In the absence of registered title, financial institutions are not likely to be interested in bearing the risks and costs associated with repossessing the land if the borrower defaults. This benefit distinguishes titling and registration from other legal tools that strengthen land rights, such as state recognition of long-term use rights.[48]

Positive environmental impacts associated with titling and registration relate to onsite improvements like terracing and tree planting that reduce degradation of the land by, for example, reducing erosion and preserving soil quality. Many onsite improvements may incidentally reduce offsite impacts—for example, terracing installed to keep soil from washing away can reduce downstream flooding. Other off-farm impacts, such as pollution of water due to agrochemical runoff, may either be unaffected by land-conserving improvements or actually be made worse if land improvements lead to more intensive production. Thus, if they allow farmers to lengthen their planning horizon and to access credit to make land-conserving improvements while simultaneously promoting more intense farming practices, titling and registration may have mixed environmental impacts.

Finally, titling and registration may not always benefit marginalized groups, especially where, as often occurs, the impetus for titling and registration takes place at the insistence of the more powerful segments of local society.[49] Titling then may result in spontaneous individualization of common-use resources, thereby depriving the poor of access to important sources of food, fodder, and fuel.

Nor do titling and registration automatically benefit women. In most cases, titling should be in the name of both husband and wife ("joint titling") to help strengthen the claims of women who are abandoned or divorced; however, joint titling is likely to be most effective where it is more or less consistent with the values contained in local custom.[50] Before embarking on titling and registration, it is critical to examine the likely impacts on the poor, women, and other marginalized groups.

---

[48] Full commoditization of land requires not only titling and registration of rights but also (1) procedures and judicial institutions sufficient to give financial institutions confidence that they can foreclose upon the forfeited collateral; and (2) local demand to purchase land (as well as the wherewithal to purchase) strong enough to make financial institutions confident they can sell the land after foreclosure.

[49] *See* chapter 5 in this book; *see also* Admassie, *supra* n. 37, at 29.

[50] *See* chapter 3 of this book.

6.4.1.2 Redistributive Land Reform

As with titling, registration, and formalization of occupation rights, a common form of redistributive land reform emphasizes the potential of the individual to care for the land and use it productively.[51] The driving goals of redistributive land reform are to provide landless and land-poor families with access to land so that they may improve their socioeconomic well-being through marketing crops to generate income, improving the quality and quantity of food consumed by the household, and improving the status of the household in the local community. An important incidental benefit of redistribution may be improved stewardship of farmed land and reduced pressure on public lands.

6.4.1.2.1 Redistributive Land Reform and Land Conservation Classic redistributive land reform is intended to grant ownership or ownership-like interests to cultivating tenants and agricultural laborers. Significant reforms were carried out beginning in the 1940s in Japan and South Korea, the 1950s in Taiwan, and the early 1970s in South Vietnam.[52] The main impetus behind classic redistributive land reform was to extend the benefits of land ownership to landless and land-poor families, not only to enhance their physical and economic health but also to give them a stake in preserving a politically stable rural society.

While land-to-the-tiller programs are not intended to change the scale or manner of farming, there is general agreement in the literature that tenant cultivators who become owners are almost certain to be better stewards of the land. Tenants cannot hope to reap all the benefits of any long-term investment in conserving the land, and the longer the anticipated term of return (the higher the present discount rate), the less likely it is that a tenant will undertake the improvement. A tenant who improves the land too much may risk having the landlord retake the land either for personal cultivation or to lease out to another tenant at a higher rent.[53]

Anticipated positive environmental impacts of redistribution are therefore likely to be similar to, and perhaps even greater than, those associated with laws that strengthen the tenure of farmers who already claim ownership-like rights.

---

[51] Redistributive land reform may also result in cooperative farms. Such farms are notoriously inefficient and have survived only when prohibitions against private farming are strictly enforced, as in Communist China and the USSR, or where there are heavy state subsidies, nonagricultural sources of income, and extreme social enthusiasm, as in the case of the Israeli kibbutz movement.

[52] In South Vietnam the noncommunist land-to-the-tiller program was implemented during 1970–1973. Concurrently, monthly communist recruitment in the South dropped by 70–85 percent (although the land reform could not affect the divisions coming down from the North) and rice production increased by 30 percent. *See* Prosterman & Reidinger, *supra* n. 4, at 139–140.

[53] *See id.* at 37.

One potential constraint to improved land conservation after redistribution, how-ever, is the ability of new owners to finance land improvements. Even if poor owners are interested in making long-term land conserving investments, they may have few resources and limited access to credit. It is therefore important, par-ticularly in lands vulnerable to erosion or other forms of degradation, for the State to support land redistribution with programs to make credit available to new landowners for land conservation.

In the former Soviet Union, it was long observed that agricultural workers worked much more intensively on their own village house plots and small garden plots than they did on the large collectively managed fields and orchards. One estimate is that individually operated plots, which account for only 5 percent of agricultural land, produce more than half of all agricultural output,[54] indicating the social preference for and value of individual cultivation.

It is not clear whether smaller farms are more environmentally friendly than larger ones. If land is redistributed to poor families, they may not have sufficient capital to make land-conserving improvements. Moreover, if smaller parcels are more intensively cultivated than larger parcels, there may be at least some danger that the use of fertilizers and biocides per unit of farmland will increase, and with it the potential for offsite water pollution.

During the 1990s several States that emerged from the former Soviet Union began redistributive land reforms that allow, but do not require, a change in the scale of farming. Moldova is an example of one of the deeper reformations in the region. Between 1992 and 2000, the government redistributed ownership of more than 1.5 million hectares of state-owned arable land to approximately 783,000 workers and retired workers of former collective and state farms. Of that number, roughly 189,000 individuals—some 25 percent of the total—had claimed their land before the government's national redistribution program began in 1996.[55] Because more than half the new owners were already retired at the time of the land redistribution, and because most younger owners could not afford to pur-chase or hire needed farm machinery, the great majority of new owners opted to lease land to former collective farm managers or others who had access to machinery. Thus, a typical commercial farmer in Moldova may lease land from as many as 500 or 1,000 owners. The scale of Moldovan farms remains extremely large by European standards, and farms of 500 or 1,000 hectares and larger are not uncommon.

---

[54] S. Osbourne & M. Trueblood, *Agricultural Productivity and Efficiency in Russia and Ukraine: Building on a Decade of Reform,* Agricultural Economic Report No. AER813, 1 (July 2002), http://www.ers.usda.gov/publications/aer813/.

[55] S. Dobrilovic & R. Mitchell, *End of Contract Report: Project to Develop Land and Real Estate Markets in Moldova* 7 (report submitted to USAID, copy on file with RDI 2000).

It is too early to know what environmental impact these changes are having. Large commercial farmers tend to sign short-term leases, which are also favored by new owners who are loathe to enter into long-term leases at the current low rents dictated by the depressed market for agricultural products. There is a risk that those leasing large farms will have incentives to "mine" the soil under these conditions, particularly because most farmers perceive the future prospects for profitable farming in the region to be uncertain. However, a significant number of new owners, including many who claimed their land before the national redistribution process, did begin farming their plots as commercial smallholders, often supplementing their own holdings by leasing in or even purchasing plots from other new owners.

6.4.1.2.2 The Potential Effect of Redistributive Land Reform on Forest Conservation   In countries where large numbers of poor farmers are crowded onto small amounts of farmland, population pressure can cause them to migrate to frontier regions to clear forests or claim marginal lands for cultivation. As Thiesenhusen observes, this occurs even in countries where a large amount of agricultural land is not used to its full productive potential, a situation he and others attribute to the practice of amassing and holding large tracts as investments rather than productive assets.[56] Such large holdings often occupy the most fertile plains, while smallholdings are relegated to less fertile slopes. Stonich, whom Thiesenhusen quotes, reports from a case study of farms in southern Honduras:

> In general, the smallest landholdings and the highest population densities were located in the highlands, the area with the least agricultural potential. Nevertheless, farmers strove to enlarge production in these marginal areas by more intensively farming land already in cultivation . . . and by farming previously uncultivated, steeper areas.[57]

Under such conditions, if large landholdings were divided and redistributed to poor farm families, the new farms could easily absorb large amounts of labor from overcrowded small landholdings. This in turn would help to reduce the pressure on poor families to deforest lands or bring marginal lands under production. To quote Thiesenhusen:

> [W]hat happens in the settled agricultural areas of the country is probably more important in curbing resource destruction than what is done physically in the nature preserve itself. . . . In Latin America, this inquiry could

---

[56] W. C. Thiesenhusen, *Implications of the Rural Land Tenure System for the Environmental Debate: Three Scenarios*, 26(1) J. Developing Areas 1, 17 (1991).

[57] *See* Stonich, *supra* n. 32, at 284.

well lead to a renewed call for land reform. Such reform could (1) increase production and employment per unit of land and discourage migration to the frontier, with its attendant environmental damage; and (2) raise incomes for reform participants, thereby lowering both family size and ultimate pressure on scarce resources. The land reform would have to be redistributionist—land already involved in agriculture would have to be involved.[58]

6.4.1.2.3 Distribution of Small Plots Classic redistributive land reform is an attempt to provide landless and land-poor families with land sufficient to operate a commercial farm that will supply the majority of the family income. Unless there are no recognized private claimants to the land (as in the former USSR), the government must either confiscate land from private owners, purchase it for something approaching a market price, or help families to purchase it at market prices. Each proposition is likely to be costly in terms of social friction or financing. One alternative to distribution of farm-size plots is government distribution of small house-and-garden plots to landless and land-poor rural families to supplement their income and nutrition while they continue to earn their primary income as laborers or otherwise.[59]

Under this approach, a one-hectare parcel that might have benefited one family under a classic land reform program might be divided into plots measuring 250–330 square meters and distributed among thirty or forty families. Relatively small house-and-garden plots that rural families use to construct a house, plant annual and perennial food crops, and raise animals for dairy and meat products can make a significant contribution to the nutrition, income, status, and overall well-being of agricultural laborers and other poor rural households.[60] Such plots also provide special benefits to women, giving them a place close to home to garden and perform other economic activities—such as tending animals, engaging in home industries, and so on—that can provide them with an important source of independent income.[61] In Indonesia, research has shown that Javanese

---

[58] *See* Thiesenhusen, *supra* n. 56, at 17.

[59] *See generally,* R. Mitchell & T. Hanstad, *Small Homegarden Plots and Sustainable Livelihoods for the Poor,* Livelihood Support Program Working Paper (FAO March 2004), http://www.fao.org/sd/dim_pe4/pe4_040905_en.htm.

[60] R. Marsh, *Building on Traditional Gardening to Improve Household Food Security,* Food, Nutr. & Ag. No. 22, 3–4 (FAO 1998); *see generally,* A. Stoler, *Garden Use and Household Economy in Rural Java,* 14 Bull. Indonesian Econ. Studs. 85 (1978).

[61] T. Hanstad, J. Brown & R. L. Prosterman, *Larger Homestead Plots as Land Reform? International Experience and Analysis from Karnataka,* RDI Reports on Foreign Aid & Dev. No. 113, 7–8 (RDI 2001).

house-and-garden plots can produce 44 percent of total food calories and 32 percent of total protein consumed by rural households.[62]

There may be several environmental benefits to small plot distribution. First, it can reduce the need to resettle rural populations away from their home villages, thus reducing the need to convert forests and wetlands to agriculture to support creation of arable land for resettled families. This is because the government can purchase or finance the private purchase of relatively small amounts of land near the home village usually for far less than is required for resettlement programs that transport families to other parts of the country. Families are likely to be better off remaining and working in areas with established social services and markets for their labor and production rather than remote areas where such services and markets are undeveloped.

Second, to the extent families can afford to improve their house-and-garden plots, the plots are likely to have positive impacts on land conservation. In the Indian State of Karnataka, of families who received plots of land from the government measuring 200–600 square meters, the majority reported increased status within the village and increased income from sale of foods and other products produced on the plot, and approximately half reported they had acquired credit as a result of becoming a landowner.[63] In a study of Scheduled Caste and Scheduled Tribe families in West Bengal, all families who were given or otherwise acquired house-and-garden plots of between 100 and 300 square meters reported having made permanent improvements to the land, including construction of walls and wells and raising the level of the land to reduce runoff.[64]

Finally, distribution of small plots to landless and land-poor households is also likely to reduce pressure on forests and may actually enhance local plant and animal biodiversity. Diversity of plant species and the layered canopy of species are the most striking features of home gardens, with all home gardens generally consisting of "a herbaceous layer near the ground, a tree layer at upper levels, and intermediate layers in between."[65] Families that produce fuel wood and fodder on

---

[62] O. Soemarwoto, *The Javanese Homegarden as an Integrated Agro-Ecosystem,* 7 Food & Nutr. Bull. 3 (U.N. Univ. Press 1985).

[63] *See* Hanstad *et al., supra* n. 61, at 22 and 24.

[64] T. Hanstad & S. B. Lokesh, *Allocating Homestead Plots as Land Reform: Analysis From West Bengal,* RDI Reports on Foreign Aid and Development No. 115, 18–19 (RDI 2002).

[65] P. K. R. Nair, *An Introduction to Agroforestry* 91 (Kluwer Academic Pub. 1993). For example, traditional Thai home gardens are reported to contain multiple and sometimes rare varieties of each planted species and represent "in-situ reservoirs for biodiversity at all levels: genetic, species, and ecological," all of which helps to prevent pest and weed outbreaks. *See* J. Gajaseni & N. Gajaseni, *Ecological Rationalities of the Traditional Homegarden System in the Chao Phraya Basin, Thailand,* 46(1) Agroforestry Sys. 3, 19 (1999). The high density of homegarden plants also provides habitat for insects, reptiles, birds, and small mammals. *See* L. Christanty, *Home Gardens in Tropical Asia, with Special Reference to Indonesia* in *Tropical Home Gardens* 9, 19 (K. Landauer & M. Brazil, eds., U.N. Univ. Press 1990).

their own plots may opt to reduce collection of fodder and fuel wood from marginal lands. Distribution of small plots may also help to reduce incentives for land-poor families to migrate and bring under cultivation ecologically sensitive areas, such as forests and marginal lands.

6.4.1.3 Zoning to Preserve Agricultural Land

Intensified cultivation of productive agricultural land near urban areas can help to reduce the need to open new land for farming in ecologically sensitive areas. In the United States, where population density is relatively low and land abundant, forty-eight of the fifty states entrust local governments with decisions whether to use zoning to preserve agricultural land; state governments generally attempt to encourage preservation through tax incentives and other less restrictive policies.[66] Where the amount of arable land per person is relatively low, as in China, the State is very concerned to limit conversion of land to nonagricultural uses.[67] Such restrictions may help to limit the need to bring marginal lands under production.

States use a variety of tools to restrict conversion of agricultural land to non-agricultural uses in order to preserve prime agricultural land. For example, Article 21(2) of the 1991 Bulgarian Constitution provides that

> Arable land shall be used for agricultural purposes only. Any change in purposes shall be allowed only in exceptional circumstances, when necessity has been proven, and on terms and by a procedure established by law.[68]

Such prohibitions are more common in national laws than in constitutions. In Taiwan, the Agricultural Development Act (1973) requires the permission of central agricultural authorities for conversion of high-grade farmland to other uses.[69] In the Netherlands, although no law strictly forbids its conversion to other uses, farmland is preserved through binding regional land use plans developed through consultation among national, provincial, and local governments.[70] Other countries achieve the same result by requiring owners to submit to cumbersome processes to obtain permits for conversion, as in Slovenia.[71]

---

[66] R. Alterman, *The Challenge of Farmland Preservation: Lessons From a Six-Nation Comparison,* 63(2) J. Am. Plan. Assn. 220, 222 (1997).

[67] G. P. Brown, *Arable Land Loss in Rural China: Policy and Implementation in Jiangsu Province,* 35(10) Asian Surv. 922, 922 (1995).

[68] Constitution of Bulgaria, art. 21(2), http://www.online.bg/law/const/const1.htm.

[69] Agricultural Development Act of Taiwan, arts. 10 and 12 (1973, last rev. February 2003), http://eng.coa.gov.tw/law/law12a/html.

[70] *See* Alterman, *supra* n. 66, at 229–30.

[71] R. Giovarelli, *Land Use Regulation,* in *Legal Impediments to Effective Rural Land Relations in Eastern Europe and Central Asia* 81, 87 (R. Prosterman & T. Hanstad, eds., World Bank 1999).

But such restrictions may be difficult to enforce, particularly where demand for residential or industrial land is high. In developing countries, urbanization outbids all other uses for land adjacent to cities, including prime cropland.[72] Between 1987 and 1991, official Chinese reports of conversions of arable land showed that "unexplained losses"—conversions of arable land to other uses without explanation of the reason for conversion—accounted for 28 percent of the arable area converted, a demonstration of the laxity in enforcement and monitoring in much of rural China.[73]

Planners must weigh the benefits of preserving agricultural land from development against the social costs to urban dwellers who face land prices that rise much faster than family incomes.[74] Well-enforced zoning rules may prevent creation of affordable housing, causing hardship to substantial numbers of less-well-off families. Where local demand for residential land makes it very difficult for the State to enforce zoning restrictions, informal settlements may appear where public infrastructure has not been built, while planners build infrastructure in areas where demand is low. In order to avoid such outcomes, zoning plans must be based on accurate information about local demand from the field, as well as a realistic assessment of the State's ability to enforce the zoning restrictions.[75]

6.4.1.4 Policies Influencing Conversion of Forest to Agricultural Use

Most land throughout the world that is potentially available for agricultural extensification is presently tropical forest.[76] The potential environmental impacts associated with conversion of native forest are significant. Against these must be weighed the potential social benefits of giving poor families access to land they can own and cultivate.

The most obvious legal tool for encouraging conversion of forest is the State grant of ownership to those who clear forest and establish farms. States may additionally provide subsidies and tax incentives to encourage settlement and conversion of forest. However, as the experience in Brazil demonstrates, unless the State policy is carefully designed, strategies intended to benefit the long-term interests of the poor may end up serving the short-term interests of powerful groups.[77]

---

[72] E. F. Lambin *et al.*, *The Causes of Land-Use and Land-Cover Change: Moving Beyond the Myths,* 11 Global Envtl. Change 261, 265 (2001).

[73] *See* Brown, *supra* n. 67, at 929.

[74] D. E. Dowall, *Benefits of Minimal Land-Use Regulations in Developing Countries,* 12(2) Cato J. 413, 415 (1992).

[75] *See id.* at 419–420.

[76] *See* Gregory *et al.*, *supra* n. 1, at 281.

[77] S. L. Barraclough & K. B. Ghimire, *Agricultural Expansion and Tropical Deforestation: Poverty, International Trade and Land Use* 50 (Earthscan Pubs. 2000).

Brazil contains the largest area of tropical forest located in a single country. Government-supported agricultural extensification has been identified as the principal driving force behind deforestation in the Amazon during the 1980s.[78] Beginning in the 1940s and then accelerating after 1964, the Brazilian government embarked on a massive campaign to encourage families to leave the poverty-stricken northeast of the country to settle in the Amazon region and convert native forest to farms and livestock ranches. Most clearing in the Brazilian Amazon is the result of burning forests rather than cutting trees for timber, because burning is an efficient method for clearing land and because neither the government nor the ranchers will invest the time and funds necessary to cut and transport timber.[79] While the Brazilian policies did result in conversion of forests, the policies did not ultimately benefit poor farmers.

Binswanger describes six Brazilian policies that encourage deforestation, of which four are described briefly here:[80]

1. Income tax laws allow individuals to exclude from taxation up to 90 percent, and corporations up to 80 percent, of agricultural income, which increased demand for agricultural land among urban investors and corporations. Poor farmers who pay no income tax do not benefit.
2. Adverse possession rules allow an individual or corporate squatter to claim up to 3,000 hectares of federal land by using it effectively for at least a year and a day, and effective use commonly equates to clearing trees to create pastures. In some regions only one third of the claimed area must be used effectively to support the claim. Since wealthy individuals and corporations have the capital to build private roads, they are able to access far more land away from public roads than are poor settlers.
3. Brazilian land taxes, although progressive in principle, are not progressive in practice due to a number of exceptions. Claimed forested land is taxed at a higher rate than pasture, for example, encouraging conversion of forest to pasture.
4. Finally, agricultural credit policies favor those whose land is titled, giving an advantage to wealthier land claimants who can afford to navigate the process of obtaining titles. The prevailing highly subsidized interest rates for agricultural credit tend to increase the demand for agricultural land, further contributing to deforestation. Such credits also encourage mechanization, which reduces employment and tenancy opportunities.

---

[78] U. Lele, V. Viana, A. Verissimo, S. Vosti, K. Perkins & S. A. Husain, *Brazil—Forests in the Balance: Challenges of Conservation with Development* 19 (World Bank 2000).

[79] M. S. Giamo, *Comment: Deforestation in Brazil: Domestic Political Imperative— Global Ecological Disaster,* 18 Envtl. L. 537, 550 (1988).

[80] H. P. Binswanger, *Brazilian Policies that Encourage Deforestation in the Amazon,* 19(7) World Dev. 821 (1991).

Thus, Brazilian policies not only contribute to deforestation on a massive scale, they have also been described as simply reproducing Brazilian socioeconomic inequalities on the Amazonian frontier rather than attempting to resolve them as they arise.[81] Many colonization projects were in areas with soils inappropriate for farming and were otherwise poorly planned and monitored. In the end, much of the cleared land intended to support smallholder farming ended up either abandoned or in the hands of large livestock ranchers.[82] The loss of forest and lack of benefit to the poor together make the Brazilian experience particularly troubling.

6.4.2   Forests

Natural forests are critical to preserving biodiversity because they provide refuge to wild animals and plants, including rare species found only in the forest. Trees—whether natural or cropped—act as a sink for carbon and help to regulate climate at the regional and global levels. Preserving such benefits is the central focus of numerous international agreements.

Forests are important for preventing soil erosion, which can cause a variety of harms to downstream users, such as diminishing the quality and quantity of water available to farmers and urban populations, reducing the useful life of reservoirs through deposit of sediment, and increasing the risk of flooding. However, the dynamics of this protection are often misunderstood. Thus, although surface erosion rates are lowest beneath undisturbed forests, leaf litter and ground cover beneath the trees protect against erosion as much as or more than the trees themselves. Mechanical harvesting of trees causes erosion not so much because it removes the tree cover but because poorly planned roads and trails disturb forest soils and groundcover.[83] Undisturbed (natural) forests therefore tend to provide better protection against erosion than mechanically harvested forests.

As compared to food-cropping systems, properly administered tree-farming systems can be sustainable for longer periods without application of fertilizers because the deeper and denser root system and perennial ground cover make them less vulnerable to soil loss and nutrient leaching.[84] This is also true of

---

[81] B. H. Millikan, *Tropical Deforestation, Land Degradation and Society: Lessons from Rondonia, Brazil,* 19(1) Latin Am. Persps. 45, 68 (1992).

[82] *See* Barraclough & Ghimire, *supra* n. 77, at 37, 40, and 42.

[83] *See* Hamilton & Pearce, *supra* n. 25, at 37–38.

[84] K. Otsuka, *Population Pressure, Land Tenure and Natural Resource Management,* ADB Institute Working Paper No. 16, 3 (ADB Inst. 2001).

natural forest. It follows that the major threat to forest viability is excessive or poorly planned removal of trees and other forest products—as the result of either harvesting or forest clearing to make way for agricultural extensification—rather than poor management of inputs.

In considering options for managing forests to protect them, it is important to keep in mind how management regimes affect the poorest of the poor. The following sections address policies aimed at managing forests to avoid externalities like species loss and loss of carbon sequestration capacity, provide a renewable source of lumber and other forest products, and ensure that the poor do not bear an unfair proportion of the associated costs.[85]

6.4.2.1   State Management of Forest Use

Many States inherited ownership of forests from former colonial governments that had nationalized the forests. State ownership of forests serves the desire of States to earn revenue from sale of timber and other products. Many private and public actors benefit from state ownership of forests, and there is a tendency for States in many developing countries to replicate colonial forestry practices in which the State takes on the role of shielding the forest against increasing usage driven by population pressures.[86]

One method of preserving forest resources is to establish protected forests in which officials restrict and closely monitor human access and harvest of forest products. This approach can significantly reduce land clearing, logging, hunting, grazing, and fire, even at average annual costs approaching $1 per hectare.[87]

Of course, the effectiveness of its forest management depends upon the State's capacity to monitor forest product harvesting and to sanction transgressions effectively. Where forests are located in areas with established communities, forestry officials often find it difficult to protect the forest from harvesting by local communities that are aware of the State's claims and prohibitions but that nevertheless feel justified in gathering food, fodder, and fuel from the forest to meet their subsistence needs, as they have for generations, especially where risk

---

[85] The most recent forest strategy document prepared by the World Bank remarks upon the need to prioritize alleviation of the poverty confronting families who depend on forests for survival. World Bank, *Sustaining Forests: A Development Strategy* 26–28 (World Bank 2004) [hereafter, *Sustaining Forests*].

[86] J. W. Bruce & L. Fortmann, *Agroforestry: Tenure and Incentives,* LTC Paper No. 135, 16 (Land Tenure Center, U. Wisconsin–Madison 1989).

[87] A. G. Bruner, R. E. Gulison, R. E. Rice & Gustavo A. B. de Fonseca, *Effectiveness of Parks in Protecting Tropical Biodiversity,* 291 Science 125, 125 (January 5, 2001) (study of 93 protected areas in 22 countries, with annual median funding of US$1.18 per hectare).

of detection is low.[88] Wily reports, for example, on the incapacity of Tanzanian central authorities to manage large forests, with the result that some forests become like unowned property that belongs "to everyone and to no one."[89] Gururani recounts practices in a village of the Kumaon Himalaya of India:

> To avoid the guard, women time their trips to the reserved forest carefully and go to the forest only after they have made sure that the forest guard has gone past their patch of the forest. The activities of the forest guard are persistently monitored and even men and women who do not go to the forest keep track of the forest guard. Discussions about the forest guard constitute a significant part of conversation among Bankhali men and women.[90]

While Bankhali villagers regarded the forest guard for the state reserve as a government employee who had no real stake in or understanding of the forest and its products, they were much more inclined to accept the authority of the guard of the village (*panchayat*) forest. Villagers were reluctant to incur humiliation by a fellow villager or risk dismissal from *panchayat* membership.[91]

Unless the State has the capacity to enforce restrictions on forest use in settled areas, degradation of the forest will depend to a high degree on the extent to which nearby communities depend upon forest products to meet their daily needs. Individuals and groups may be more efficient in monitoring use and applying sanctions, as explored in the following sections.

Lack of state enforcement capacity has been identified as a serious threat to conservation of protected forests in Brazil.[92] Where state enforcement capacity is lacking, some have suggested, environmental objectives could be advanced by

---

[88] J. I. O. Abott & R. Mace, *Managing Protected Woodlands: Fuelwood Collection and Law Enforcement in Lake Malawi National Park,* 13(2) Cons. Biol. 418 (1999).

[89] L. A. Wily, *The Legal and the Political in Modern Property Management: Re-Making Communal Property in Sub-Saharan Africa with Special Reference to Forest Commons in Tanzania* 4 (1998), http://dlc.dlib.indiana.edu/archive/00000188/00/wily.pdf. For a comprehensive treatment of the Tanzanian case, *see* L. A. Wily, *Community-Based Land Tenure Management: Questions and Answers about Tanzania's New Village Land Act, 1999,* IIED Issue paper No. 120 (Intl. Inst. for Env. & Dev. 2003), http://www.iied.org/drylands/pubs/documents/dry_ip120eng.pdf.

[90] S. Gururani, *Regimes of Control, Strategies of Access: Politics of Forest Use in the Uttarakhand Himalaya, India* in *Agrarian Environments: Resources, Representations, and Rule in India* 170, 177–178 (A. Agrawal & K. Sivaramakrishanan, eds., Duke U. Press 2000).

[91] *See id.* at 187.

[92] C. A. Peres & J. W. Terborgh, *Amazonian Nature Reserves: An Analysis of the Defensibility Status of Existing Conservation Units and Design Criteria for the Future,* 9(1) Cons. Biol. 34, 37 (1995).

rezoning the Amazon forest to allow commercial tree harvesting in some areas while reducing the bounds of the protected area to the territory the State is prepared to protect in fact.[93]

6.4.2.2 Group Tenure and Management

Historically, forestry legislation has generally provided little scope for involving local communities in the management and allocation of forest resources,[94] but a growing trend in developing countries is to involve local communities in management of forests, particularly of depleted forests.[95] (See Box 6–3.) It is useful to distinguish between two conditions under which groups exercise rights to forests: (1) cases in which the State recognizes the group's traditional right to manage the forest, based in law or fact; and (2) cases in which the State asserts the right to manage the forest but invites groups to help it do so. We first address the former case in the context of providing groups with ownership or ownership-like tenure in forest land.

6.4.2.2.1 Grant of Ownership or Ownership-like Tenure to Groups

Groups who claim rights to trees and other forest products may be particularly efficient in guarding against unplanned harvesting of trees and forest products, especially where the group has traditionally regarded the forest as its common property resource. Natural forests may provide more benefits to local users than uniform tree stocks; replacement of natural forest with monocrop tree plantations may disrupt the many uses that local community members previously made of the forest, such as collecting plants for food and medicine, hunting forest animals, and forage for domestic animals.[96] Whereas uniform tree stocks can be managed effectively in smaller woodlots, maintaining multispecies forests usually requires keeping the forest intact.[97]

---

[93] A. Verissimo, C. A. Junior, S. Stone & C. Uhl, *Zoning of Timber Extraction in the Brazilian Amazon,* 12(1) Cons. Biol. 128 (1998).

[94] Food and Agriculture Organization, chapter titled "Forestry," in *FAO Legal Trends, supra* n. 18, at 294, citing J. W. Bruce, *Legal Bases for the Management of Forest Resources as Common Property,* FAO Community Forestry Note 14 (FAO 1999).

[95] *See* "Forestry," *supra* n. 94, at 293–96.

[96] C. O. Delang, *Deforestation in Northern Thailand: The Result of Hmong Farming Practices or Thai Development Strategies?,* 15 Soc. & Nat. Res. 483, 494 (2002).

[97] J. E. M. Arnold, *Managing Forests as Common Property,* FAO Forestry Paper 136, 42–43 (FAO 1998), citing L. N. Rasmussen & R. Meinzen-Dick, *Local Organizations for Natural Resource Management: Lessons from Theoretical and Empirical Literature,* EPTD Discussion Paper No. 11 (IFPRI 1995).

Box 6–3. Environmental Stewardship—a Relative Concept

In the absence of extreme economic pressure or economically attractive alternative uses for forested land, a group that has effective control of the forest is likely to manage the forest sustainably if its tenure is secure against encroachments from outsiders and confiscation by the State. But the concept of "sustainability" is elastic: it depends upon what exactly is being sustained. Sustainability may refer to long-term maintenance of economic returns from the resource, prevention of erosion of forest soil, preservation of the quality of products emerging from the forest, preservation of a minimum stock of trees as a carbon sink, or preservation of natural forest as habitat for wild animals and plants. The World Bank's 1991 forest-planning strategy contained three definitions for sustainability of forests:

- The continuous flow of timber products and services, some of which may be essential for sustaining the livelihood of indigenous people
- The continued existence of the current ecosystem
- The long-term viability of alternative uses that might replace the original ecosystem.[98]

Thus, the interests of the group in sustainably managing the forest as an economic resource may not coincide with the aims of the State—or the international community—in preserving the forest as an environmental resource. For example, groups managing forests in the upper watershed cannot be expected to bear the costs of management decisions that benefit only downstream users. In many cases, the State must find ways to provide incentives to groups to manage forests in ways that satisfy environmental goals of the broader society. Outsiders—such as downstream water users—may find it useful to negotiate incentives to groups to adopt management practices that help to preserve the downstream benefits of healthy forests. The alternative to providing incentives to the group for managing the forest so as to satisfy broader environmental goals is for the State to mandate conservation practices. High enforcement costs, particularly in remote areas, may make this alternative unaffordable in some countries.

Source: Adopted and summarized by the author from various authorities.

---

[98] *See* Lele, *supra* n. 78, at 57, summarizing *A World Bank Policy Paper: The Forest Sector* (World Bank 1991). *See also Sustaining Forests, supra* n. 85, at 26–28.

Even where the State might prefer to manage forests directly, group management may be a better alternative for preserving threatened forests when state administrative capacity is not adequate at the local level, or where groups who have *de facto* control of the resource actively resist state administration.

Where an indigenous group has historically managed the forest, the forest is of modest size and its area sufficiently delimited, and management is exercised by an indigenous institution, the State may simply recognize the indigenous property rights of the community.[99] Conversely, the State may be unwilling to recognize such rights where the forest is very large, its area is not clearly delimited, other groups claim rights to parts of the same forest, or there is no indigenous institution that the State can recognize.

6.4.2.2.2 Legal Bases for Group Recognition One fundamental requirement for implementing group tenure is legislation that provides a process by which the State can legally recognize the membership and management structure of the group, including indigenous groups. It is not necessary for the State to record the informal laws of the group; this may in fact be counterproductive since it may unnaturally constrain the ability of the group to modify its informal laws in response to changing circumstances. But it is necessary for the State to identify and acknowledge the membership of the group as well as the group's internal method for making decisions about management of land and natural resources. This is important so that the State and other outsiders know that individuals who purport to represent the group have the legitimate support of the group.

Tanzania provides an interesting model for granting local control rights over forests. A stated objective of the 1998 National Forest Policy is the promotion of community-owned and managed forests. This objective is greatly aided by the fact that Tanzanian villages are legally recognized and registered entities comprised of a list of households living within a delimited area.[100] A village may own land and may sue and be sued in its corporate capacity. An elected village council is authorized by law to provide social infrastructure (roads, water, education, health, and other local needs) and its governance functions become more important during periods when the national government has been unable to meet such needs.[101] Villages have therefore begun managing nearly a third of the country's 580 forest reserves as "local authority forest reserves."[102]

---

[99] *See* Bruce, *supra* n. 94, at 51.

[100] *See* Wily, *supra* n. 89, at 11.

[101] *See id.* at 15.

[102] *See id.* at 8.

The 1997 Mozambique Land Law, mentioned earlier in the context of individual land claims, also allows groups to assert claims to land. Under the law, communities may define themselves, delimit the boundaries of the resource, and negotiate with neighboring communities about shared resources. In Uganda, the Land Act, 1998, requires a group that seeks customary tenure to create a communal land association, select officers to act as the "body corporate," and apply to the State to obtain certification as a group. Article 20(3) of the Ugandan law authorizes the officers to hold title to the land on behalf of the community but disallows any transaction with the land without majority approval:

> Where land is held on a certificate of customary ownership or a freehold or leasehold title by the Managing Committee on behalf of an Association, no transactions of any kind in respect of the land or any part of the land shall be entered into or undertaken or concluded by the Managing Committee unless and until a majority convened for the purpose to approve the specific transactions which are the subject of the meeting and any transaction which is concluded which does not comply with this subsection shall be null and void and shall give rise to no rights or interest in the land.[103]

In Papua New Guinea (PNG) the Land Groups Incorporation Act 1974 provides a procedure by which customary groups can apply to the State to be recognized as an "incorporated land group" based upon the group's customary structure, and to receive authorization to manage traditional land according to customary law.[104] Once incorporated, the land group may acquire, hold, or dispose of customary land and rights in customary land.[105] Similarly, the Native Title Act 1993 (Cth) of Australia allows the Federal Court to rule on the validity of claims to traditional land made by an aboriginal group. The Aboriginal Councils and Association Act 1976 (Cth) provides a mechanism for group

---

[103] Land Act of Uganda (Act No. 16 of 1998), sec. 20(3), http://faolex.fao.org/docs/pdf/uga19682.pdf.

[104] Land Groups Incorporation Act of Papua New Guinea (1974), http://www.paclii.org/pg/legis/consol_act/ lgia1974292/. For an overview of the law, *see* J. S. Fingleton, *Legal Recognition of Indigenous Groups,* FAO Legal Papers Online (1998), http://www.fao.org/Legal/prs-ol/lpo1.pdf, 11–13 (last accessed March 30, 2005). *See also* D. Lea, *Individual Autonomy, Group Self-Determination and the Assimilation of Indigenous Cultures,* North Australia Research Unit Discussion Paper No. 18/2000 (2000); H. Holzknecht, *Policy Reform, Customary Tenure and Stakeholder Clashes in Papua New Guinea's Rainforests,* Rural Dev. Forestry Network Paper No. 19c (1996); P. Brown & A. Ploeg, *Introduction: Change and Conflict in Papua New Guinea Land and Resource Rights,* 7 Anthropological Forum 507 (1997).

[105] Land Groups Incorporation Act of Papua New Guinea, art. 13 (1974) (also providing that the incorporated group may acquire, hold, and dispose of rights to other land).

incorporation.[106] In passing on the validity of the group claim, the court may also decide that the aboriginal associations shall hold the land in trust and manage it in the interest of the group.[107]

6.4.2.2.3 Defining the Group   To be effective in preserving forest resources, group tenure must be enforced by a group institution.[108] The structure of the institution is likely to be related to the complexity of the group's management goals. Although a relatively simple organizational form is needed to simply protect the forest against encroachment by outsiders and to control use by members of the group, the structure must be more complex if the group will attempt to produce and market products collectively.[109]

The institutional structure of the group may also become more complex if the group is internally differentiated, with user subgroups having different resource claims and environmental preferences.[110] Although smaller groups may be more cohesive than larger groups comprised of subgroups, a larger group may be better able to defend the group against outsiders, including the State.[111] If a larger group is selected, enforcement is likely to be more effective if it provides incentives to subgroups that rely upon the resource, including the poor and women.

While it is possible for the State to mandate participation of women and marginalized subgroups in the group institution charged with managing the forest, it is difficult for the State to ensure that such participation indeed happens. In India, rules of the Forest Department require that one of five members of the *panchayat* (village governing body) be a woman. Gururani reports that in three *panchayats,* although a woman is listed as a member, none has ever attended a meeting or participated in any decision, while males who are not *panchayat* members

---

[106] The 1993 Act followed the historic ruling in *Mabo v. State of Queensland,* (No. 2) [1992] HCA 23; (1992) 175 CLR 1 F.C. 92/014 (3 June 1992), in which the High Court of Australia rejected the concept of "terra nullius" (according to which Australian land was said to be owned by no one before the British colonialists arrived) and ruled that the Aboriginal natives continue to own all land to which they have maintained a traditional relationship since the time of British sovereignty, provided that the Crown has not granted the land to settlers in ownership and has not otherwise used it in ways inconsistent with the ownership of Aboriginals. The 1993 Act was amended in 1998 after the High Court decision in *Wik Peoples v. State of Queensland and Ors,* [1996] HCA 40 (23 Dec. 1996), in which the court held that pastoral leases may coexist with native title where lease rights are not fundamentally inconsistent with Aboriginal claims. I am grateful to Shéhan de Sayrah for clarifying my understanding of these statutes and case holdings.

[107] *See* Fingleton, *supra* n. 103, at 28.

[108] *See* Bruce & Fortmann, *supra* n. 86, at 13.

[109] *See* Bruce, *supra* n. 94, at 51.

[110] *See* Leach, *supra* n. 5, at 230.

[111] *See* Arnold, *supra* n. 97, at 43.

frequently attend and participate in deliberations.[112] Village women say village custom forbids them from even speaking to male members of the *panchayat*. Even where outside agents are present to insist that marginalized groups participate in decision making, mere participation does not result in empowerment, which must be sought outside the process.[113]

6.4.2.2.4 Delimiting Group Territory Where the State has not previously adjudicated boundaries of territories claimed by groups, disputes among groups that claim the same territory may be brought to a head through the group titling process. Claims are likely to overlap, for example, where groups that inhabit the forest tend to use different parts of the forest during different years, or a group claims areas that it does not use often but that have ritual or other important significance to the group's identity.

Uganda's Land Act, 1998, provides that after the Land Board issues the customary certificate to the communal land association, the Land Committee must demarcate the boundaries of the certified land, taking note of any prior or coexistent rights to the land, such as easements, leases, use rights, or other encumbrances.[114] The committee not only demarcates the boundaries, it is also responsible for applying customary law to adjudicate any disputes that arise out of the application for certification. Early on the Ugandan government initiated a targeted "sensitization program" to make landholders aware that they hold secure rights even though government offices had not yet been created to provide land certificates.[115]

Outsiders, including communities living near the forest, may also feel they have a vested interest in protecting their past uses of the forest, even if such uses might be reasonably characterized as encroachments under the law. It is not uncommon to find competition between "indigenous" groups that claim ancient association with a place and local communities who claim longstanding, though not ancient, attachment to the same place.[116] Unreasonably high transaction costs for negotiating the claims of various users may ultimately require authorities to legitimize the claims of core users and deny other claims.[117] The process of resolving competing claims is intensely political and may take years.

---

[112] *See* Gururani, *supra* n. 90, at 182.

[113] *See* Admassie, *supra* n. 37, at 47.

[114] Land Act of Uganda, arts. 7 and 8 (1998), http://www.fao.org/Legal/pub-e.htm.

[115] Government of Uganda, *Report of the Land Act Implementation Study* (1999).

[116] H. Rangan & M. B. Lane, *Indigenous Peoples and Forest Management: Comparative Analysis of Institutional Approaches in Australia and India,* 14 Soc. & Nat. Res. 145, 149 (2001), citing B. Kingsbury, *"Indigenous Peoples" in International Law: A Constructivist Approach to the Asian Controversy,* 92(3) Am. J. Intl. L. 414, 425 (1998).

[117] *See* Bruce, *supra* n. 94, at 53.

6.4.2.3 Cooperative Agreements for Group Management of Forests

Where the State is unwilling to grant a group ownership or ownership-like rights to forest land, it may decide to grant usufruct rights to a group in exchange for the group's managing the forest. Banana and Gombya-Ssembajjwe recount the example of a state forest in Uganda where state administrators gave a Pygmy tribe that lived within the forest special permission to harvest forest products and residents of nearby local communities much more restricted permission to harvest.[118] The resident tribe very efficiently monitored the harvesting activities of neighboring communities, effectively eliminating the overuse that plagued other forests in the district. The tribe was motivated to preserve the resource for its own use, and because the tribe lived apart from and had little interaction with outsiders, its members had little fear of reprisals.

More complex and organized versions of this concept have been applied in India under joint forest management programs. The first such arrangement arose spontaneously from the efforts of forest-dwelling communities to protect their access to what they traditionally regarded as communal resources.[119] In the early 1980s the government of West Bengal began working with local communities to share management of state forests, and the national government embraced joint forest management beginning in 1990. The programs are consistent with a general shift in Indian forest management policy from revenue generation to greater emphasis on conservation and local community requirements for forest products.[120] Although the reports vary considerably, it has been estimated that more than 36,000 community groups in 22 states currently manage as much as 10.2 million hectares of state forest lands—roughly 17 percent of total forest cover in India.[121] According to program principles, a local community is granted the right to manage

---

[118] A. Y. Banana & W. Gombya-Ssembajjwe, *Successful Forest Management: The Importance of Security of Tenure and Rule Enforcement in Ugandan Forests,* in *People and Forests: Communities, Institutions and Governance* 89, 95 (C. C. Gibson, M. A. McKean & E. Ostrom, eds., MIT Press 2000).

[119] S. R. Harrison, A. S. Ghose & J. L. Herbohn, *Lessons from Social and Community Forestry in the Tropics, with Particular Reference to India and the Philippines,* in *Sustainable Farm Forestry in the Tropics* 227, 230 (S. R. Harrison & J. L. Herbohn, eds., Ed. Elgar Pub. 2001).

[120] S. Saigal, *Beyond Experimentation: Emerging Issues in the Institutionalization of Joint Forest Management in India,* 26(3) Envtl. Mgt. 269, 270 (2000).

[121] N. N. C. Saxena, *Research Issues in Forestry in India,* 55(3) Indian J. Agric. Econs. 359, 366 (2000). *See also Sustaining Forests, supra* n. 85, at 27 (noting need to incorporate into collaborative forest management programs "safeguard measures aimed at minimizing the risk of more powerful members of the community or outside commercial interests appropriating non-timber forest products on which the poorest depend").

state forest lands in exchange for the grant of usufruct rights to specified forest products. The program has met with varied success in different villages.

Similar agreements have been used in the Philippines since 1995 under a program to provide renewable leases to community groups that agree to manage state forest reserve land.[122] Pursuant to the Community-Based Forest Management Agreement, the State provides a community group with the exclusive right to possess, cultivate, and enjoy the products of the land for twenty-five years (renewable for another twenty-five years). Because upland communities typically do not have sufficient capital to begin the forest enterprise, the State often advances some operating costs and may maintain a minority share in the timber rights.[123] The process of concluding the agreement and incorporating the community group has been criticized as overly complicated.[124] It has also been criticized as reinforcing state jurisdiction over forest areas long used by local communities and promoting timber production by restricting farming and other activities practiced by such communities.[125]

There is no guarantee that a group management agreement will improve the relative position of marginalized subgroups who depend upon the forest, and it is likely that an agreement will regularize existing arrangements that may be inequitable.[126] In India, subgroups that are most dependent on forest products—women, members of lower castes, and the landless—are often missing entirely from the local institution that implements the joint forest management agreement, and the poor often incur the brunt of any decision to "close" part of the forest to collection of wood products or grazing to allow regrowth of the forest.[127] Summarizing a number of recent studies of joint forest management in India, Saxena concludes in part that:

> Poverty alleviation, tribal welfare and women's empowerment have neither been stressed nor monitored in government programmes, hence not achieved. Benefits to the poor beyond wages are limited.[128]

---

[122] *See* Bruce, *supra* n. 94, at 40.

[123] *See* Harrison *et al., supra* n. 118, at 234.

[124] *See* Bruce, *supra* n. 94, at 40, citing O. J. Lynch & K. Talbott, *Balancing Acts: Community-Based Forest Management and National Law in Asia and the Pacific* (World Resources Inst. 1995).

[125] J. M. Pulhin, Presentation, *Community Forestry in the Philippines: Paradoxes and Perspectives in Development Practice* (Eighth Biennial Conf., Intl. Assoc. Study of Common Prop., Bloomington, Indiana, May 31–June 4, 2000), http://dlc.dlibindiana. edu/documents/dir0/00/00/05/75/dlc-00000575-00/pulhinj061300.pdf.

[126] *See* Arnold, *supra* n. 97, at 45–46.

[127] *See* Saigal, *supra* n. 119, at 271–72.

[128] *See* Saxena, *supra* n. 120, at 369.

Time-limited group management agreements represent a middle ground between a grant of perpetual group tenure and state management of forest land. They are unlikely to be effective unless the forest and the community are in close proximity, the community is highly dependent upon the forest and perceives the resource to be scarce, and the community has an effective structure for managing resources.[129] The signatory village must have the capacity and motivation to monitor the forest and prevent overuse by its own members as well as use by residents of other villages.

In addition to fashioning agreements that effectively preserve forest resources, it is critical to design them so as to ensure that they do not worsen the position of poorer segments of the community. Saigal offers several suggestions for this, including the following: (1) ensure that all community subgroups are represented on the local management committee; (2) require the forest management plan expressly to recognize and protect the interests of the poorest and most forest-dependent segments of the community; and (3) introduce training and orientation programs to sensitize state forest department staff to these equity issues.[130]

A further approach, one the Bolivian National Park Service has implemented in a number of protected forests, is for the State to invite representatives of local communities to participate with park officials on management committees tasked with defining policies for development of the area, planning activities, overseeing plan implementation, and creating a forum for resolving disputes. The Bolivian committees are consultative bodies; state officials retain ultimate authority to make decisions.[131] Researchers report that where management committees actually meet regularly, they have tended to help central planners understand the local social and economic environment, have led to greater local acceptance of the protected area, and have contributed to formation of relationships between the community and park service officials.[132]

6.4.2.4   Industrial Timber Harvesting

Even where a State recognizes that one or more customary groups own a section of naturally forested land, the law may not give them full control over timber resources. Hunt provides an interesting account of forest management practices in

---

[129] *See* Arnold, *supra* n. 97, at 29, citing M. Sarin, *From Conflict to Collaboration: Local Institutions in Joint Forest Management*, Joint Forest Mgmt. Wkg. Paper No. 14 (SPWD 1993).

[130] *See* Saigal, *supra* n. 119, at 277.

[131] D. Mason, M. Baudoin, H. Kammerbauer, L. Maria Calvo, Z. Lehm & F. Heinrich, *Integrating Local People and Institutions into Protected Area Management: Lessons Learned from Bolivia* 4, http://www.earthlore.ca/clients/WPC/English/grfx/sessions/PDFs/session_3/Mason.pdf.

[132] *See id.* at 5–7.

Papua New Guinea, where the Forestry Act 1991 and the Forestry (Amendment) Act 1993 authorize the Forestry Authority to acquire timber rights from customary owners through forest management agreements.[133]

PNG law does not authorize customary landowners to decide whether the forest will be logged or who will log it—those decisions are taken by the Forestry Authority, which allocates timber rights to private logging concessionaires. Concessionaires pay a log export tax to the central government, which shares a portion of the revenues with the customary landowners, sometimes in the form of local development initiatives that are subject to mismanagement. Though the system provides substantial revenues to concessionaires and the government, landowners receive at most only about 12 percent of the market value of exported logs—a highly inequitable distribution.[134]

PNG Forest Management Agreements are intended to achieve a "sustained yield" so that the resource will continue to produce throughout the term of the agreement. Thus, if the forest is believed to regenerate on a forty-year cycle, the agreements provide that the concessionaire can harvest and replant one-fortieth of the concession area annually. In this way, the first harvested area will be ready to harvest again at the end of the forty-year cycle. Hunt identifies a number of factors that undermine realization of this model in practice: (1) The government does not accurately estimate timber volumes in concession areas. (2) The government lacks capacity to enforce either harvesting limits or guidelines requiring sound harvesting methods. (3) Landowners whose lands are scheduled to be harvested near the end of the agreement are unwilling to wait forty years before receiving compensation. (4) There are no adequate controls to ensure that deforested areas will be replanted rather than converted by landowners to other uses as opportunities arise. (5) There is a high risk that the forest will not regenerate by the end of the planned cycle. If the concessionaire is not confident that it will

---

[133] Hunt's assessment is sobering:

Under current conditions it is difficult to see how industrial harvesting of timber will ever get on to a sustainable footing in Papua New Guinea. This is true even if 'sustainable' is defined in the narrow sense of managing forests such that profitable yields of timber can be harvested in perpetuity. If we add other dimensions of sustainability, such as the conservation of biological diversity and other forest goods and services, or the development of vibrant and equitable rural economies, then the goal of sustainable forest management in PNG seems even more remote.

C. Hunt, *Executive Summary* [hereafter, *PNG Forestry Summary*] in *Production, Privatisation and Preservation in Papua New Guinea Forestry* iii (C. Hunt, ed., Intl. Inst. Env. & Dev. 2002) [hereafter, *PNG Forestry*].

[134] *See id.* at iv.

have access to the same forest at the end of the regeneration cycle, it is likely to reharvest the regenerating stand prematurely.[135]

Hunt recommends that the State cede much greater control to customary landowners to determine whether to allow timber to be harvested on their land or to make some alternative use of the land, such as selling conservation easements to those willing to finance forest preservation.[136] Although this would not increase the attractiveness of forest preservation unless the financial rewards were competitive with other uses, it would at least make preservation an option. Such proposals are likely to be resisted by PNG government bureaucrats, whose incomes and authority are linked to maintaining a large log export industry. If landowners choose to allow timber harvesting, Oliver recommends that the law allow landowners to contract directly with concessionaires, as is currently done in PNG for oil palm plantations on customary land.[137] This proposal may be less objectionable to the bureaucrats who benefit from timber exports.

Such changes in the law would primarily address imbalances in benefit distribution in the current system but would probably do little to address the environmental consequences of harvesting. Hunt therefore recommends that, in addition to the current export tax based on the value of the exported logs, the State impose a fixed tax denominated in local currency to help offset the adverse environmental impacts of logging, which are conservatively estimated to be kina 50 per cubic meter of wood (approximately US$14 at 2001 exchange rates). Because the fixed tax would not be affected by changes in log export prices or exchange rates, it would be more stable than taxes based on the dollar-denominated market value of exported logs.[138]

6.4.2.5   *Individual Ownership or Control of Trees*

6.4.2.5.1 Individual Ownership or Control of Forest   Where forest use or environmental goals do not depend upon maintaining a wide diversity of plant species, and where the forest does not provide important benefits to local poor, it may be appropriate under certain conditions to manage the forests as individual woodlots. This approach may be particularly appropriate in efforts to reforest wasteland.

---

[135] C. Hunt, *Industrial Harvesting: Problems and Proposals,* in *PNG Forestry, supra* n. 133, at 32–34.

[136] *See PNG Forestry Summary, supra* n. 133, at vii.

[137] N. Oliver, *Lease, Lease-Back—An Instrument for Forestry?* in *PNG Forestry, supra* n. 133, at 59 and 60–62.

[138] *See* Hunt, *supra* n. 135, at 51 (calculation based on 2001 currency exchange rate, kina = US$0.28).

China provides an interesting example of different approaches to local management of forests. "Nonstate" forests account for an estimated 60 percent of forest area nationally in China, and in southern provinces the proportion is as high as 90 percent.[139] In the 1980s China introduced the "Two Mountain" policy, pursuant to which the State allocated "Freehold Mountain" land to use of individual households and forested "Responsibility Mountain" land to use of local collectives.[140] Through the Freehold Mountain policy, the State granted use rights free of charge to households that agreed to plant trees on wasteland and degraded land. Holders of Freehold Mountain land do not become its owners but instead enjoy the right to plant trees and harvest any trees planted. Between 1981 and 1984, when such allocations ended, the State granted more than 31 million hectares of land to households under the Freehold Mountain policy.[141]

Through the Responsibility Mountain policy, the State granted use rights to collectives that agreed to manage existing forests. The collectives have the right to plant and harvest trees on Responsibility Mountain land and use various methods to manage planting and harvesting. Although some collectives choose to manage the forest directly, the most common practice is for the collective to contract with households to manage sections of the forest.[142]

China's Forestry Law, which was substantially amended in 1998, provides in Article 26 that a State or collective that owns barren hills or wasteland may sign afforestation contracts with individuals and collectives to replant such areas.[143] Article 27 provides that, unless the contract specifies otherwise, the planter owns the tree:

> If the collective or private individual contracts for state-owned or collectively owned waste mountains and land suitable for tree planting, the trees planted after the contract shall be owned by the contracting collective or private individual; if the contract has other provisions, those contractual provisions shall be followed.[144]

---

[139] D. Liu, *Tenure and Management of Non-State Forests in China Since 1950: A Historical Review*, 6(2) Envtl. Hist. 239, 240 (2001).

[140] B. Schwarzwalder, P. Li, B. Zheng, Y. Su & L. Zhang, *Tenure and Management Arrangements for China's Forestland and Grassland Resources: Fieldwork Findings and Legal and Policy Recommendations* 3 (unpublished ms. 2001) (copy on file with RDI).

[141] *See* Liu, *supra* n. 139, at 247 (470 million mu [1 mu = 1/15 hectare] distributed), citing Ministry of Forestry, *China Forestry Year, 1949–1986* 479 (China Forestry Pub. 1987).

[142] *See* Liu, *id.* at 249.

[143] Forestry Law of the People's Republic of China (1984, last revised April 1998), art. 26, http://www.novexcn.com/forestry_1998.html.

[144] *See id.* art. 27.

Article 7 explicitly protects the rights of individuals and collectives to resist interference in their management of forests under contract:

> The State protects the legitimate rights and interests of collectives and private individuals who have contracted for forestation; no organization and private individual shall encroach upon the ownership of trees and other legitimate rights and interests entitled according to the law to the collectives and private individuals who have contracted for forestation.[145]

Such contracts, which range in length from 30 to 100 years, reportedly give households sufficient security to encourage them to invest in tree planting.[146] To reduce the cost of managing fragmented plots scattered on more than one hill, households in some areas have pooled their forest use rights to share both management and proceeds, with costs and returns based on the proportionate contribution of each household.[147]

6.4.2.5.2 Tree Planting on Arable Land

Farmers may plant trees on existing arable land for several reasons: to diversify crops (including by timber production), to protect against soil loss from wind or water, and to strengthen tenure claims to the land. Farmers may also plant trees on unused lands (including degraded lands and wastelands) to produce food crops and timber, often under the auspices of a government program of land reclamation. With proper planning, such programs can make land more productive and create environmental benefits. In China, reforestation has been used to reduce surface waterlogging, making land beneath the trees available for interplanting annual crops.[148]

The species of tree and the product to be produced will determine how long the farmer must wait before harvesting the products of a tree (apples, for example) or cutting it for timber. Where the farmer plants the tree, on land to which the farmer has secure tenure, the waiting period represents one of the farmer's opportunity costs because the area planted with trees cannot produce other crops during this period. The farmer bears other costs, including the cost of the seedling and the time invested in planting and caring for the tree, all of which might otherwise be spent on cultivating crops or earning wages from off-farm employment. Tree planting, therefore, much more resembles a permanent improvement like digging a well than it resembles planting of annual crops.[149]

---

[145] *See id.* art. 7.

[146] *See* Liu, *supra* n. 139, at 250.

[147] *See id.* at 252–53.

[148] *See* Hamilton & Pearce, *supra* n. 25, at 47.

[149] *See* Bruce & Fortmann, *supra* n. 86, at 3.

Farmers who plant trees on unused lands and wastelands bear similar costs, except that the waiting period does not represent an opportunity cost because they are not using owned land. However, if the planted area is not close to the farmer's residence, as is likely in the case of wastelands, the farmer must presumably incur additional costs in terms of time spent traveling to the site and guarding the trees (or the cost of hiring others to do so).

We would expect to find that property rights to the land and the trees are likely to affect a farmer's propensity to plant trees. If state law or local custom denies farmers the right to cut and sell the wood of trees, the trees are much less valuable to the farmer. Yin and Newman studied the effects of different government policies pursued in northern and southern provinces of China during the period 1978–1988.[150] They found that farmers in northern provinces had increased tree planting dramatically in response to stable government policies that respected individual tenure over planted trees, did not require harvesting permits, and applied low taxes; farmers in southern provinces were unwilling to plant trees in the face of fluctuating government policies on the security of individual tenure over trees, requirements for harvesting permits, and requirements that farmers sell timber to state companies at half the market price. Even a small possibility of losing the land makes investment in long-lived assets unattractive compared with less sustainable activities that yield more immediate gains.[151] Other studies have found that farmers are more likely to plant trees on land they own while planting annual crops on land they lease.[152] While the propensity to plant trees of any kind is likely to be affected by the stability of long-term tenure rights, this may be especially true with regard to trees that are planted primarily for their value as timber.

The situation is more complicated where law or custom gives the tree planter a claim to the land on which the tree is planted. Where trees are used to strengthen land tenure claims, farmers may be willing to bear relatively high costs in order to acquire the tenure-strengthening benefits of tree planting. However, others who claim tenure rights to the same land may seek to prevent the farmer from planting trees on the contested land.[153]

By giving farmers full rights to cut trees planted on government-owned wastelands, the government would encourage efforts to make the land productive, which would presumably reduce the pressure to harvest natural forests. On the

---

[150] R. Yin & D. H. Newman, *Impacts of Rural Reform: The Case of the Chinese Forest Sector,* 2 Envt. & Dev. Econs. 291, 294–95 (1997).

[151] R. Mendelsohn, *Property Rights and Tropical Deforestation,* 46 Oxf. Econ. Papers, New Series 750, 753 (1994).

[152] *See* Bruce & Fortmann, *supra* n. 86, at 3.

[153] *See id.* at 6.

other hand, in some settings land that the government regards as "wasteland" may supply important resources to the poor, who may gather fodder, fuel, and food from it.[154] Reforestation of such land may therefore deprive marginalized families of access to critical resources. Laws that allow farmers to plant trees on unused lands and wastelands should include a requirement that before authorizing tree planting on such lands, the State first assess the extent to which families currently rely upon the land to supply fodder and other household goods.

Moreover, to enhance the environmental benefits of tree-planting on unused lands and wastelands in areas that are at risk of soil erosion, the law should specify tree-farming procedures that will protect the land against erosion. In particular, in any area where land slope exposes the soil to risk of erosion, lawmakers should consider requiring land users to plant groundcover. Lawmakers should also prescribe the method of harvest to ensure that construction of roads and trails does not disturb groundcover. Although a discussion of forest-harvesting techniques is beyond the scope of this chapter, where there is not enough administrative capacity to closely regulate harvesting, policymakers mighty consider forbidding clear cutting and requiring farmers to harvest mature trees from one site over several years.

Different considerations arise for tree tenure and land tenure policy near natural forests. A law that allows farmers to cut trees they plant and to claim land beneath such trees may actually encourage farmers to cut trees in natural forest and replace the natural forest with tree crops. Evidence from Sumatra and Ghana indicates that where access to natural forest is unrestricted and the law grants strong individual rights on cleared land, clearing of forests will be excessive.[155] It is important that laws and policies designed to encourage tree planting not increase pressure for removal of natural forest.

6.5   Conclusion

Increased farming on existing farmland or land newly opened to farming may give rise to a number of negative environmental impacts, most of which relate to soil erosion and changes in the quality and quantity of water within watersheds but which may also involve loss of biodiversity. Deforestation—whether caused by opening of new farmland and rangeland or by increased demand for timber—may cause numerous negative impacts, including loss of wild animal and plant species and reduction of global capacity to sequester greenhouse gases.

---

[154] T. Beck & M. G. Ghosh, *Common Property Resources and the Poor: Findings from West Bengal,* Econ. & Political Wkly. 147, 147–148 (January 15, 2000).

[155] *See* Otsuka, *supra* n. 84, at 4, citing T. L. Anderson & P. J. Hill, *The Race for Property Rights,* 16 J. Econ. Hist. 16 (1973).

Land and resource management policies implemented through laws and regulations can play an important role in preserving and facilitating sustainable use of forests, arable lands, and rangelands. Of equal importance, they can influence the extent to which the poor and marginalized groups share in the benefits of land use. This is especially true in developing countries, where most families earn their living from agriculture and where a sizable proportion of families are economically vulnerable.

The likelihood that a legal rule will be implemented and enforced should be a threshold consideration in the design and adoption of laws intended to conserve land and other natural resources. Laws and other legal tools may be enforced through a variety of means and actors. In evaluating the appropriateness of legal tools regulating land and resource use, policymakers should consider the scale of resource exploitation, whether the resource is exploited by individuals or groups (and the size of the group), and whether exploitation of the resource by one group poses costs on other groups or the larger society. State political and administrative capacity to implement desired policies is likely to influence greatly the options that are available to the State for managing resource use.

Legal tools that substantially rely upon individual assertion of control rights are more likely to be effective in promoting resource use in which individual management of inputs plays an important role, such as sedentary farming. Tools that may usefully encourage land conservation include those that strengthen land tenure, such as rules that provide secure rights to land users based upon long-term occupation of land or that provide for certification and registration of land rights. Certification and registration, though much more expensive, provide a basis for making formal credit available to landowners.

Redistribution of existing farmland to landless and land-poor farm families holds some promise not only for enhancing the welfare of poor households and allowing them to become more productive but also for reducing pressures that cause poor families to deforest lands and bring marginal lands under production. Distribution of small plots (up to 300 square meters) to village households *in situ* may be an especially affordable alternative where population pressure is high and the government can afford to purchase or finance the private purchase of only small amounts of land for redistribution. Individual tenure, including long-term use rights to state wastelands, may also give households enough security to encourage tree planting.

Legal tools that rely upon group assertion of control rights are more likely to be useful in promoting protection of common resources, such as forests, that are important to a number of users and for which preventing overuse is more important than management of inputs. Even where the State might prefer to manage forests directly, group management of forests may be an attractive alternative where state administrative capacity is inadequate at the local level or where groups that have *de facto* control of the resource actively resist its administration by the State.

One fundamental requirement for implementing group tenure is adoption of legislation that provides a process by which the State can legally recognize the membership and management structure of groups, including indigenous groups. Care must be taken to ensure that group management of common resources, whether through recognition of group tenure or through management contracts similar to the joint forest management agreements used in India, does not undermine access to the resources by subgroups that are most dependent on forest products, which often include women, members of lower castes, and the landless.

It is also important to keep in mind that the interests of the group in sustainably managing the forest as an economic resource may not coincide with the aims of the State, or the international community, in preserving the forest as an environmental resource. Legal tools that rely upon individual or group assertion of control rights are less likely to be effective in discouraging negative externalities associated with resource use, such as loss of species, siltation of reservoirs, or pollution affecting downstream users. Legal tools that rely primarily on proactive state reservation of control rights or restriction of private control rights may therefore be necessary with respect to environmental and other factors that affect the interests of the broader society.

CHAPTER 7

Conclusion

John W. Bruce

As the development community moves further into the new millennium, land law reform must find ways to contribute to the reduction of severe poverty, the advancement of gender equity, and the creation of conditions for sustainable resource use. Drawing upon the many specific needs discussed in the previous chapters, let us look at the key challenges for land law reform in the developing world.

First, proposed changes in land law must be evaluated specifically in terms of their impact on poverty. Property systems have welfare as well as efficiency underpinnings, and recognition of the welfare side calls for a clearer focus on the short-term impacts of land law reforms on the poor. As several chapters urge, land law reforms must be informed by poverty-reduction strategies. Often, programs designed to support growth are simply relabeled as poverty-reducing. The relabeling is true in one sense: The larger "pie" produced by economic growth is in the long run critical to poverty reduction. But the poor need to survive and better their lot in the short and intermediate run. Reforms whose designers have their eyes fixed too exclusively on the far horizon of development can easily neglect the immediate needs and vulnerability of the poor. Growth and poverty reduction are compatible objectives, but the demands of poverty reduction need to be on the table when land law reforms are discussed. Then the necessary balance can be struck, in full awareness of what the landless and the land-poor will gain and lose.

Second, the gendered impacts of reforms in the law relating to land deserve far more attention than they have received. Women and their children are among the most vulnerable members of society. The rules relating to inheritance of land and distribution of marital property in land upon divorce directly affect whether or not, in critical life transitions such as widowhood and divorce, women and their children fall into desperate poverty. Women's land rights are not a minority issue; they affect the well-being of half the population of the developing world. Often the difficulties of cultural change are cited as obstacles to reform, and these are very real. But even when governments today are granting new property rights, for instance in countries in transition, or are otherwise writing on a relatively clean slate, for instance in resettlement schemes, they often fail their women citizens badly. Where whole new national property systems are created, as in the formerly communist nations, men too often end up owning nearly all the land. Failure in creating gender equity is often rooted in the assumption that laws that are gender-neutral on their face are sufficient. In societies where strong patriarchal values continue to dominate, they are not. Proactive legal reforms are needed. Those reforms need to be culture-sensitive, but solutions must be found.

Third, there is a need to examine more critically and systematically the legal mechanisms used for redistributive land reform and the legal consequences of land reform. The World Bank has affirmed land reform as a potentially critical tool in the struggle against poverty. The movement of productive assets to the poor allows them to provide for their future. Yet little has been written about the legal dimensions of land reform in recent years. There are new models of land reform that call for attention because they rely on quite different legal mechanisms than the older models. For example, land reform that relies on use of market mechanisms to acquire land for redistribution depend on the law affecting land transactions, while older compulsory acquisition models relied on the law of eminent domain or some special variant of it.

There is also a need to reaffirm land reform as a process that can take place within the law. Often, land reform has been an extralegal event. Beneficiaries have been left in an ambiguous legal position, with old rights not extinguished by law and new rights not affirmed in law. Society is then left with the painful task of reestablishing respect for property rights in the wake of the reform. Because of the importance of land reform to the poor, these issues need to be examined more systematically and ways found to better protect their interests.

Fourth, an adequate poverty-reduction approach to law reform requires reexamination of the divergence between the legal frameworks for agricultural land and for natural resources. The poor usually rely on both sets of resources, but disproportionately on the grazing and forest commons. Yet often government agencies, such as forestry departments, that manage production-cum-protection regimes for natural resources that are critical to the poor fail to recognize community-based rights in such resources or, where the resource is state-owned, to give community users clear rights. Land laws must provide a solid legal framework for property rights in common lands and legal personality for the communities that use them. Internationally funded land administration projects commonly fail to register such rights, focusing too exclusively on rights in agricultural and residential land—often because a clear legal framework for recognizing community property rights does not exist in national law. Such projects need to feature this issue in their legal reform agendas; failure to deal with it results in the anomaly of village temples, football fields, and pastures being registered as state land.

Fifth, there is a need to examine the often flawed interfaces between the law governing farmland and the law governing protected areas. The poor are often disadvantaged by the inappropriate classification of land under protection regimes. For instance, large areas of land long used for farming may be gazetted as forest land, the result of land-grabbing by forestry agencies that is unrelated to past use or the future potential of the land for forestry. This can mean that users of that land have no way to secure tenure. There is a need to bring land in the different use categories under a single land policy and land law umbrella so that classifications can be more rationally defined and perverse outcomes avoided.

Sixth, the law reform needs of landholders under customary tenure need renewed attention. The assertion of state ownership of land in much of Africa, for example, which is an artifact of the colonial era or a reflection of socialist aspirations, has often placed in legal limbo culturally grounded customary systems of private property—even though those systems, *de facto,* govern most land use in Africa. Today, much land law reform is concerned with formalization of "informal" land rights, and this formulation is itself risky. Customary systems are not "informal"; rather, they represent an alternative formality, reflecting substate social systems of political importance. Their legal recognition by the State will often be the first step toward the creation of solid property rights systems in land; it will set the stage for reform of those systems to increase transparency, accountability, and gender equity.

Seventh, the law on compulsory acquisition of land by the State (the power of eminent domain) requires new attention. While it is not often recognized, the poor suffer disproportionately when governments appropriate land without compensation for dubious public purposes. Their land is targeted because they are weak and lack influence and clear property rights. The law on compulsory acquisition has to some extent been a blind spot in land law reform. Legal reforms can provide landholders with long-term, robust property rights but leave in place a law on public acquisition of land that provides excessively broad grounds for taking land with inadequate compensation. There is a reluctance to acknowledge that in many countries the State itself—pursuing not just public purposes but the private purposes of the influential—is the primary threat to land tenure security. Reforms should narrow the grounds for takings to specified public purposes and should provide fair compensation that is related to market value. The eminent domain power is a necessary component of any system of private property but it must be carefully drawn.

In meeting these needs, our efforts at law reform should be informed by a more adequate model of land law and its role in providing a legal basis for security of tenure. This is not a matter that concerns only the poor, but their needs will be better addressed if we work with an adequate model. In the past, it was sometimes assumed that land registration itself provided security of tenure. In fact, land registration is simply a superior method of proof of rights. Similarly, robust property rights alone will not suffice. Security of tenure—the secure expectation of continued enjoyment of the right—requires long-term, relatively complete property rights; an effective way to prove rights (for example, land registration); reliable rights enforcement mechanisms (courts or mediation institutions); restrained use of the eminent domain power; and a rule-of-law environment. No single initiative will deal with all of these, but it is important not to lose sight of the full array of needs for establishing security of tenure. The task of meeting them all for the poor, especially the rural poor, is challenging.

Still, there are real opportunities for the World Bank, among others, to more adequately address these issues as it moves into more development policy lending and away from investment projects. In policy lending, the potential for more holistic approaches to land law reform and delivery of property rights is greater. Whereas a generation of land administration projects focused heavily on the legal framework for land registration itself, PRSPs and PRSCs can address the need for security of tenure more holistically. Given the more liberal time frame of the policy lending context, there should also be more scope for a solid law reform process: research-based policy-making and public consultation on law reforms, which will provide an opportunity for better understanding of the law reform needs of the poor. This will be important for serious inquiry into the potential impact of proposed reforms on the poor and other disadvantaged groups. If investment projects tend to define legal reform needs too strictly in terms of project purposes, policy lending poses the opposite danger: use of generic legal reform targets grounded in theory rather than the situation and needs of the poor in the client country.

In the end, the real challenge for all of us, whether in international institutions, governments, or civil society organizations, is to focus relentlessly upon how legal reforms impact the poor, the disadvantaged, and the environment. The challenge is to refuse to be satisfied with easy assumptions and optimistic scenarios and instead to demand and provide clear and convincing evidence and analysis for pro-poor impacts before land law reforms are enacted.

Selected Bibliography

Abdildina, Zhanar & Jaime Jaramillo-Vallejo, *Streamlining Conditionality in World Bank—and International Monetary Fund—Supported Programs*, in *Conditionality Revisited Concepts, Experiences, and Lessons* (Stefan Koeberle, Harold Bedoya, Peter Silarszky & Gero Verheyen, eds., World Bank 2005).

Abott, J. I. O. & R. Mace, *Managing Protected Woodlands: Fuelwood Collection and Law Enforcement in Lake Malawi National Park*, 13(2) Cons. Biol. 418 (1999).

Admassie, Y., *Twenty Years to Nowhere: Property Rights, Land Management and Conservation in Ethiopia* (Red Sea Press 2000).

Agarwal, Bina, *Gender, Environment, and Poverty Interlinks: Regional Variations and Temporal Shifts in Rural India 1971–1991*, 25(1) World Dev. 23 (1997).

———, *A Field of One's Own: Gender and Land Rights in South Asia* (Camb. U. Press 1994).

Ajani, I. & U. Mattei, *Codifying Property Law in the Process of Transition: Some Suggestions from Comparative Law and Economics*, 19 Hastings Int'l & Comp. L. Rev., 117 (1995).

Alterman, R., *The Challenge of Farmland Preservation: Lessons From a Six-Nation Comparison*, 63(2) J. Am. Plan. Assn. 220 (1997).

Anderson, T. L. & P. J. Hill, *The Race for Property Rights*, 16 J. Econ. Hist. 16 (1973).

Appleton, S., *Women-Headed Households and Household Welfare: An Empirical Deconstruction for Uganda*, 24(12) World Dev. 1811 (1996).

Appu, P. S., *Land Reforms in India* (Vikas Publg. H. Pvt. Ltd. 1996).

Arnold, J. E. M., *Managing Forests as Common Property*, FAO Forestry Paper 136 (FAO 1998).

Arun, S., *Does Land Ownership Make a Difference? Women's Roles in Agriculture in Kerala, India* in *Women, Land, and Agriculture* (Caroline Sweetman, ed., Oxfam 1999).

Ashby, J. A., E. B. Knapp & H. M. Ravnborg, *Involving Local Organizations in Watershed Management*, in *Agriculture and the Environment: Perspectives on Sustainable Rural Development* (E. Lutz, ed., World Bank 1998).

Australian Agency for International Development (AusAID), *Improving Access to Land and Enhancing the Security of Land Rights: A Review of Land Titling and Land Administration Projects*, Quality Assurance Series No. 20 (AusAID 2000).

Aziz, A. & S. Krishna, *Land Reforms in India: Karnataka Promises Kept and Missed* (Sage Publications 1997).

Baland, J., F. Gaspart, F. Place & J. Platteau, *Poverty, Tenure Security, and Access to Land in Central Uganda: The Role of Market and Non-Market Processes* (World Bank 1999).

Baland, J., F. Gaspart, F. Place & J. Platteau, *The Distributive Impact of Land Markets in Central Uganda*, Working Paper (Centre de Recherche en Economie du Développement (CRED), Dept. of Econs., U. Namur 2000).

Banana, A. Y. & W. Gombya-Ssembajjwe, *Successful Forest Management: The Importance of Security of Tenure and Rule Enforcement in Ugandan Forests*, in *People and Forests: Communities, Institutions and Governance* (C. C. Gibson, M. A. McKean & E. Ostrom, eds., MIT Press 2000).

Barbier, E. B., *The Farm-Level Economics of Soil Conservation: The Uplands of Java*, 66(2) Land Econs. 199 (1990).

Barraclough, S. L. & K. B. Ghimire, *Agricultural Expansion and Tropical Deforestation: Poverty, International Trade and Land Use* (Earthscan Publications 2000).

Beck, T. & M. G. Ghosh, *Common Property Resources and the Poor: Findings from West Bengal*, Econ. & Political Wkly. 147 (Jan. 15, 2000).

Becker, E., *Far From Dead, Subsidies Fuel Big Farms*, N.Y. Times A1 (May 14, 2001).

Benin, S. & J. Pender, *Impacts of Land Redistribution on Land Management and Productivity in the Ethiopian Highlands*, 12 Land Degradation & Dev. 555 (2001).

Besley, T., *Property Rights and Investment Incentives: Theory and Evidence from Ghana*, 103(5) J. Political Econ. 903 (1995).

Binswanger, H. P., *Brazilian Policies that Encourage Deforestation in the Amazon*, 19(7) World Dev. 821 (1991).

Binswanger, H., K. Deininger & G. Feder, *Power, Distortion, Revolt, and Reform in Agricultural Land Relations,* in *Handbook of Development Economics*, vol. III (J. Behrman & T. N. Srinivasan, eds., Elsevier Sci. 1995).

Bird, R. M., *Taxing Agricultural Land in Developing Countries* (Harv. U. Press 1974).

Black's Law Dictionary (Bryan A. Garner, ed., 2d pocket ed., West Group 2001).

Bledsoe, D. & C. Pinto, *Republic of Angola: Land Law and Policy Assessment* (USAID 2002).

Brasselle, A., F. Gaspart & J. Platteau, *Land Tenure Security and Investment Incentives: Puzzling Evidence from Burkina Faso*, 67 J. Dev. Econs. 373 (2002).

Brown, G. P., *Arable Land Loss in Rural China: Policy and Implementation in Jiangsu Province*, 35(10) Asian Survey 922 (1995).

Brown, J., *Ejidos and Comunidades in Oaxaca, Mexico: Impact of the 1992 Reforms*, Rural Dev. Inst. Reports on Foreign Aid & Dev. #120 (RDI 2004).

Brown, J., K. Ananthupur & R. Giovarelli, *Women's Access and Rights to Land in Karnataka, India*, Rpts. Foreign Aid & Dev., No. 114 (RDI 2002).

Brown, P. & A. Ploeg, *Introduction: Change and Conflict in Papua New Guinea Land and Resource Rights*, 7 Anthro. Forum 507 (1997).

Bruce, J., *Property Rights Issues in Common Property Regimes for Forestry*, in *World Bank Legal Review: Law and Justice for Development*, vol. 1 (World Bank 2003).

————, *Legal Bases for the Management of Forest Resources as Common Property*, FAO Community Forestry Note 14 (FAO 1999).

————, *Country Profiles of Land Tenure: Africa 1996*, Land Tenure Ctr. Res. Paper No. 130 (Land Tenure Center, U. Wisconsin–Madison. 1998).

————, *Land Tenure Issues in Project Design and Strategies for Agricultural Development in Sub-Saharan Africa* (Land Tenure Center, U. Wisconsin–Madison 1986).

Bruce, J. & R. Mearns, *Natural Resource Management and Land Policy in Developing Countries: Lessons Learned and New Challenges for the World Bank*, IIED Issue Paper No. 115 (Intl. Inst. Env. & Dev. 2002).

Bruce, J. W. & L. Fortmann, *Agroforestry: Tenure and Incentives,* LTC Paper No. 135 (Land Tenure Center, U. Wisconsin–Madison 1989).

Bruner, A. G., R. E. Gulison, R. E. Rice & G. A. B. de Fonseca, *Effectiveness of Parks in Protecting Tropical Biodiversity*, 291 Science 125 (2001).

Bush, R., *More Losers Than Winners in Egypt's Countryside: The Impact of Changes in Land Tenure*, in *Counter-Revolution in Egypt's Countryside: Land and Farmers in the Era of Economic Reform* (Ray Bush, ed., Zed Books Ltd. 2002).

Byamugisha, F., *How Land Registration Affects Financial Development and Economic Growth in Thailand*, Policy Res. Working Paper Series No. 2241 (World Bank 1999).

Carothers, T., *The Rule of Law Revival*, 77 Foreign Affairs 95 (1998).

Carter, M. R., *Designing Land and Property Rights Reform for Poverty Alleviation and Food Security*, Land Reform, Land Settlement & Cooperatives (2003/2).

Carter, M. R. & R. Salgado, *Land Market Liberalization and the Agrarian Question in Latin America* in *Access to Land, Rural Poverty, and Public Action*

(Alain de Janvry, Jean-Philippe Platteau, Gustavo Gordillo & Elisabeth Sadoulet, eds., Oxf. U. Press 2001).

Carter, M. R. & E. Zegarra, *Land Markets and the Persistence of Rural Poverty: Post-Liberalization Policy Options*, in *Rural Poverty in Latin America* (R. Lopez & A. Valdez, eds., MacMillan Press, Ltd. 2000).

Carter, M. & E. Katz, *Separate Spheres and the Conjugal Contract: Understanding the Impact of Gender-Based Development* in *Intrahousehold Resource Allocation in Developing Countries: Models, Methods, and Policy* (L. Hadaad, J. Hoddinott & H. Alderman, eds., Johns Hopkins U. Press for Intl. Food Policy Res. Inst. 1992).

Chauveau, J., *The Land Question in Côte d'Ivoire*, Issue Paper No. 95, Drylands Program (Intl. Inst. Env. & Dev. 2000).

Childress, M., *East Asia and Pacific Region: Regional Study on Land Administration, Securitization, and Markets* (World Bank 2003).

Childress, M., R. Giovarelli, R. Shimarov & K. Tilekeyev, *Rapid Appraisal of Land Reform in the Kyrgyz Republic* 22 (USAID 2003).

Chluba, K. & E. Schmidt-Kallert, *Strategy for Land Consolidation and Improved Land Management in Armenia* (FAO 2001).

Christanty, L., *Home Gardens in Tropical Asia, with Special Reference to Indonesia* in *Tropical Home Gardens* (K. Landauer & M. Brazil, eds., U. N. U. Press 1990).

Clarke, D. C., *Economic Development and the Rights Hypothesis: The China Problem,* 51 Am. J. Comp. L. 89 (2003).

Coldham, S., *The Effect of Registration of Title upon Customary Land Rights in Kenya,* 22(2) J. Afr. Law 91 (1978).

Consultative Group to Assist the Poorest (CGAP), *Assessing the Relative Poverty of Microfinance Clients* (CGAP 1999).

Dale, P. F. & J. D. McLaughlin, *Land Administration* (Oxf. U. Press 1999).

David, R., *A Civil Code for Ethiopia: Considerations on the Codification of the Civil Law in African Countries*, 37 Tul. L. Rev. 189 (1963).

Davis, S. & N. Rukuba-Ngaiza, *Meaningful Consultation in Environmental Assessment*, Social Dev. Note 39 (World Bank 1998).

de Janvry, A., G. Gordillo, J. Plateau & E. Sadoulet, eds., *Access to Land, Rural Poverty and Public Action* (Oxf. U. Press 2001).

———, *Access to Land and Land Policy Reforms*, in *Access to Land, Rural Poverty, and Public Action* (Alain de Janvry, Jean-Philippe Platteau, Gustavo Gordillo & Elisabeth Sadoulet, eds., Oxf. U. Press 2001).

de Janvry, A., *The Agrarian Question and Agrarian Reformism in Latin America* (Johns Hopkins U. Press 1981).

de Soto, H., *The Mystery of Capital: Why Capitalism Triumphs in the West and Fails Everywhere Else* (Basic Books 2002).

Deere, C. D. & M. León, *Empowering Women, Land and Property Rights in Latin America* 3 (U. Pitt. Press 2001).

———, *Who Owns the Land? Gender and Land-Titling Programmes in Latin America*, 1(3) J. Agrarian Change 440 (2001).

Deininger, K., *Land Policies for Growth and Poverty Reduction*, World Bank Policy Research Report (World Bank & Oxf. U. Press 2003).

———, *Making Negotiated Land Reform Work: Initial Experience from Brazil, Colombia, and South Africa*, World Bank Policy Research Working Paper No. 2040 (World Bank 1999).

Deininger, K. & H. Binswanger, *The Evolution of the World Bank's Land Policy* in *Access to Land, Rural Poverty and Public Action* (Alain de Janvry, Gustavo Gordillo, Jean-Philippe Plateau & Elizabeth Sadoulet (Oxf. U. Press 2001).

———, *The Evolution of the World Bank's Land Policy: Principles, Experience, and Future Changes*, 14(2) World Bank Res. Observer 260 (World Bank 1999).

Deininger, K. & G. Feder, *Land Institutions and Land Markets*, World Bank Policy Research Working Paper No. 2014 (World Bank 1998).

Deininger, K. & S. Jin, *The Impact of Property Rights on Households' Investment, Risk Coping, and Policy Preferences: Evidence from China*, World Bank Policy Research Paper 2931 (World Bank 2002).

Deininger, K., G. Feder, G. Gordillo de Anda & P. Munro-Farure, *Land Policy to Facilitate Growth and Poverty Reduction*, Land Reform, Land Settlement and Cooperatives (2003/3 spec. ed.).

Dekker, H., *The Invisible Line: Land Reform, Land Tenure Security, and Land Registration*, Ashgate Intl. Land Mgmt. Series (Ashgate Publishing Ltd. 2003).

Delang, C. O., *Deforestation in Northern Thailand: The Result of Hmong Farming Practices or Thai Development Strategies?* 15 Soc. & Nat. Res. 483 (2002).

Demsetz, H., *Toward a Theory of Property Rights*, 57 Am. Econ. Rev. 347 (1967).

Dept. for International Development (DFID), *Better Livelihoods for Poor People: The Role of Land Reform* (DFID 2003).

Deutsche Gesellschaft für Technische Zusammenarbeit (GTZ) GmbH, *Land Tenure in Development Cooperation* (GTZ 1998).

Development Workshop, *Terra Firme: Oportunidades e Constrangimentos para uma Gestão Apropriada da Terra Urbana em Angola* (Dev. Wkshp. 2003).

Dey-Abbas, J., *Gender Asymmetries in Intrahousehold Resource Allocation in Sub-Saharan Africa: Some Policy Implications for Land and Labor Productivity* in *Intrahousehold Resource Allocation in Developing Countries: Models,*

Methods, and Policy (L. Hadaad, J. Hoddinott & H. Alderman, eds., Johns Hopkins U. Press for Intl. Food Policy Res. Inst. 1992).

di Leva, C. E., *The Conservation of Nature and Natural Resources Through Legal and Market-Based Instruments*, 11(1) Rev. European Community & Intl. Envtl. L. 84 (2002).

Diagne, A. & M. Zeller, *Access to Credit and its Impact on Welfare in Malawi*, Intl. Food Policy Res. Inst. Res. Rpt. (Intl. Food Policy Res. Inst. 2001).

Dobrilovic, S., *Ukraine Land Titling Initiative: Monthly Report for April 2004* (Chemonics Intl. 2004).

Dobrilovic, S. & R. Mitchell, *Project to Develop Land and Real Estate Markets in Moldova: End of Contract Report* (USAID/ Booz Allen & Hamilton 2000).

Dolzer, R., *Expropriation and Nationalization,* in *Encyclopedia of Public International Law*, vol. II (Rudolf Bernhardt, ed., 1992).

Dowall, D. E., *Benefits of Minimal Land-Use Regulations in Developing Countries,* 12 Cato J. 413 (1992).

Ellickson, R. C., *Property in Land*, 102 Yale L. J. 1315 (1993).

Fafchamps, M. & A. Quisumbing, *Control and Ownership of Assets Within Rural Ethiopian Households*, Food Consumption & Nutr. Div. Disc. Paper No. 120 (Intl. Food Policy Res. Inst. 2001).

Faruqee, R. & K. Carey, *Land Markets in South Asia: What Have We Learned?* World Bank Policy Research Working Paper No. 1754 (World Bank 1997).

Faudez, J., *Legal Reform in Developing and Transition Countries; Making Haste Slowly,* in *Comprehensive Legal and Judicial Development: Towards an Agenda for a Just and Equitable Society in the 21st Century* (Rudolf V. Van Puymbroeck, ed., World Bank 2001).

Feder, G., *Land Policies and Farm Productivity in Thailand* (Johns Hopkins U. Press 1988).

Feder, G. & A. Nishio, *The Benefits of Land Registration and Titling: Economic and Social Perspectives*, 15(1) Land Use Policy 25 (1999).

Feder, G. & D. Feeny, *Land Tenure and Property Rights: Theory and Implications for Development Policy*, 5(1) World Bank Econ. Rev. 135 (1991).

Feder, G., T. Onchan, Y. Chalamwong & C. Hongladarom, *Land Policies and Farm Productivity in Thailand* (Johns Hopkins U. Press 1988).

Fiflis, T., *English Registered Conveyancing: A Study in Effective Land Transfer*, 59 Nw. U. L. Rev. 470 (1964).

Finan, F., E. Sadoulet & A. de Janvry, *Measuring the Poverty Reduction Potential of Land in Mexico*, CUDARE Working Papers, No. 983 (U. Cal., Berk. 2002).

Firestone, D., *Black Families Resist Mississippi Land Push*, N.Y. Times A20 (September 10, 2001).

Firmin-Sellers, K., *The Politics of Property Rights*, 89(4) Am. Political Sci. Rev. 867 (1995).

Foltz, J., B. Larson & R. Lopez, *Land Tenure, Investment, and Agricultural Production in Nicaragua*, Dev. Disc. Papers: Ctr. Am. Project Series (Harv. Inst. Intl. Dev. 2000).

Fong, M., *Gender Analysis in Sector Wide Assistance in Agriculture Productivity* in *Women Farmers: Enhancing Rights, Recognition and Productivity*, Dev. Econs. & and Policy, vol. 23 (P. Webb & K. Weinberger, eds., Peter Lang Publishing 2001).

Food and Agriculture Organization of the United Nations, *Law and Sustainable Development Since Rio: Legal Trends in Agriculture and Natural Resource Management*, FAO Legislative Study No. 73 (FAO 2002).

———, *Good Practice Guidelines for Agricultural Leasing Arrangements*, FAO Land Tenure Studies 2 (FAO 2001).

———, *Women, Agriculture, and Rural Development: A Synthesis Report of the Near East Region* (FAO 1995).

Freestone, D., *Incorporating Sustainable Development Concerns into the Development and Investment Process—the World Bank Experience* in *Exploitation of Natural Resources in the 21st Century* (M. Fitzmaurice & M. Szuniewicz, eds., Kluwer Law Intl. 2003).

Gajaseni, J. & N. Gajaseni, *Ecological Rationalities of the Traditional Homegarden System in the Chao Phraya Basin, Thailand*, 46(1) Agroforestry Sys. 3 (1999).

Galal, A. & O. Razzaz, *Reforming Land and Real Estate Markets*, World Bank Policy Research Working Paper No. 2616 (World Bank 2001).

Gavian, S. & M. Fafchamps, *Land Tenure and Allocative Efficiency in Niger*, 78(2) Am. J. Agric. Econs. 460 (1996).

Gaynor, R. & D. Bledsoe, *Evaluation of the Albania Land Market Project* (USAID/ARD 2000).

Giamo, M. S., *Comment: Deforestation in Brazil: Domestic Political Imperative— Global Ecological Disaster*, 18 Envtl. L. 537 (1988).

Gilborn, L. Z., R. Nyonyintono, R. Kabumbuli & G. Jagwe-Wadda, *Making a Difference for Children Affected by AIDS: Baseline Findings from Operations Research in Uganda* (Pop. Council Inc. 2001).

Giovarelli, R., *Mortgage in the Bulgarian Agricultural Sector*, Rural Dev. Inst. Report on Foreign Assistance & Dev. No. 104 (RDI 2000).

———, *Land Use Regulation,* in *Legal Impediments to Effective Rural Land Relations in Eastern Europe and Central Asia* (R. Prosterman & T. Hanstad, eds., World Bank 1999).

————, *Women and Land* in *Legal Impediments to Effective Rural Land Relations in Eastern Europe and Central Asia*, World Bank Technical Paper No. 436 (R. Prosterman & T. Hanstad eds., World Bank 1999).

Giovarelli, R. & D. Bledsoe, *Land Reform in Eastern Europe: Western CIS, Transcaucasis, Balkans, and EU Accession Countries*, Sust. Dev. Dept., SD dimensions (FAO 2004/2001).

Giovarelli, R., C. Aidarbekova, J. Duncan, K. Rasmussen & A. Tabyshalieva, *Women's Rights to Land in the Kyrgyz Republic* (World Bank 2001).

Giovarelli, R., L. Rolfes, Jr., B. Schwarzwalder, J. Duncan & D. Bledsoe, *Legal Impediments to Effective Rural Land Relations in Eastern Europe and Central Asia*, World Bank Technical Paper No. 436 (R. Prosterman & T. Hanstad, eds., World Bank 1999).

Gopal, G., *Gender-Related Legal Reform and Access to Economic Resources in Eastern Africa*, World Bank Discussion Paper No. 405 (World Bank 1999).

Gorton, M., *Agricultural Land Reform in Moldova*, INTAS Research Project, INTAS99-00753 (U. Newcastle 2000).

Government of the United Republic of Tanzania (Ministry of Lands, Housing and Urban Development), *Report of the Presidential Commission of Inquiry into Land Matters*, vol. I (Scandinavian Inst. Afr. Studies 1994).

Government of Uganda, *Report of the Land Act Implementation Study* (1999).

Green, K. M. & A. Raphael, *Third Environmental Assessment Review (FY 96–00)*, Environment Department (World Bank 2002).

Gregory, P. J., *et al.*, *Environmental Consequences of Alternative Practices for Intensifying Crop Production*, 88 Agric., Ecosystems & Env. 279 (2002).

Gururani, S., *Regimes of Control, Strategies of Access: Politics of Forest Use in the Uttarakhand Himalaya, India* in *Agrarian Environments: Resources, Representations, and Rule in India* (A. Agrawal & K. Sivaramakrishanan, eds., Duke U. Press 2000).

Hamilton, L. S. & A. J. Pearce, *Biophysical Aspects in Watershed Management*, in *Watershed Resources Management: Studies from Asia and the Pacific* 33 (K. W. Easter, J. A., Dixon & M. M. Hufschmidt, eds., Inst. Southeast Asian Studies 1991).

Hanstad, T. & S. B. Lokesh, *Allocating Homestead Plots as Land Reform: Analysis From West Bengal*, RDI Reports on Foreign Aid & Dev. No. 115 (RDI 2002).

Hanstad, T., *Introduction to Agricultural Land Law Reform* in *Legal Impediments to Effective Rural Land Relations in Eastern Europe and Central Asia: A Comparative Perspective*, World Bank Technical Paper No. 436 (Roy Prosterman & Tim Hanstad, eds., World Bank 1999).

————, *Designing Land Registration Systems for Developing Countries*, 13(3) Am. U. Intl. L. Rev. 647 (1998).

Hanstad, T. & J. Brown, *Land Reform Law and Implementation in West Bengal: Lessons and Recommendations*, Rural Dev. Inst. Reports on Foreign Aid & Dev. #112 (RDI 2001).

Hanstad, T. & L. Ping, *Land Reform in the People's Republic of China: Auctioning Rights to Wasteland*, 19 Intl. & Comp. L. J. 545 (1997).

Hanstad, T., J. Brown & R. L. Prosterman, *Larger Homestead Plots as Land Reform? International Experience and Analysis From Karnataka*, RDI Reports on Foreign Aid & Dev. No. 113 (RDI 2001).

Harrison, S. R., A. S. Ghose & J. L. Herbohn, *Lessons from Social and Community Forestry in the Tropics, with Particular Reference to India and the Philippines,* in *Sustainable Farm Forestry in the Tropics* (S. R. Harrison & J. L. Herbohn, eds., Edward Elgar Pub. 2001).

Haverfield, R., *Hak Ulayat and the State: Land Reform in Indonesia* in *Indonesia: Law and Society* (Timothy Lindsey, ed., Federation Press 1999).

Hayes, J., M. Roth & L. Zepeda, *Tenure Security, Investment and Productivity in Gambian Agriculture: a Generalized Probit Analysis*, 79(2) Am. J. Agric. Econs. 369 (1997).

Hedley, K., *Law and Development in Russia: A Misguided Enterprise?* 90 Am. Soc, Intl. Law Proceedings 237.17 (1996).

Hilhorst, T., *Women's Land Rights: Current Developments in Sub-Saharan Africa* in *Evolving Land Rights, Policy and Tenure in Africa* 181, 186 (C. Toulmin & J. Quan, eds., DFID/IIED/NRI 2000).

Holden, S. & H. Yohannis, *Land Redistribution, Tenure Insecurity, and Intensity of Production: A Study of Farm Households in Southern Ethiopia*, 78(4) Land Econs. 573 (2002).

Holzknecht, H., *Policy Reform, Customary Tenure and Stakeholder Clashes in Papua New Guinea's Rainforests*, Rural Dev. Forestry Network Paper No. 19c (1996).

Inter-American Development Bank, *Paraguay Cadastre and Property Registry Program Loan Proposal* (IADB 2002).

International Fund for Agricultural Development (IFAD), *Rural Poverty Report 2001: The Challenge of Ending Rural Poverty* (Oxf. U. Press 2001).

———, *Rural Poverty Report 2000/2001 Fact Sheet: Assets and the Rural Poor* (IFAD 2001).

International Land Coalition (ILC), *Towards a Common Platform on Access to Land: The Catalyst to Reduce Rural Poverty and the Incentive for Sustainable Natural Resource Management* (ILC 2003).

Irving, D. K., *Should the Law Recognize the Acquisition of Title by Adverse Possession?* 2 Australian Prop. L. J. 1 (1994).

Izumi, K., *Liberalisation, Gender, and the Land Question in Sub-Saharan Africa* in *Women, Land, and Agriculture* 9 (C. Sweetman, ed., Oxfam 1999).

Judd, M. & J. Dulnuan, *Women's Legal and Customary Access to Land in the Philippines* (World Bank 2001).

Kahn, M. H., *Rural Poverty in Developing Countries: Issues and Policies*, IMF Working Paper WP/00/78 (Intl. Monetary Fund 2000).

Katz, E. & J. S. Chamorro, *Gender, Land Rights, and the Household Economy in Rural Nicaragua and Honduras* (USAID BASIS/CRSP 2002).

Kevane, M. & L. C. Gray, *A Woman's Field Is Made at Night: Gendered Land Rights and Norms in Burkina Faso*. 5(3) Fem. Econs. 1 (1999).

Kigula, J., *Land Disputes in Uganda: An Overview of the Types of Land Disputes and the Disputes Settlement Fora* (Makere Inst. Soc. Research, Kampala, Uganda & Land Tenure Center, U. Wisconsin–Madison 1993).

Kingdom of Lesotho, *Report of the Land Policy Review Commission* (Govt. Printer 2000).

Kingsbury, B., *"Indigenous Peoples" in International Law: A Constructivist Approach to the Asian Controversy*, 92(3) Am. J. Intl. L. 414 (1998).

Koch, E., J. M. Massyn & A. van Niekerk, *The Fate of Land Reform in Southern Africa: The Role of the State, the Market, and Civil Society*, in *Whose Land? Civil Society Perspectives on Land Reform and Rural Poverty Reduction* (K. Ghimire, ed., Intl. Fund Agric. Dev. 2001).

Kumar, K., *Land Use Rights and Gender Equality in Vietnam*, Engendering Development No. 1 (World Bank 2002).

Kunich, J. C., *Fiddling Around While the Hotspots Burn Out*, 14 Geo. Intl. Envtl. L. Rev. 179 (2001).

Lambin, E. F., *et al., The Causes of Land-Use and Land-Cover Change: Moving Beyond the Myths*, 11 Global Envtl. Change 261 (2001).

Land Law in Comparative Perspective (Maria Elena Sanchez Jordan & Antonio Gambaro, eds., Kluwer Law Intl. 2002).

Lastarria-Cornheil, S., *Impact of Privatization on Gender and Property Rights in Africa*, 25(8) World Dev. 1317 (1997).

Lastarria-Cornheil, S., S. Agurto, J. Brown & S. E. Rosales, *Joint Titling in Nicaragua, Indonesia, and Honduras: Rapid Appraisal Synthesis* (Land Tenure Center, U. Wisconsin–Madison 2003).

Lastarria-Cornhiel, S. & R. Wheeler, *Gender, Ethnicity and Landed Property in Albania*, Working Paper No. 18, Albania Series (Land Tenure Center, U. Wisconsin–Madison 1998).

Latin American Land Reforms in Theory and Practice: A Retrospective Analysis (U. Wis. Press 1992).

Law and Sustainable Development since Rio: Legal Trends in Agriculture and Natural Resource Management, FAO Legislative Study 73 (FAO 2002).

le Prestre, P. G., *The CBD at Ten: the Long Road to Effectiveness*, 3(5) J. Intl. Wildlife L. & Policy 269 (2002).

Lea, D., *Individual Autonomy, Group Self-Determination and the Assimilation of Indigenous Cultures*, North Australia Research Unit Discussion Paper No. 18/2000 (2000).

Leach, M., R. Mearns & I. Scoones, *Environmental Entitlements: Dynamics and Institutions in Community-Based Natural Resource Management*, 27(2) World Dev. 225 (1999).

Ledec, G., *Effects of Kenya's Bura Irrigation Settlement Project on Biological Diversity and Other Conservation Concerns*, 1(3) Cons. Biol. 247 (1987).

Lele, U., V. Viana, A. Verissimo, S. Vosti, K. Perkins & S. A. Husain, *Brazil— Forests in the Balance: Challenges of Conservation with Development* (World Bank 2000).

Lemel, H., *Land Titling: Conceptual, Empirical, and Policy Issues*, in *Land Use Policy* (Butterworth & Co. 1988).

Lerman, Z., *Comparative Institutional Evolution: Rural Land Reform in the ECA Region*, World Dev. Report Background Paper (World Bank 2001).

Lerman, Z. & A. Mirzakhanian, *Private Agriculture in Armenia* (Lexington Books 2001).

Li, Z., *The Lao People's Democratic Republic: Preserving Women's Rights in Land Titling*, in *Agricultural Investment Sourcebook*, Ag. & Rural Dev. Dept. (World Bank 2004).

———, *Women's Land Rights in Rural China: A Synthesis* (Working Paper for the Ford Foundation 2002).

Li, Z. & J. Bruce, *Gender, Landlessness and Equity in Rural China* in *Developmental Dilemmas: Land Reform and Institutional Change in China* (Peter Ho, ed., Routledge 2005).

Liu, D., *Tenure and Management of Non-State Forests in China Since 1950: A Historical Review*, 6(2) Envtl. History 239 (2001).

Lok-Dessallien, R., *Review of Poverty Concepts and Indicators*, SEPED Series on Poverty Reduction (UNDP 2001).

Lopez, R. & A. Valdez, *Fighting Rural Poverty in Latin America: New Evidence and Policy*, in *Rural Poverty in Latin America* (R. Lopez & A. Valdez, eds., MacMillan Press, Ltd. 2000).

Lopez, R. & T. S. Thomas, *Rural Poverty in Paraguay: The Determinants of Farm Household Income*, in *Rural Poverty in Latin America* (R. Lopez & A. Valdez, eds., MacMillan Press, Ltd. 2000).

Lynch, O. J. & K. Talbott, *Balancing Acts: Community-Based Forest Management and National Law in Asia and the Pacific* (World Resources Inst. 1995).

Lynch, O. J. & K. Talbott, *Balancing Acts: Community-Based Forestry Management and National Law in East Asia and the Pacific* (World Resources Inst. 1995).

Mackinnon, J. & R. Reinikka, *Lessons from Uganda on Strategies to Fight Poverty* (Centre for Study Afr. Econs. & World Bank 2000).

Maggio, G. F., *Recognizing the Vital Role of Local Communities in International Legal Instruments for Conserving Biodiversity*, 16 UCLA J. Envtl. L. & Policy 179 (1997).

Making Development Work: Legislative Reform for Institutional Transformation and Good Governance (Ann Seidman, Robert B. Seidman & Thomas W. Wilde, eds., Kluwer Law Intl. 1999).

Marsh, R., *Building on Traditional Gardening to Improve Household Food Security,* Food, Nutr. & Ag. No. 22 (FAO 1998).

McAuslan, P., *Bringing the Law Back In: Essays in Land, Law and Development* (Ashgate Publishing Ltd. 2003).

———, *Only the Name of the Country Changes: The Diaspora of "European" Land Law in Commonwealth Africa*, in *Bringing the Law Back In: Essays in Land, Law and Development* (Patrick McAuslan, ed., Ashgate Publishing Ltd. 2003).

Mearns, R., *Access to Land in Rural India: Policy Issues and Options*, World Bank Working Paper No. 2123, 31 (World Bank 1999).

Meinzen-Dick, R. S., L. R. Brown, H. S. Feldstein & A. S. Quisumbing, *Gender, Property Rights, and Natural Resources*, 25(8) World Dev. 1303 (1997).

Mendelsohn, R., *Property Rights and Tropical Deforestation,* 46 Oxf. Econ. Papers, New Series 750 (1994).

Migot-Adholla, S., *et al.*, *Security of Tenure and Land Productivity in Kenya* in *Searching for Land Tenure Security in Africa* (John Bruce & Shem Migot-Adholla, eds., Kendall-Hunt Pub. 1993).

Migot-Adholla, S. E., S. P. Hazell, B. Blorel & F. Place, *Indigenous Land Rights in Sub-Saharan Africa: A Constraint on Productivity*, 5.1 World Bank Econ. Rev. (World Bank 1991).

Millikan, B. H., *Tropical Deforestation, Land Degradation and Society: Lessons from Rondonia, Brazil*, 19(1) Latin Am. Persps. 45 (1992).

Ministry of Forestry, *China Forestry Year, 1949–1986* (China Forestry Pub. 1987).

Ministry of Lands, Housing, and the Environment of Botswana, *Review of Botswana National Land Policy, Final Report* 80 (January 31, 2003).

Mitchell, R. & T. Hanstad, *Small Homegarden Plots and Sustainable Livelihoods for the Poor*, Livelihood Support Programme Working Paper (FAO 2004).

Moguel, P. & V. M. Toledo, *Review: Biodiversity Conservation in Traditional Coffee Systems of Mexico*, 13(1) Cons. Biol. 11 (1999).

Moock, P., *The Efficiency of Women as Farm Managers: Kenya*, 58 Am. J. Agric. Econ. (1976).

Muhereza, F. & D. Bledsoe, *Final Report—Land Sector Analysis: Common Property Resources Component* (Govt. Uganda 2002).

Mushunje, M., *Women's Land Rights in Zimbabwe*, Report of Land Tenure Ctr. 11 (Land Tenure Center, U. Wisonsin-Madison 2001).

Mwebaza, R. & R. Gaynor, *Final Report—Land Sector Analysis: Land Market, Land Consolidation, and Land Re-adjustment Component* (Govt. Uganda 2002).

Nair, P. K. R., *An Introduction to Agroforestry* (Kluwer Academic Publishers 1993).

Nelson, G., W. Stoebuck & D. Whitman, *The Law of Property* (West Group Pub. 2002).

Ng'weno, B., *On Titling Collective Property, Participation, and Natural Resource Management: Implementing Indigenous and Afro-Colombian Demands: A Review of Bank Experience in Colombia* (2000).

Nichols, P. M., *The Viability of Transplanted Law: Kazakhstani Reception of a Transplanted Foreign Investment Code*, 18 U. Pa. J. Int'l Econ. L. 1235 (1997).

Norway Ministry of Foreign Affairs, *Agriculture—A Way out of Poverty* (Norway 2002).

Olinto, P., B. Davis & K. Deininger, *Did the Poor Benefit from Land Market Liberalization in Mexico? Panel-Data Evidence of the Impact of the Ejido Reforms* (World Bank 1999).

Oliver, N., *Lease, Lease-Back—An Instrument for Forestry?* in *Production, Privatisation and Preservation in Papua New Guinea Forestry* (C. Hunt, ed., Intl. Inst. Env. & Dev. 2002).

Olsen, P. C., *Adverse Possession in Oregon: The Belief in Ownership Requirement*, 23(4) Envtl. L. 1297 (1993).

Oppenheim's International Law (Robert Jennings & Arthur Watts, eds., 9th ed., Longman 1992).

Osbourne, S. & M. Trueblood, *Agricultural Productivity and Efficiency in Russia and Ukraine: Building on a Decade of Reform*, Agricultural Economic Report No. AER813 (July 2002).

Otsuka, K., *Population Pressure, Land Tenure and Natural Resource Management*, ADB Institute Working Paper No. 16 (Asian Dev. Bank Inst. 2001).

Pagiola, S., *Economic Analysis of Rural Land Administration Projects*, Land Policy & Admin. Thematic Team (World Bank 1999).

Parnwell, M. J. G., *Rural Poverty, Development and the Environment: The Case of North-East Thailand*, 15(1) J. Biogeography 199 (1988).

Peres, C. A. & J. W. Terborgh, *Amazonian Nature Reserves: An Analysis of the Defensibility Status of Existing Conservation Units and Design Criteria for the Future*, 9(1) Cons. Biol. 34 (1995).

Perez-Arteaga, A., K. J. Gaston & M. Kershaw, *Undesignated Sites in Mexico Qualifying as Wetlands of International Importance*, 107 Biol. Cons. 47 (2002).

Platteau, J., *Does Africa Need Land Reform?* in *Evolving Land Rights, Policy and Tenure in Africa* (C. Toulmin & J. Quan, eds., IIED & Natural Res. Inst. 2000).

Pretty, J. N., J. I. L. Morison & R. E. Hine, *Reducing Food Poverty by Increasing Agricultural Sustainability in Developing Countries*, 95 Agric. Ecosystems & Envt. 217 (2003).

Production, Privatisation and Preservation in Papua New Guinea Forestry (C. Hunt, ed., Intl. Inst. Env. & Dev. 2002).

Prosterman, R. L. & L. Rolfes, Jr., *Review of the Legal Basis for Agricultural Land Markets in Lithuania, Poland, and Romania*, in *Structural Change in the Farming Sectors in Central and Eastern Europe*, World Bank Technical Paper No. 465 (Csaba Csaki & Zvi Lerman, eds., World Bank 2000).

Prosterman, R. L. & J. M. Reidinger, *Land Reform and Economic Development* (Johns Hopkins U. Press 1987).

Prosterman, R., B. Schwarzwalder & J. Ye, *Implementation of 30-Year Land Use Rights for Farmers Under China's 1998 Land Management Law: An Analysis and Recommendations Based on a 17 Province Survey*, 9(3) Pac. Rim L. & Pol'y J. 507 (2000).

Prosterman, R., T. Hanstad, B. Schwarzwalder & L. Ping, *Legal and Institutional Reforms in China's Rural Land System* (unpublished report, RDI 2001).

Quan, J., *Land Tenure, Economic Growth and Poverty in Sub-Saharan Africa* in *Evolving Land Rights, Policy and Tenure in Africa* (C. Toulmin & J. Quan, eds., IIED & Natural Res. Inst. 2000).

Rangan, H. & M. B. Lane, *Indigenous Peoples and Forest Management: Comparative Analysis of Institutional Approaches in Australia and India*, 14 Soc. & Nat. Res. 145 (2001).

Rasmussen, L. N. & R. Meinzen-Dick, *Local Organizations for Natural Resource Management: Lessons from Theoretical and Empirical Literature*, EPTD Discussion Paper No. 11 (IFPRI 1995).

Republic of Rwanda, *Land Assessment Report* 36 (Natural Res. Inst. U. Greenwich 2004).

Republic of Uganda, *Land Sector Strategic Plan: 2001–2011* (Repub. Uganda 2002).

Rwabahungu, M., *Tenurial Reforms in West and Central Africa: Legislation, Conflicts, and Social Movements*, in *Whose Land? Civil Society Perspectives on*

Land Reform and Rural Poverty Reduction (K. Ghimire, ed., Intl. Fund Agric. Dev. 2001).

Rygnestad, H., *Land Administration and Gender Issues Portfolio Review* (prepared for the World Bank Group 2004).

Sadoulet, E., R. Murgai & A. de Janvry, *Access to Land via Rental Markets*, in *Access to Land, Rural Poverty, and Public Action* (Alain de Janvry, Jean-Philippe Platteau, Gustavo Gordillo & Elisabeth Sadoulet, eds., Oxf. U. Press 2001).

Saha, U. S. & M. Saha, *Case Study. Regulating the Sharecropping System: Operation Barga* in *Access to Land, Rural Poverty, and Public Action* (Alain de Janvry, Jean-Philippe Platteau, Gustavo Gordillo & Elisabeth Sadoulet, eds., Oxf. U. Press 2001).

Saigal, S., *Beyond Experimentation: Emerging Issues in the Institutionalization of Joint Forest Management in India*, 26(3) Envtl. Mgt. 269 (2000).

Sarin, M., *From Conflict to Collaboration: Local Institutions in Joint Forest Management*, Joint Forest Management Working Paper No. 14 (SPWD 1993).

Saxena, N. N. C., *Research Issues in Forestry in India*, 55(3) Indian J. Agric. Econs. 359 (2000).

Schwarzwalder, B., R. L. Prosterman, J. Ye, J. Riedinger & P. Li, *An Update on China's Rural Land Tenure Reforms: Analysis and Recommendations Based on a Seventeen-Province Survey*, 16 Colum. J. Asian L. 143 (2002).

Searching for Agrarian Reform in Latin America (William C. Thiesenhusen, ed., Unwin Hyman 1989).

Searching for Land Tenure Security in Africa (J. W. Bruce & S. E. Migot-Adholla, eds., Kendall/Hunt 1994).

Sebina-Zziwa, A., *et al., Land Act Monitoring Exercise I* (DFID & Ugandan Ministry of Water, Lands & Env. 2000).

Seidl-Hohenveldern, I., *International Economic Law* (3d rev. ed., Kluwer Law Intl. 1999).

Seidman, A. & R. B. Seidman, *Beyond Contested Elections: The Processes of Bill Creation and Fulfillment of Democracy's Promises to the Third World*, 34 Harv. J. on Legis. 1 (1997).

Seidman, A. & R. B. Seidman, *Drafting Legislation for Development: Lessons from a Chinese Project*, 44 Am. J. Comp. L. 101 (1996).

Seidman, A., R. B. Seidman & N. Abeyesekere, *Legislative Drafting for Democratic Social Change; A Manual for Drafters* (Kluwer Law Intl. 2001).

Shipton, P., *The Kenyan Land Tenure Reform: Misunderstandings in the Public Creation of Private Property,* in *Land and Society in Contemporary Africa* (R. E. Downs & S. P. Reyna, eds., U. New Hampshire Press 1988).

Shivji, I. G., *Not Yet Democracy: Reforming Land Tenure in Tanzania* (Intl. Inst. Env. & Dev. 1998).

Simpson, S., *Land Law and Registration* (Camb. U. Press 1976).

Skinner, J., *If Agricultural Land Taxation Is So Efficient, Why Is It So Rarely Used?* 5 World Bank Econ. Rev. 113 (World Bank 1991).

Soemarwoto, O., *The Javanese Homegarden as an Integrated Agro-Ecosystem*, 7(3) Food & Nutr. Bull. 3 (U. N. University Press 1985).

Stamm, V., *The Rural Land Plan: An Innovative Approach from Cote d'Ivoire,* Issue Paper No. 91, Drylands Program (Intl. Inst. Env. & Dev. 2000).

Stevenson, C. G., *Common Property Economics: A General Theory and Land Use Applications* (Camb. U. Press 1991).

Steyn, L. & M. Aliber, *Resources and Finances Required for the Implementation of a New Land Act in Lesotho*, Lesotho Land Policy & Law Harmonization and Strategic Plan Project, Agricultural Policy and Capacity Building Project (DFID 2003).

Stoler, A., *Garden Use and Household Economy in Rural Java*, 14 Bull. Indonesian Econ. Studs. 85 (1978).

Stonich, S. C., *Dynamics of Social Processes and Environmental Destruction: A Central American Case Study*, 15 Pop. & Dev. Rev. 284 (1989).

Strachan, L., *Assets-Based Development: The Role for Pro-Poor Land Tenure Reform* (Discussion Paper, Canad. Intl. Dev. Agency 2001).

Strickland, R., *To Have and to Hold, Women's Property and Inheritance Rights in the Context of HIV/AIDS in Sub-Saharan Africa*, ICRW Working Paper (ICRW June 2004).

Thiesenhusen, W. C., *Implications of the Rural Land Tenure System for the Environmental Debate: Three Scenarios*, 26 J. Developing Areas 1 (1991).

Troutt, E., *Rural African Land Markets and Access to Agricultural Land: The Central Region of Uganda* (Makere Inst. Soc. Research, Kampala, Uganda & Land Tenure Center, U. Wisconsin–Madison 1994).

United Nations Department of Economic & Social Affairs, *1999 World Survey on the Role of Women in Development: Globalization, Gender and Work* (UN 1999).

United Nations Economic Commission for Europe (UNECE), *Key Aspects of Land Registration and Cadastral Legislation, Part 1 of 2* (UNECE 2000).

United States Agency for International Development, *Armenia: Real Estate Market Reform and Title Registration* (USAID 2001).

Verissimo, A., C. A. Junior, S. Stone & C. Uhl, *Zoning of Timber Extraction in the Brazilian Amazon*, 12 Cons. Biol. 128 (1998).

Wachter, D., *Farmland Degradation in Developing Countries: The Role of Property Rights and an Assessment of Land Titling as a Policy Intervention*, Land Tenure Ctr. Paper No. 145 (U. Wis. 1992).

Wade, T. W. & J. L. Gunderson, *Legislative Reform in Transition Economies: A Short-Cut to Social Market Economy Status*, in *Making Development Work* (A. Seidman, R. B. Seidman & T. W. Wade, eds., Kluwer Law Intl. 1999).

Watson, Alan, *Aspects of the Reception of Law*, 44(2) Am. J. Comp. L. 335 (1996).

Weiss, E. B., *Understanding Compliance with International Environmental Agreements: The Baker's Dozen Myths*, 32 U. Rich. L. Rev. 1555 (1999).

Wiley, Liz, *Finding the Right Legal and Institutional Framework for Community-Based Natural Forest Management: The Tanzania Case*, CIFOR Special Publication (CIFOR 1997).

Williams, Paula, *Draft Evaluation Summary, Evaluation of Three Pilot Models for Participation Forest Management: Village Involvement in Production Forestry in Lao PDR* (World Bank 2000).

World Bank, *Gender Issues and Best Practices in Land Administration Projects, A Synthesis Report* (World Bank 2005).

———, *Sustaining Forests: A Development Strategy* (World Bank 2004).

———, *Land Policies for Growth and Poverty Reduction*, World Bank Policy Research Report (World Bank 2003).

———, *Reaching the Rural Poor: A Renewed Strategy for Rural Development* (World Bank 2003).

———, *Land Policy and Administration, Module IX: Land Administration, Policy, and Markets—Overview* (World Bank 2003).

———, *World Bank Lending Instruments; Resources for Development* (World Bank 2003).

———, *World Development Report 2002: Building Institutions for Markets* (World Bank 2002).

———, *World Development Report 2000/2001, Attacking Poverty; Opportunity, Empowerment and Security* (World Bank 2001).

———, *Thailand Land Reform Areas Project and Second Land Titling Project Performance Audit Report* (World Bank 1998).

———, *India: Achievements and Challenges in Reducing Poverty* (World Bank 1997).

———, *The World Bank and Legal Technical Assistance: Initial Lessons*, vol. 1, Policy Research Working Paper No. WPS 1414 (Legal Department) (World Bank 1995).

———, *A World Bank Policy Paper: The Forest Sector* (World Bank 1991).

World Bank & Klaus Deininger, *Land Policies for Growth and Poverty Reduction*, World Bank Policy and Poverty Reduction Report (World Bank & Oxf. U. Press 2003).

Yavlinsky, Grigory, *"Good Tsar" as a Risk Factor,* 46 Moscow News 5 (November 20–26, 2002).

Yin, R. & D. H. Newman, *Impacts of Rural Reform: The Case of the Chinese Forest Sector*, 2 Envt. & Dev. Econs. 291 (1997).

Zhu, L. & Z. Jiang, *Gender Inequality in the Land Tenure System of China, in Women Farmers, Enhancing Rights, Recognition and Productivity Women Farmers: Enhancing Rights, Recognition and Productivity*, Dev. Econs. & Policy, vol. 23, 203 (P. Webb & K. Weinberger, eds., Peter Lang Publishing 2001).

Index